Readings
Primary School M

**NORTH DEVON
TEACHERS'
PROFESSIONAL
CENTRE**

For Pam, Ben and Dad

Readings in Primary School Management

Edited by
Geoff Southworth

 The Falmer Press

(A member of the Taylor & Francis Group)
London New York and Philadelphia

UK	The Falmer Press, Falmer House, Barcombe, Lewes, East Sussex, BN8 5DL
USA	The Falmer Press, Taylor & Francis Inc., 242 Cherry Street, Philadelphia, PA 19106–1906

© Selection and editorial material G. Southworth 1987

All rights reserved. No part of this publication may be reproduced, stored in a retrieval system, or transmitted in any form or by any means, electronic, mechanical, photocopying, recording or otherwise, without permission in writing from the Publisher.

First published 1987

Library of Congress Cataloging-in-Publication Data
Readings in primary school management.
    Includes index.
    1. Education, Primary—Great Britain. I. Southworth, Geoff.
LA633.R4 1987   372.12′00941   87-15578
ISBN 1-85000-245-2
ISBN 1-85000-246-0 (pbk.)

Jacket design by Caroline Archer

Typeset in 10½/12 Caledonia
Imago Publishing Ltd, Thame, Oxon

*Printed & bound in Great Britain by
Redwood Burn Limited, Trowbridge, Wiltshire.*

Contents

Acknowledgements vii

Introduction 1
Geoff Southworth

Section 1: Roles and Responsibilities 13

Introduction 14

Recruitment and Management Development for 16
Primary Headship
Alan A. Coulson

One Finger, One Thumb: A Case Study of the Deputy 30
Head's Part in the Leadership of a Nursery/Infant School
Jennifer Nias

The Role of the Curriculum Postholder 54
Jim Campbell

Primary School Headteachers and Collegiality 61
Geoff Southworth

Section 2: Roles and Relationships 77

Introduction 78

Are Primary Teachers Primarily People? 80
Robin Yeomans

Learning the Job while Playing a Part: Staff Development in the 90
Early Years of Teaching
Jennifer Nias

Staff Selection or By Appointment? A Case Study of the 105
Appointment of a Teacher to a Primary School
Geoff Southworth

Contents

Leading the Team, Belonging to the Group? *Robin Yeomans*	128
Section 3: Curriculum Management	**141**
Introduction	142
Perspectives on the Primary Curriculum *Geoff Southworth*	144
'The Curriculum from 5 to 16': Background, Content and Some Implications for Primary Education *Colin Richards*	160
Further Perspectives on the Primary Curriculum *Geoff Southworth*	171
Section 4: Evaluation and Effectiveness	**189**
Introduction	190
Learning and Teacher Appraisal: The Heart of the Matter *Marion Dadds*	192
Key Factors for Effective Junior Schooling *ILEA Research and Statistics Branch*	201
Making it Count: Evaluation for the Developing Primary School *Peter Holly*	208
Endpaper *Geoff Southworth*	238
List of Contributors	241
Index	242

Acknowledgements

The publishers are grateful to the following for permission to reproduce copyright material:

The editor and publishers of *School Organization* for COULSON, A.A. (1985) 'Recruitment and management development for primary headship', SOUTHWORTH, G.W. (1987) 'Primary headteachers and collegiality'.

Falmer Press and RICHARDS, C. (1985) *The Study of Primary Education : A Source Book, Vol. 3* for CAMPBELL, R.J. 'The role of the curriculum postholder'.

The editor and publishers of *Education 3–13* for YEOMANS, R. (1985) 'Are primary teachers primarily teachers'; and RICHARDS, C. (1986) 'The Curriculum from 5 to 16'.

The editor and publishers of *Educational Review* for parts of NIAS, J. 'Learning the job and playing the part' which originally appeared in NIAS, J. (1984) 'Learning and acting the role: In-school support for primary teachers'.

The editor and publishers of *Cambridge Journal of Education* for SOUTHWORTH, G.W. (1985) 'Perspectives on the primary curriculum'; and SOUTHWORTH, G.W. (1985) 'Further perspectives on the primary curriculum'.

The ILEA for 'Key Factors for Effective Junior Schooling' from *'The Junior School Report'* ILEA Research and Statistics Branch, 1986.

Introduction

Geoff Southworth

The idea of managing a school has been taken up to such an extent that a new growth industry has been created. There are now numerous in-service courses devoted to management and there has been a corresponding upsurge in the literature. This book plays a part in maintaining this trend. However, although this book continues the trend it seeks to question the direction of the trend.

Despite the fact that there are now many books on school management there are not all that many which specifically focus on primary schools. Even fewer of the books concerned with primary schools are able to provide a match between management theory and the primary school as a living organization. All too frequently one feels that management is simply a matter of doing things to people who will then respond and conform to the neat and tidy patterns described on the school's organizational chart. Perhaps, because of this outlook very little attention has been devoted to the particular and distinctive characteristics of primary schools as organizations and cultures. This book will try to keep in view and explore the *distinctive* characteristics of primary schools and the adults who work and live in them. Moreover, the book aims to raise questions about the *application* and *appropriateness* of organization and management theories which are not grounded in primary schools.

Some Thoughts on Management

Management is the field of study which is concerned with the operation of an organization, in our case the operation of a primary school. Management is therefore a practical activity since it is to do with making and helping the school 'work'. When described in this way management appears to be quite straightforward. However, management involves many things because a school is never a singular entity. A school is a composite of many components. The components of a school can be illustrated by listing the children, teachers, non-teaching staff, governors, parents, buildings, materials and equipment. Other components might be the arrangement of children into classes, curricular plans and policies, staff roles and responsibilities, and timetables, to say nothing of the values which underpin these things. Schools, even so called small schools, are therefore quite complex organizations. This is further supported by recognizing that a school is not just complex because of the number of components that comprise a school but also because the components interrelate and interpenetrate in subtle and diverse ways.

This view of the school as an organization owes much to organizational theory. One feature of school management has been the way in which it has been influenced by mainstream organization theory which is typically developed from research based upon commercial and industrial companies. There have been certain gains from this but there are also dangers which raise the need to check out the appropriateness of management theory when applied to school settings. Handy (1984), for one, has noted that whilst schools share similarities with other organizations there are also four differences.

First, there is a lack of time for management in schools. Teachers are teachers first and managers when there is time. Teaching heads are most aware of this and so too are nearly all deputy heads in primary schools. Second, unlike industry, the aims of education are broad, imprecise, not always agreed on and difficult to measure. Third, teachers have to switch roles a lot. In the course of a single day a teacher can be an authority figure in the classroom, an adult among equals in the staffroom, a subordinate in a staff meeting and an expert and leader in a working party. Fourth, there are the children. Working with young children is both rewarding and demanding. The principle of 'loco parentis' requires particular skills in liaison and communication between home and school and sometimes other agencies (eg. social services, health). Schools are also densely populated places. Walk into a school during the working day and you will find many children and adults. Yet the sheer number of these children is only one part of the picture, another is their diversity. A primary school may well have children who range in age from three to eleven years and whose abilities, development, backgrounds and attitudes can be very varied. Schools are not simply faced with a lot of children, they cater for a lot of *individual* children.

Additional to Handy's four differences I think there is one other. This fifth feature is that primary schools are individually different. For one thing primary schools vary in size; some schools have less than thirty pupils whilst others have more than 600 pupils. Next, the age range of a school varies: there are Infant, Junior, 5–11 Primaries, lower/first schools and middle schools deemed primary. Furthermore many schools now have nursery units/classes attached to them as well as four-year-olds in reception classes. Another way in which schools differ is in terms of environmental context (eg. urban, suburban, rural). Finally primary schools can be designated community schools and be controlled by the LEA or church or a combination of both.

Implications

Taken together these five differences contain at least four *implications* for the management of primary schools. First, as a consequence of this diversity management is often contingent upon the effects exerted by the school's context. Managing a 'small' school in an affluent rural setting is significantly different to managing a very large school in a depressed, urban setting.

A second implication is that because primary schools are complex organizations so too will the management of them be a complex task. Further, since primary schools are also different from other organizations it may be possible to say that the management of primary schools needs to be different. Given the components and contextual differences of primary schools management is not only a matter of administrative, technical and interpersonal decisions. Primary school management is do with defining and prioritizing the school's aims, the construction of a total pattern of education for children of all ages and abilities between three and eleven years and the determining of a set of moral and behavioural norms for a variegated community of children and adults (Alexander, 1984). As Alexander goes on to say, these decisions require competences which are essentially conceptual, judgmental and ethical. Taken together these competences constitute a formidable set of expectations concerning the skills of primary teachers and headteachers.

Third, because there are many larger organizations around in our society, for example a teaching hospital, car factory, or a 2000-place comprehensive school, primary schools are judged to be simple because they are small. Typically, primary schools as organizations are regarded as 'little organizations'. By comparison with some organizations primary schools *are* little but in accepting that we should perhaps try to understand them as *little* and *different*. Quite frequently primary schools are seen as little big-organizations: primary schools are *not* little big-schools. All too often approaches which work for larger organizations are made to fit primary school contexts. Do primary schools as little organizations *match* the solutions workable in larger and different organizational contexts? A number of articles in this reader suggest that this question of match or appropriateness needs to be treated more seriously than at present.

Fourth, managerial decisions are not just made about each issue as it arises. Rather, any one decision must be seen in relation to all the other components. For example, the distribution of areas of the curriculum to teachers acting as curriculum co-ordinators needs to be linked to the co-ordinator's knowledge of four to eleven year olds, to equipment and resources available, to teacher and curriculum development plans, to the use of time and the interpersonal skills of the co-ordinator. Primary school management is therefore a *synthetic* activity in the sense of keeping many things in view at any one time and being able to synthesize all the elements into a *whole school*. In part this is a perceptual skill. Also, in bringing together different parts it may well be that disparate and even inconsistent parts are brought together which means that 'managers' will have to accept ambiguity. Furthermore, the idea of establishing a whole school means that the staff group will need to work together. Currently there is considerable emphasis being placed on 'whole school policies', the development of the 'whole curriculum' and teamwork. Much of this is expressed under the guise of teachers working collaboratively. However, collaboration is currently prescribed without sufficient attention being paid to the tact and diplomacy which will be needed to resolve the micropolitical dimensions connected with coalitions, relationships and differences which seem to be an everpresent feature of groups.

Primary school management is therefore complex in both the scale of the task and the scope of skills needed to ensure the decisions are put into operation. This book will attempt to elaborate on this view. Each contribution adds a distinctive perspective to these issues, whilst collectively some general themes emerge in each of the four sections and across the book. Next I will outline the sections of the book, then offer a brief overview of each chapter and lastly sketch out some of the themes.

The Four Sections of the Book

Having said that primary school management is a complex task it needs to be admitted that this book does not cover every and all aspects of management practice. Some aspects have been omitted such as external relations, finance and communication. Nevertheless the four sections focus on some of the key issues.

Section one, roles and responsibilities, considers the formal side of the school as an organization. The roles of headteacher, deputy, and curriculum postholder are considered in the four chapters. In each case the demands of the role are highlighted and the implications of the role are noted, both for the person playing the role, and the school where those roles are performed.

Section two focuses more closely on the informal aspects of schools. The implications of teachers working together, which are signposted at the end of section one, are now more carefully considered. The issue of how teachers sustain their individuality whilst working collaboratively with their colleagues is raised. Section two also develops another issue identified in section one, namely that in primary schools the notion of 'wholeness' appears to mean that primary teachers do not distinguish between the teacher-as-a-professional and the teacher-as-a-person. The two are seen as connected for all teachers.

Section three considers contemporary issues to do with curriculum management. Attention is devoted to the ideas and language now being employed to describe the primary school curriculum. The scale and pace of curricular change is also considered. This section should be seen alongside the first two sections and not as separate from them because curriculum management relies upon teachers so that their roles, responsibilities and relationships as discussed in sections one and two, need to be consistent with the curriculum tasks identified in this section. This also applies to school evaluation and effectiveness as discussed in section four.

Section four presents aspects of school evaluation, self-evaluation, teacher appraisal and the main findings of research into school effectiveness in ILEA junior schools. Issues of school and teacher development, curriculum change and support are focused on as well as the kinds of formal and informal structures and climate needed to create a 'developing school'.

Taken together a number of themes can be identified as well as a long agenda of action points for schools to be thinking about. However, before listing these things the specific focus of each contribution should be noted.

The Chapters in this Reader

Alan Coulson: *Recruitment and management development for primary headship*

Coulson looks at two interlinked areas of concern; career development for teachers and management training. In a carefully organized chapter Coulson argues that the primary headteacher's work should be closely analyzed and he provides one such analysis. Also, that the effects of each school's unique characteristics on the head's tasks should be taken into account when management courses are devised. Moreover, because a head's management practice is based upon the head's personal assumptions, values and attitudes then professional development of heads necessarily involves personal development. Recognizing this personal aspect of management development means that the nature of management courses may have to alter. At one and the same time Coulson accepts the centrality of the head's role and reviews the implications this creates for headteacher development and school development, since the article ends with a brief consideration of a collegial approach to school management.

Geoff Southworth

Jennifer Nias: *One finger, One thumb*

This chapter examines the part played by the deputy head in a highly successful head-deputy partnership in a Group 4 nursey-infant school. Over thirteen years they had evolved a tacitly understood system in which, within the unchallenged, overall leadership of the head both served 'instrumental' and 'expressive' functions in respect of the rest of the staff. Moreover, both also performed these functions for each other. This results in overlap, duplication and ambiguity which gave the leadership of the school a kind of 'slack' in human resources which enabled all the staff successfully to withstand the stress, and uncertainty which is a feature of life in school.

Jim Campbell: *The role of the curriculum postholder*

The chapter provides a concise overview of the curriculum postholder's role. Although the title of postholder is likely to be overtaken by notions of curriculum leader or co-ordinator, and by alterations to salary structure and status, Campbell's two-fold classification of the role, with five subdivisions, is likely to remain pertinent for some time. One part of the classification identifies interpersonal skills as a key feature. Certainly these are skills all teachers increasingly need since collaboration, if not collegiality, is being prescribed. The chapter conveys the complex nature of the role and suggests that curriculum change is more likely to be developmental than dramatic. Although the chapter highlights some of the conflicts in the role, particularly in terms of authority and esteem, there is also recognition of the achievements of postholders. Curriculum development is undoubtedly largely dependent upon the skills, motivations and energies of these teachers.

Geoff Southworth: *Primary school headteachers and collegiality*

In this chapter I look at two sets of messages which primary schools are receiving; those to do with leadership and those to do with collegiality. Leadership is closely associated with headship (see also Southworth, 1986) and the first part of the chapter looks at primary headteachers. The idea of a psychology of headship is offered, whilst notions of example, values, loyalty, influence, headteacher succession and the role of the deputy are introduced. One conclusion is that heads need greater support and like Coulson I propose that the head's personal development should not be ignored. Moving onto collegiality, the advocates of collegiality are cited and this is then discussed in terms of the key components of collegiality: the implications for role relations, the need for pre-conditions, interpersonal and group dynamics, and the disturbance collegiality may create

Introduction

for both formal and informal school processes. The conclusion draws attention to the implications which collegiality has for teacher and headteacher development.

Robin Yeomans: *Are primary teachers primarily people?*

This chapter asks some penetrating and awkward questions. It takes on the notion that teachers are both professionals and persons and illustrates, sometimes with a sense of piquancy, the dilemmas of being both. Yeomans offers a way forward by suggesting that the staff group could be developed as an effective task group and support group. In this sense Yeomans adds to the discussion about collegiality. By drawing on social psychology and the theory of groups Yeomans brings a fresh perspective to the idea of teachers in primary schools working collaboratively. However, in offering this help he also makes the case for greater awareness and understanding of group processes in primary staff groups. More than anything he calls for research into primary school groups and relationships.

Jennifer Nias: *Learning the job while playing a part: Staff development in the early years of teaching*

How do teachers learn the job and develop as teachers in schools? This chapter explores these questions using concepts drawn from social psychology. Data from ninety-nine novitiate teachers is examined and a number of significant issues are illuminated. These issues are of importance to teacher, curriculum and school development. The data begin to show how teachers learn the job, feel isolated, gain access to colleagues, survive in the classroom and are helped by professional parents. The influence of the staffroom and membership groups are also discussed. Whilst much of the evidence demonstrates how new teachers use colleagues as exemplars and for guidance, practical assistance and moral support, the chapter goes on to argue that teachers also sustain a sense of personal identity. The picture Nias presents is one where new teachers are offered support by colleagues but because of their personal values these new teachers are selective of the help on offer in order to defend and preserve their individual identity.

Geoff Southworth: *Staff selection or by appointment?*

This is a case study of the appointment of a teacher to a primary school. As such it provides some fresh and, hopefully, valuable data on a little researched aspect of management. The case study demonstrates how for the teachers in the appointing school the process of staff selection is informal. Also the study reveals how these teachers are concerned to find

7

Geoff Southworth

out about the teacher-as-a-person as well as teacher-as-a-professional. The chapter provides insights into teachers working collaboratively and how one head involves and consults staff. There is a review of the literature on staff selection and the chapter ends by asking some questions about how we presently regard the appointment of teachers.

Robin Yeomans: *Leading the team, belonging to the group?*

In this, his second chapter, Robin Yeomans develops some of the ideas in his first chapter, particularly those to do with the staff operating as a group. However, Yeomans also considers what the contemporary reports are advocating and what this means for heads and teachers, particularly curriculum postholders (or co-ordinators as they now look to be called). He looks carefully at a number of important concepts — leadership, membership, roles, and collegiality. In so doing Yeomans picks up many of the ideas presented in sections 1 and 2 and weaves them into his argument. He draws on a range of ideas, some of which are only presently emerging and being applied to primary schools (eg. Primary School Staff Relationship Project; Cambridge Institute of Education 1985–7). The picture which Yeomans draws is of primary schools where the roles of leaders and members are blurred, where *team* does not necessarily equate with *group*, and where interactions between individuals are subtle, complex and ambiguous. Although never intended as such, the chapter could act as a synthesis of many of the ideas in sections one and two.

Geoff Southworth: *Perspectives on the primary curriculum*

The chapter reviews many of the documents published in the early 1980s. A critical stance is taken in respect of how accurately and sensitively classroom issues and children's learning are reflected (or ignored) in the documents. The article asks four questions: What do children need to come to know?; What are the best means of helping children come to know these things?; How do we know the children have learned something? and How do we let those outside school know what the children are doing? These are four questions which seem to me to be also pertinent to managing the curriculum. The conclusion makes the point that school development and management should not seek to eventually 'end up' with improvements in the classroom, as if the classroom were the terminal destination, rather, we should never leave the classroom.

Colin Richards: *The Curriculum from 5 to 16*: Background, content and some implications for primary education.

Colin Richards HMI, offers a very readable summary of what is an important document from HM Inspectors. Richards focuses on the

Introduction

primary years and puts forward both a concise description and some explanation of HM Inspectors' ideas. The section on implications is significant and a number of management issues are raised. For example, demands on classteachers, collegial approaches, conscious planning and evaluation, and staff development. Richards suggest that HM Inspectors are offering 'The Curriculum from 5 to 16' as an attempt to provide a common language and some common markers which enable a national framework to be constructed. Readers may find it useful to link Richard's chapter to the two other articles in this section.

Geoff Southworth: *Further perspectives on the primary curriculum*

In this chapter I try to review HM Inspectors' 'The Curriculum from 5 to 16' and the DES White Paper 'Better Schools'. Readers might like to set my comments concerning the HMI paper alongside Colin Richards' views. Also, since this is a companion chapter to the first chapter in this section, readers will find that the discussion initiated in that chapter continues in this. Once again a critical stance is adopted. Towards the end of the chapter a list of how schools can proceed towards 'getting better' is presented based upon the ideas and prescriptions in the literature. I call it a DIY list for primary school and curriculum management. Readers might consider this list in the light of all the other chapter in this reader. Far from being straightforward I feel it looks increasingly problematical.

Marion Dadds: *Learning and teacher-appraisal: The heart of the matter*

This chapter takes a critical look at teacher appraisal. Marion Dadds asks a series of pertinent and probing questions concerning the contribution appraisal might make to the children's learning and the teacher's development. Why are we getting involved? Who is appraisal for? What are *they* going to do with it when it's done? If appraisal does not treat seriously such key words as 'children', 'teachers', 'learning', 'classrooms', 'support' and 'development' should we be devoting hard-pressed resources to it? Throughout the chapter learning theory is applied to teacher appraisal because the writer regards appraisal as a process whereby teachers should learn about their teaching and the children's development. Hopefully, appraisal should provide opportunities for teachers to talk about and share their concerns and reflections on their teaching. Essentially the nature and effectiveness of appraisal rests on the quality of the relationships that exist in the school.

ILEA: *Key factors for effective junior schooling*

This is an extract from the summary of the main report and presents twelve key factors of effectiveness which the research team identified.

Prior to offering these twelve factors there is a review of those features which appear to make it easier to create an effective school. These include all age primary schools, schools with less than 160 pupils, class size, a good physical environment, and a stable staff group. Readers might like to look at the ILEA findings and see if they are consistent with their own experiences in school. You might also like to use the twelve factors to check against the chapters in this book and see where our emphases lie and if our ideas in any way match ILEA's criteria for effectiveness.

Peter Holly: *Making it count: Evaluation for the developing primary school*

This chapter surveys the main trends in self evaluation in primary schools. Classroom self evaluation, LEA schemes and school self evaluation are included in this overview but the chapter finds all these approaches to have some drawbacks in terms of their ability to fuse individual with institutional development. Consequently, Peter Holly begins to explore what an alternative model of self evaluation might have to look like to bring about meaningful development in the primary school. The chapter revisits and develops a number of the themes which occur across the other readings and which are drawn together in the Endpaper.

Themes

Arising from these contributions a number of themes can be identified. It is not the intention, ahead of the contributions, to make explicit the fine detail of these themes, rather it is merely the intention to present them as an outline list so that the reader might bear them in mind when reading the chapters.

The first theme is *development*. Running through each section is the idea of development : the development of teachers, management, curriculum and schools. All of this is to do with improvement and effectiveness. Yet, when it is all added together, for example the development of curriculum areas, headteachers, evaluation strategies, and the development of participative management, then the scope of development can be seen as considerable not least because of the interactions triggered in all the others by developing any single area.

The second theme is *people* and this is closely connected with development. The development of the curriulum relies on the development of teachers. This is now well known. It is less well recognized that, as a number of the contributions highlight, the development of primary teachers does not simply mean the development of those teachers as professionals but also as *people* since primary teachers make little distinction between person and professional.

Introduction

The third theme is *values*. Primary schools are not just densely populated places because of the number of children and adults who work there, they are also intensely value-populated places. Teachers have strong values, feelings, beliefs and attitudes about their job, their role, the curriculum and the purposes of education. Developing teacher-as-persons logically means that the values which teachers subscribe to must be recognized.

A fourth theme concerns *teachers working together*. The idea of collegial school and of participative management means that formal and informal relationships should be given explicit attention. The implications of teachers working together for the staff as a group, internal relationships, leadership, curriculum development and appraisal should be more widely identified and addressed.

The fifth theme is the *agenda for change*. Almost all the contributors imply developments and changes for primary schools. By no means do these chapters encapsulate the full force of changes bearing down on primary schools. Many other changes could be added: the increasing number of four-year-olds in reception classes, information technology, conditions of employment, and parental involvements are but a few. The size of the agenda for change is huge. When the agenda for change is juxtaposed with the low level of resourcing which primary schools experience then it may be no surprise that the agenda appears overwhelming. Quantitatively, the list is worrying yet, as the contributors consistently portray, the changes are also qualitative in the sense of being to do with personal values and understandings. In other words the agenda for change for primary schools is in *scale* both broad and deep, and in *scope* both professional and personal. Any pairing of these requires sensitive support. To experience all four requires considerable help and support. To be sure 'management' matters and has a part to play, but so too do others and these changes cannot be supported on a shoe-string budget however good the management.

The last theme is the appropriateness of management theory to primary schools. The pressure to take management seriously is considerable. Management can make a difference. However, the writers here appear to see management less as the pronouncement of prescriptive systems and policies than as an invitation to enquire into how a school, and the people therein, 'work'. Perhaps 'managers' in their 'own' primary schools should approach the task of management as a kind of school-based enquiry possibly using these questions:

PURPOSE   What is done?
                      Why is it done?
                      What *else* might be done?
                      What *should* be done?

PLACE	*Where* is it done?
	Why is it done *there*?
	Where *else* might it be done?
	Where *should* it be done?
SEQUENCE	*When* is it done?
	Why is it done *then*?
	When *might* it be done?
	When *should* it be done?
PERSON	*Who* does it?
	Why does *that* person do it?
	Who *else* might do it?
	Who *should* do it?
MEANS	*How* is it done?
	Why is it done *that* way?
	How *else* might it be done?
	How *should* it be done?

(International Labour Office (1978) pp. 101–20)

In using these, or other questions of your own making, school management will become more to do with being curious, imaginative and active. If all staff in the school ask these questions both separately and collectively then management will make a significant and positive contribution to the work of the school.

Hopefully the questions will trigger thoughts and issues which help teachers contemplate their own teaching, the children's learning and set a tone whereby teachers can learn about their own teaching and ways of working together.

References

ALEXANDER, R. (1984) *Primary Teaching*, London, Holt, Rinehart and Winston.
HANDY, C. (1984) *Taken for Granted? Understanding Schools as Organizations*, York, Schools Council/Longman.
INTERNAL LABOUR OFFICE (1978) *Introduction to Work Study*, Geneva, pp. 101–20.
SOUTHWORTH, G. (1986) 'The primary head's burden', *Education*, 1 August, p. 109.

Section One
Roles and Responsibilities

Introduction

This section looks at some of the management roles in a primary school. The focus is restricted to headteachers, deputy heads and curriculum post holders (or co-ordinators as they are likely to be called in the future). The chapters seek to illuminate the nature and demands of these roles, both for those who occupy them and for the schools where the roles are performed.

Alan Coulson begins by providing a careful analysis of the primary head's role. The analysis is a valuable addition to our conception of the primary head's job. Coulson also considers how management training for headship should be approached, both before and after appointment. A major criticism of existing approaches to management development and training is that the focus remains on the individual head's role and their performance of that role, whereas Coulson believes that it is the person of the head, their perceptions and values, which are of essential concern. Finally, Coulson suggests that what is needed is the development of a professional collegial approach to primary school management.

Jennifer Nias' chapter looks at the partnership which has developed between a head and deputy in an Infant and Nursery school. The major focus is on the deputy head. Nias considers the partnership in terms of 'instrumental' and 'expressive' functions and she provides some rich data to illustrate these functions. Because this case study is constructed from data collected over a school year the argument is illuminated by a fund of day-to-day observations. Moreover, being a case study the concluding discussion is based upon what actually took place. Since rather a lot of contemporary management literature and argument is based on less concrete analysis this case study adds greatly to what we know about the head/deputy partnership. This is valuable in two ways. Obviously it helps us understand what this deputy does. Secondly, the case study reveals how a partnership *works*. If teachers are to work together collaboratively, if not collegially, then we need to know rather more about those who are already working collaboratively.

Introduction

Jim Campbell's chapter is also based on research although this time looking at the role of the curriculum postholder. Campbell produces a two-fold classification of the postholders' role. This classification is useful because it helps to show the dimensions of the role and suggests that post holders need to be competent both in their designated curricular area and in terms of interpersonal skills with colleagues. This chapter relates closely to Robin Yeomans article in section two and all the chapters in section three.

My chapter looks at the two sets of messages that are being broadcast to primary schools; those to do with leadership and those to do with collegiality. Because management training for primary schools is largely devoted to primary headteachers this chapter looks at the nature of primary headship. I draw attention to the belief in loyalty, influence and example which heads hold. The implications of these for headteacher succession and deputy heads are also examined. Collegiality is discussed first by citing those who advocate it and then in terms of the components of collegiality — role relations, interpersonal and group dynamics, and the disturbances collegiality may trigger. I conclude by looking at the implications collegiality has for teacher and headteacher development.

It can be seen from these four chapters that primary school management should be less prescriptive and more cautious. What is needed is rather more research and evidence on which to base analysis and diagnosis.

Recruitment and Management Development for Primary Headship

Alan A. Coulson

Introduction

One of the major recent developments in educational planning has been the infusion of funding into programmes of training in management with a consequential increase in provision by institutions of higher education. A wide variety of courses has been provided as a consequence of DES Circular 3/83 and they represent an enormous variety of approaches to the matter. It is clear that there is as yet no general consensus as to what education management is about and there is certainly little agreement on appropriate training approaches. In some ways this is no bad thing because an oversimplified and unitary approach is unlikely to suit the needs of differing sectors and clients. However, some of the provision has been hasty and ill-considered, based on no sound or coherent theories of management or adult learning. Furthermore, it would seem that without a clear understanding of the bases on which training courses are considered, little valid evaluation can take place.

If management courses are to have a chance of fulfilling the expectations now being held out for them — of increasing the confidence and managerial competence of heads and teachers, and thereby improving the schools — there is an urgent need to examine in depth the whole issue of management education for school people. Analyses of key positions may provide starting-points for assessment of training needs, and it is hoped this article will make a contribution to a sound basis for understanding not only what school people need to learn about management, but also how they learn.

Two interlinked areas of concern will be considered here: career development for teachers, especially recruitment to headship, and management training (though the terms management 'education' or 'development' may be preferred as sounding less archaic and authoritarian). Within the latter, modification of the framework of expectations and demands of headship which shape and constrain how headteachers may carry out their functions, is considered an essential complement to the preparation of individuals for management posts.

1 Recruitment

Morgan, Hall and Mackay (1983) recently reported extensive research on the recruitment of secondary heads. They conclude that there are many major deficiencies in the procedures at present employed and suggest improvements. The centrality of the headteacher in school effectiveness is generally accepted and the appointment of heads is acknowledged by LEAS as 'The most important thing we do' (Morgan et al., 1983). Since there is no reason to suppose these points do not apply with equal force at primary as at secondary level, recommendations for the improvement of headteacher recruitment deserve the closest consideration.

As a basis for evaluation of the extent of matching between selection procedures and the nature of the post a full analysis of the job of the primary head is needed. Morgan and Hall (1982) took concepts from Katz's 'Skills of an Effective Administrator' (1974) as their starting-point for looking at the secondary head's job; more recently (Coulson, 1985) a similar task has been undertaken in regard to the primary head's job, employing Mintzberg's *The Nature of Managerial Work* (1973) as the basis of the conceptual framework (see figure 1).

At present (1985), considerable attention is being given to the management training of heads already in post. However, Fiedler (1967), Fiedler *et al.* (1977) and others have for many years been arguing that since the leadership styles and motivational patterns of leaders or managers are relatively stable characteristics of the individual, training based on modifying leadership behaviour (especially *after* appointment) may be of limited value. What is likely to be more effective, according to Fiedler, is more careful matching of person to situation; in other words, a person is more likely to succeed when put into situations which call for his particular management style. If there is validity in this claim, post-appointment training for heads is unlikely to pay substantial dividends in terms of managerial improvement or school effectiveness. All the more reason then for careful attention to be paid to analysis of the work of headship and refinement of recruitment procedures. Increased attention to the overall management needs of schools might also lead away from the present primary school management model of over-dependence on an omnipresent and all-providing head, and towards the recruitment and development of balanced teams of professionally experienced peers. These could contribute a range of complementary capacities and skills towards the management of the schools.

This is not to say that management education has not a valuable part to play in school improvement. But, for success, training needs to be integrated into an overall management development strategy for the teaching profession as a whole, with suitable programmes available to staff at different career stages and levels of seniority. This approach is also advocated by Craig (1982) in the report of his survey of primary heads' perceived training needs. (As far as is known, ILEA is the only local authority which has such a scheme for primary school staff.) Education for different positions within schools, including headship, would best precede teachers' appointment to managerial positions and prepare them for these jobs; it would also be linked to advancement procedures and provide further support, guidance, and development after promotion.

Figure 1 Summary of the head's managerial roles

Chief executive roles

Roles	Description	Representative activities
Interpersonal		
Figurehead	Symbolic head, performing routine legal or social duties	Assembly; signing reports and authorizations
Leader/Supervisor	Responsible for the motivation and coordination of subordinates' work	Embodied in virtually all managerial activities involving subordinates: classroom visits, discussions, etc.
Liaison	Maintenance of network of outside contacts	Correspondence; external committee work; links with LEA people and governors
Informational		
Monitor	Seeks and receives wide variety of information to develop understanding of organization and environment; emerges as nerve centre of internal and external information	Handling mail and contacts concerned primarily with receiving information (eg. observational tours of school; LEA and government circulars and memoranda)
Disseminator	Transmits information to members of staff: some information factual, some involving interpretation and integration of diverse value positions from outsiders	Directing mail and other material to teachers for informational purposes; verbal contacts involving information flow to subordinates
Spokesman	Transmits information to outsiders on schools plans, policies, actions, results, etc: serves as education 'expert' to general public	Governors' meetings; handling contacts involving transmission of information to outsiders

Roles	Description	Representative activites
Decisional		
Entrepreneur	Searches school and its environment for opportunities to initiate change through 'improvement projects'	Reviews of curriculum and policy involving initiation of 'improvement projects'
Disturbance Handler	Responsible for corrective action when school faces unexpected disturbances	*Ad hoc* coping with breakdown of school facilities, unwelcome visitors; discipline
Resources	Responsible for the allocation of school resources of all kinds — in effect the making or approval of all significant decisions	Distribution of human and material resources in accordance with head's 'philosophy' and scale of priorities; timetabling; budgeting
Negotiator	Representing the school at negotiations	Promoting or defending the interests of the school

Leading professional roles

Roles	Description	Representative activities
Goalsetter and Evaluator	Determining the overall character of the school and overseeing progress towards this as a goal	Shaping curriculum and organization; formulating statements of aims (eg. in school prospectus); school self-evaluation
Curriculum Co-ordinator and Developer	Making final decisions as to emphases to be given among curriculum subjects and materials	Keeping informed of curriculum developments; chairing meetings; allocating posts of responsibility for curriculum areas; choice and purchase of materials; classroom supervision of teachers
Teacher	The head's time in classrooms: personal teaching or working alongside teacher colleagues	Scheduled teaching of classes or groups; covering for absent teachers
Exemplar of Professional Values	Displaying behaviours valued by teachers and seen by them as exemplifying 'professionalism'	Willingness to teach; 'commitment' to school; reliability, efficiency, concern for children and teachers; solidarity with teachers' interests

Alan A. Coulson

2 Approaches to Management Development for Heads and Teachers

(a) Introduction and Critique of Present Provision

Despite steady growth over the last couple of decades, school management development in Britain is yet in its infancy. The subject is a very wide and complex one so it is acknowledged that the following account, though derived from twenty years work in schools and many years of attendance and teaching at school management courses, remains a personal and selective one.

First, a brief critique is presented of the general character of many of the courses so far offered and of the orientation of students towards them. Second, four main elements essential to a programme of management for school people are identified: these relate to the individual's conceptual, professional, and personal development, and to his leading role in articulating the school and its environment.

Experience of both attending and contributing to a large number of courses, particularly short courses, for primary school heads and senior staff suggests that these courses are initially attractive for three principal reasons: because of concern with finding ways of coping with new and changing demands in contemporary education, because they offer an opportunity to share ideas and practices with colleagues, and because the course participant, if he is not already a head, hopes that attendance at such a course will aid promotion.

Unfortunately, many of the participants in such programmes seem to come to them mainly in search of factual knowledge and in the hope of learning how to display certain behaviours which have come to be associated with 'leadership'. In other words, the implicit assumption persists that leadership can be trained into people; that a leadership style can be assumed and performed. The person who takes this approach to learning about his relations with colleagues, and particularly subordinates, tends to think in terms of shaping his behaviour in accordance with some kind of leadership 'model'; he seeks to join the ranks of that section of the educational community which is seen as demonstrating proper leadership. The shortcoming of this is its incompleteness. In an unstable context where pluralistic and conflicting demands are made upon schools and the people who manage them, heads (and other colleagues) can no longer simply *perform*, they must continually *learn* and change. Jentz and Wofford (1979), writing of their work with American school principals, conclude that the critical outcome of a leadership development program is not particular new knowledge or behaviour, rather it is trust in the capacity to make new sense, to create new forms of action, and to take action in a context of doubt and uncertainty.

Courses for heads in the United Kingdom normally embrace a variety of activities such as hearing about how other heads run their schools, learning about theories of organization and of management, receiving the advice and direction of experienced practitioners, inspectors and advisers, and, possibly, working on case studies or simulation exercises. Now all these have undeniable value; yet all are schematized, generalized and largely unconnected with the head as a *person*, as an individual.

Employing traditional educational methods such as lectures, discussions, and exercises, most of these courses seem to carry two implications: first, that the course participant is defined as a recipient; he is the object, not the subject, of the endeavour; second, that it is all right to discuss tactics, strategies, policies and practices while only peripherally taking into account the persons involved. In other words, the focus remains upon the individual's professional role-facade. Attention is concentrated upon socializing the individual into the leadership role, the acquisition of ideas and knowledge which heads 'should' have, and upon the displaying of appropriate 'head-like' attitudes and behaviours. The emphasis is on *performing* the role adequately.

In contrast to this is the standpoint adopted by Jentz and Wofford (1979) and argued for here, which is that the *person* of the head, his perceptions and values, are of primary concern. Thus management development needs to make a serious attempt to attend to the personal growth needs of the individual and, at the same time, to integrate this with efforts to increase his sense of professional competence and effectivness.

Argyris (1976, 1982) has shown the crucial difficulty of bringing about significant change among managers by a skills-learning approach unless the new skills are accompanied by a new set of governing values. He concludes:

> Luckily, people judge the credibility of human skills by evaluating what values they serve. This means that those who learn the new skills as gimmicks and tricks will be discovered. It means further that those who wish to gain credibility not only must learn the new skills but also must internalize a new set of values (Argyris, 1982).

Thus no amount of new knowledge acquisition and skill-training will in themselves effect much difference in the practice of headship in schools. Management development also has the task of enabling heads and would-be heads to expose to scrutiny the values underlying their present practices and to help them to adopt values genuinely consonant with the practices and processes they hope to instigate.

As Argyris again has emphasized many times, it is not enough for management development to make executives aware of alternative courses of action and to see their desirability, it is also necessary to help them to learn to produce those actions.

(b) Aspects of Management Development

As suggested at the beginning of the previous section, preparation for headship may be divided into conceptual, professional, personal and environmental aspects. The first two categories will be mentioned only briefly here, and attention is reserved mainly for the personal aspect and the part an adept head may play in shaping the school's environment as well as responding to it.

Conceptual. Management development programmes for heads and teachers need to convey relevant management concepts and strategies drawn from management theory and research outside education as well as inside it. This will lead trainees to acquire the capacity to conceptualize and deliberate upon school issues from a management perspective as well as from the educational standpoint to which they are more accustomed. Moreover, it is important for school people to be able to draw inferences from management experience in other settings, for school management is in many ways similar to management in other spheres as well as in many ways different from it.

Professional. Though it is related to other fields of management, school management is in many respects a special case (Campbell, 1958; Morgan, 1976). Management preparation programmes for school people therefore need to be professionally slanted to take adequate account of the particular features of the school as an organization and the culture of schools and teachers.

Personal. A head's management practice is closely identified with and therefore inseparable from, his personal assumptions, values, perceptions and attitudes. Hence, development by the individual of conceptual and management skills, and the acquisition of deeper understanding of school and teacher culture needs to be accompanied by, and integrated with, his personal development. Professional and conceptual knowledge will be of little avail unless the head can develop working relationships of mutual trust with the wide range of adults with whom he comes into contact, relationships which lie at the very heart of his job.

Personal growth work involves the development of self-confidence, self-awareness and sensitivity to interpersonal processes. It necessitates two potentially threatening elements for some people: intensive feedback to individuals about how they are perceived and experienced by others, and the disturbance or destructuring of each person's established assumptions and expectations in order to enable new perceptions and learning to occur. Because of sensitivity about these issues, development of the person is, as Evans (1983) comments in his report on School Leader Education in Sweden, the most challenging element of management training. Though some otherwise interested or ambitious heads and teachers may seek to avoid the feelings of discomfort or insecurity which may be engendered by the personal development aspect of training, continued neglect of this element will considerably dilute the potential of school management courses to have much real effect. After all, the less open to new experiences and to self-questioning the person is, and the more defensive he tends to be of his present attitudes and practices, the less able he is to benefit from training (Gray and Coulson, 1982).

After three years' experience of the Swedish School Leader Education Programme a substantial number of participants reported personal and attitude change, and Evans (1983) concludes: 'In seeking to define and meet their [British heads'] management development needs the Swedish School Leader Education Programme may have some significant pointers to offer, not least perhaps in its powerful stress upon self-knowledge-personal, professional and institutional (p. 199).'

Since a substantial proportion of the head's managerial actions spring in a fairly spontaneous and *ad hoc* fashion from his way of being — his deeply held values and attitudes — rather than occurring as part of a systematic, well-planned, rational-analytic strategy, the need to focus development at the pre-appointment stage, and upon the *head as a person* is underlined. If school management courses are to contribute to educational creativity and renewal they will need to establish learning situations which can re-create the key features of the trainees' back-at-school work life and provide them with intensive feedback on their performance. Through this process they may be helped to a better understanding of their work and enabled to make 'new sense' of it *experientially* rather than intellectually; then, within the relative 'safety' of the training situation, they may be enabled to risk devising new ideas and experimenting with new forms of action.

'Know thyself' is also the first maxim for managers according to Patrick Nugent (1981). He is not, however, referring to the manager's personal development in quite the same way as has been discussed so far, but to the need for managers to become more aware of whether they prefer the rational mode of thought or the intuitive mode, or whether they feel equally at ease with both. Many teachers and heads are conventionally sceptical about the value of teacher education programmes, including management courses, on the grounds that most are 'all right in theory but no good in practice'. This theory-practice dichotomy is illuminated by recent research on brain function. A number of writers (eg. Ornstein, 1977; Blakeslee, 1980) report research which shows that the left hemisphere of the brain emphasizes sequential, verbal, logical, and analytical information processing, whereas the right hemisphere processes images and spatial relationships simultaneously, making intuitive connections non-verbally. Whereas the left brain clarifies, analyzes and categorizes in order to make meanings explicit, the right unifies (or makes *Gestalts*), works in metaphors, and maintains sensed or implicit meanings. It is suggested, then, that many of the activities of teaching and school management rely more on right than left brain functions, or require integration of the functions of both hemispheres. Thus the 'knowing by experience' of 'flying by the seat of the pants' elements of the head's work remain unarticulated because they are outside verbal consciousness; they may in fact be interpreted as a form of cultivated intuition. The nature of much of the head's work: fragmented, varied, unpredictable, and full of activities of short time duration, is conductive to rapid, intuitive, spontaneous, and even seemingly 'irrational' modes of reaction rather than systematically thought out, planned and analytical responses.

Until recently most management courses, and certainly those for school personnel, have been based almost solely on cognitive, rational models of thought and action (essentially left brain activities). Lack of satisfaction with many of the existing courses, which tend to present tidied-up, abstracted, and conceptualized formulations of school 'reality' ('theory'), results from their inability to reflect adequately the untidy, rapid-paced immediacy of the 'reality' experienced by heads and teachers in schools ('practice'). Nugent's (p. 46) contention that 'many managers tend to be more at ease with the intuitive mode of thought in their everyday functioning, and this leads to their discomfort when they are forced into rational management science approaches', fits closely the situation of many heads and teachers on management courses and has a good deal of pertinence for those responsible for headship training. Furthermore, it is also suggested that Mintzberg's (1976) conclusion that, whereas planning is a left brain activity, the important policy-level processes required to manage an organization rely to a considerable extent on the faculties identified with the brain's right hemisphere, has considerable relevance for preparation of school management staff. There can be little doubt, however, that outstanding heads are the ones who can couple effective right-hemisphere processes (hunch, judgment, synthesis, and so on) with effective processes of the left (articulateness, logic, analysis, and so on). It may be concluded then that for headteachers and managers undergoing training, just as for learners in other spheres of education, 'Significant learning combines the logical and the intuitive, the intellect and the feeling, the concept and the experience, the idea and the meaning. When we learn in that way then we are whole' (Rogers 1983, p. 20).

A number of forward-looking management decision-making courses, such as that described by Taggart, Robery and Taggart (1982), have attempted to engage students' left *and* right hemispheres in order that more complete understanding of management processes may take place. It is suggested that serious consideration be given to similar approaches to be employed on courses for school staff.

Environmental. At the same time as a wider variety of interest groups among the general public are becoming more engaged in educational matters, particularly the work of school, the whole educational enterprise is increasing in complexity and accelerating its rate of change. It has therefore become more difficult even for those professionally involved in education to keep abreast of the rapid flow of information being generated. It requires considerable time and effort to be able to digest the information and to maintain a grasp on the varied, complex and often subtle issues of educational decision-making.

Therefore, courses for heads and other would-be education managers certainly have a major part to play in informing school staff of administrative and legislative matters affecting them and in helping them to explore ways of responding to the demands imposed by various external constituencies. However, in addition to this re-active aspect of relations with the individuals and agencies who constitute the school's environment, courses would do well to help trainees to be more pro-active in relation to these same persons and groups.

A professionally well-informed and personally secure head who can gain and retain reciprocal trust and mutual confidence with the officers of his local authority, parents, governors and other key figures can play a significant educational role external to the school by creating the social and psychological climate in which it may flourish. In many of his managerial roles, *Figurehead, Liaison, Disseminator, Spokesman, Negotiator* and *Goalsetter and Evaluator* (see Figure 1) for instance, he has continual opportunities to adjust, influence and re-shape the framework of expectations held for the school by outsiders. In the process too he can interpret and negotiate his own version of the headship role with the significant members of his role-set (governors, parents, advisers and so on).

The head's previous career as a classroom teacher is unlikely to have prepared him for much that he will need to do as a head — the school's manager. Work with a variety of adults, both individually and in groups, within the loosely organized context of the school and its environment, calls for flexibility, a high tolerance of ambiguity, and particular skills. Such work puts a premium on what Kaplan (1982) has called 'reticular competence'. The word reticular means 'weblike' or 'like a network', and reticular competence is defined as the ability to work effectively in social networks — that is, in settings larger than a group and considerably more complex and disconnected. It involves not only the possession of a diverse set of contacts in an inter-group network, but also the knowledge of when to call upon them and in what configuration.

Similarly, the head's own functions or roles as indicated earlier (see figure 1) may be seen as components in his own personal, internal, loosely-organized system. Management development may assist the individual in identifying and activating those aspects of his role in which he is less competent and in learning to evoke all aspects in more appropriate configurations.

Also vital to the head is political competence to fathom the value-laden conflicts of interest in the loosely-organized system of the school and its environment, and to manage his own values and functions amidst these conflicts (Brown, 1980).

Provision for education likely to aid the development of reticular and political skills needs to be built into the design of headship development programmes, As McCall (1976) has pointed out in regard to leadership training in general, to be effective, training situations and simulations need to capture the important elements of the target organization and the management roles within it. A similar approach is required to that discussed earlier in relation to evoking and integrating both the left and right brain functions.

(c) Development of a Professional Collegial Approach to Primary School Management

Some years ago it was argued that for the sake of the organizational health of schools and the professional status of teachers, as well as for the welfare of heads themselves, it is desirable to modify the traditional paternal model of primary school headship (Coulson, 1976). The increased demands placed upon schools and their heads since then make this shift increasingly a necessity as well as a desirable state of affairs. Though the bulk of responsibility for the school remains with the head, less and less confidence can be placed in the capacity of a single individual to adequately carry out all the steadily proliferating tasks of school management.

The case for wider sharing of the duties normally associated with headship does not rest only upon the desirability of sparing conscientious heads from becoming overburdened and strained, but also upon the growing realization that in the present-day school situation any individual, even the head, has, on his own, limited powers to effect change. Referring to curriculum, for example, Taylor, Reid, Holley and Exon (1974: 67) suggest that:

> effective strategies can be developed only if we set about the task of studying schools in terms of 'roles and relationships, [the] interlocking ideas, practices, values and expectations that are the "givens" not requiring thought or deliberation' (Sarason, 1971). For too long it has been assumed that the shortcomings and failures of educational systems can be understood in terms of the inadequacies, obstinacies and motivations of individuals — both those who exert their influence within the system and those who bring it to bear from outside. More trust can be placed in approaches which, while recognizing the contribution of personal

characteristics, lay their major emphasis on the ways in which individuals are constrained by the role which the structure and traditions of the system define for them.

It seems desirable then to direct management development towards a focus on organization development (OD) for the school as a whole as well as towards individuals in, or destined for, senior positions. The traditional insitutionalized supremacy of the head might then increasingly give way to the potentially much more exacting task of building, managing, and coordinating within the school a peer group of colleagues, and outside it leading the colleague group in dialogue with the local authority and the public on the subject of their discharge of the school's responsibilities (Eliott, 1979).

Summary

(a) Given that the head is generally accepted as the hub of the school, recruitment procedures for this vital position need to be much more rigorous and sophisticated.

(b) Close analysis of the nature of the head's work is seen as a prerequisite to improvement in recruitment processes.

(c) Primary school headship is not reducible to a set of prescriptive statements or a body of knowledge. Thus the diversity and subtle nature of much of the head's work make it difficult to introduce improved working practices through traditional training methods with a mainly cognitive basis.

(d) For management development to succeed it is essential for heads to try to learn continuously about their own situations in order to make 'new sense' of them. Futhermore, if training programmes are to have any significant effect on the schools, self-study and personal development are considered the most significant element to concentrate upon.

(e) Following Argyris (1982), it is proposed that particular emphasis in training be given to critical scrutiny of the governing values which underpin the present practice of headship.

(f) In the course of teaching school people to employ concepts and analyses from management as well as from education to their work, training programmes must take careful account of the occupational culture of teachers and the special character of schools as organizations.

(g) Left and right brain processes need to be attended to in order to cater for training in the more intuitive and spontaneous elements of headship as well as those of a rational-analytic nature.

(h) The notion of 'recticular competence' is introduced to highlight the need for heads to develop skills related to working effectively through diverse contacts with individuals and social networks.

(i) Finally, it is suggested that the training of individuals upon or after appointment to headship is much less likely to pay useful dividends than management and organization development directed towards the workgroup or staff as a whole. Pre-appointment preparation and ongoing development opportunities for heads and others could be effectively integrated into this broader framework.

References

ARGYRIS, C. (1976) Theories of action that inhibit individual learning, *American Psychologist*, Vol. 31, No. 9, pp. 638–54.

ARGYRIS, C. (1982) The executive mind and double-loop learning, *Organizational Dynamics*, Autumn, pp. 5–22.

BLAKESLEE, T.R. (1980) *The Right Brain: A New Understanding of the Unconscious Mind and its Creative Powers* New York, Anchor Press/Doubleday.

BROWN, L.D. (1980) Planned change in underorganized systems, in CUMMINGS, T.G. (Ed.), *Systems Theory for Organizational Development*, New York, Wiley.

CAMPBELL, R.F. (1958) What peculiarities in educational administration make it a special case? in HAPLIN, A.W. (Ed.), *Administrative Theory in Education*, University of Chicago.

COULSON, A.A. (1976) The role of the primary head, in PETERS, R.S. (Ed.) *The Role of the Head* London, Routledge and Kegan Paul, pp. 92–108. Reprinted in BUSH, T., GLATTER, R., GOODEY, J., and RICHES, C. (Eds.), *Approaches to School Management*, London, Harper and Row.

COULSON, A.A. (1985) The managerial behaviour of primary school heads, *Collected Original Resources in Education* (CORE) Vol. 9, No. 1.

CRAIG, I. (1982) Training needs of primary headteachers, *Educational Management and Administration*, Vol. 10, No. 1, pp. 17–22.

EVANS, H.K. (1983) A report on School Leader Education in Sweden (1976–83), *School Organization*, Vol. 3, No. 2, pp. 191–204.

ELLIOTT, J. (1979) The case for school self-evaluation, *Forum*, Vol. 22, No. 1, pp. 23–5.

FIEDLER, F.E. (1967) *A Theory of Leadership Effectiveness*, New York, McGraw-Hill.

FIEDLER, F.E., CHEMERS, M.M. and MAKER, L. (1977) *Improving Leadership Effectiveness: The Leader Match Concept*, (revised edition) New York, Wiley.

GRAY, H.L. and COULSON, A.A. (1982) Teacher education, management and the facilitation of change, *Educational Change and Development*, Vol. 4, No. 1, pp. 17–35.

JENTZ, B.C. and WOFFORD, J.W. (1979) *Leadership and Learning: Personal Change in a Professional Setting*, New York, McGraw-Hill.

KAPLAN, R.E. (1982) Intervention in a loosely organized system: An encounter with non-being, *Journal of Applied Behavioural Science*, Vol. 18, No. 4, pp. 425–32.

KATZ, R.L. (1974) Skills of an effective administrator, *Harvard Business Review*, No. 52, pp. 90–102.

McCall, M.W. (1976) Leadership research: Choosing gods and devils on the run, *Journal of Occupational Psychology*, Vol. 49, pp. 138–53.

Mintzberg. H. (1973) *The Nature of Managerial Work*, London, Harper and Row.

Mintzberg, H. (1976) Planning on the left side and managing on the right, in Kolb, D.A., Rubin, I.M. and McIntyre, J.M. (Eds.), *Organizational Psychology: A Book of Readings*, New York, Prentice-Hall.

Morgan, C. (1976) *Management in Education — Dissimilar or Congruent?* Course E321, Unit I. Open University

Morgan, C., Hall, V. and Mackay, H. (1983) Selecting heads: the Post Project 1 and 2. *Education*, 8 July and 23 September.

Nugent, P.S. (1981) Management and modes of thought, *Organizational Dynamics*, Spring, pp. 44–59

Ornstein, R.E. (1977) *The Psychology of Consciousness*, New York, Harcourt Brace, Jovanovich, 2nd edition.

Rogers, C. (1983) Learning to be free, *Times Educational Supplement* (September 30) pp. 20–1.

Sarason, S.R. (1971) *The Culture of the School and the Problem of Change*, Boston, MA, Allyn and Bacon.

Taggart, W., Robey, D. and Taggart, B. (1982) Decision Styles Education: An Innovative Approach, *Exchange*, Vol. 7, No. 2, pp. 17–24.

Taylor, P.H., Reid, W.A., Holley, B.J. and Exon, G. (1974) *Purpose, Power and Constraint in the Primary School Curriculum*, Basingstoke, Macmillan.

One Finger, One Thumb: A Case Study of the Deputy Head's Part in the Leadership of a Nursery/Infant School

Jennifer Nias

Discussing the appointment of her deputy, the head said 'I actually chose another candidate, the Governors chose Julia. Julia knows this'.

The deputy said:

> I desperately wanted to be a head, desperately. I planned to be a head by the time I was 40, that was my ambition. I was 36 when I got the job and I reckoned that four years was a fair time to give to a school ... I then started to apply for jobs which just happened to coincide with numbers falling and there were very few suitable jobs available ... I did get very frustrated at one stage and found it quite hard to cope with. Realizing also that I was getting older and they wanted younger people. Very few jobs came up. I got interviews for all that I applied for ... but obviously I was not what they were looking for. It's an easy excuse, I suppose, to try not to feel such a failure ... It was quite hard, it's hard to go back and actually face the staff because they're super, but you know, they must think, well, she can't be any good. Your own image begins to fail.

After thirteen years and six interviews she is still at the school. Yet as a participant observer in the school I constantly noted instances of collaboration, mutual support or friendship between the head and deputy. As the year progressed I became more and more aware that the partnership between them was an immensely productive one, enabling each of them to enhance her own and the other's contribution to the school. This chapter is an attempt to analyze the deputy's part in this relationship, using Etzioni's (1964) notion that leadership has both instrumental and expressive dimensions (where 'instrumental' refers to task definition and achievement and 'expressive' encompasses the affective and pastoral aspects of interactions within the organization). I argue that both head and deputy had an instrumental and expressive part to play in the school (that is there was none of the 'splitting' advocated by Burnham, 1968). Moreover, though the precise nature of the functions each carried out reflected a division of labour based upon the nature of their two personalities and upon the head's unchallenged responsibility for and therefore authority in the school, the differentiation between them in management terms was neither tightly defined nor rigid. In the parts that they played in the adult community each could, and often did, stand in for the other, creating a structure in which ambiguity went hand in hand with flexibility and resilience. Further, head and deputy each played both types of role in respect of each other, thereby increasing the capacity of both to meet the instrumental and expressive demands of pupils, parents, administrators and colleagues. The resulting strength of their relationship enhanced the self-confidence of each of them in dealing with management problems, reduced the strain upon them and, because it was a source of pleasure to them both, increased their job satisfaction.

Had this relationship been an exclusive one it could, of course, have had the effect of splitting the two teachers charged with responsibility for the management of the school from the rest of the staff, thereby opening the door to any number of weaknesses in, for example, its communication and decision making systems. It lies beyond the scope of this chapter to show that this was not the case, but evidence presented elsewhere (Nias 1987) demonstrates that interdependence was a characteristic of the whole staff and not just of one unit within it. Nor is it the purpose of this chapter to comment on the effectiveness of the school or its management. Rather my concern has been to understand and document the partnership between head and deputy and to explain how it was formed and sustained. It is however relevant that this was one of the six schools selected by the Cambridge Institute of Education's Primary Schools Staff Relations Project as offering a 'positive model of adult relationships'.

There is no available evidence to show whether or not an effective partnership between head and deputy is unusual in primary schools. There has been little empirical research on the head and very little of that is qualitative (see Coulson 1980; Management and the School Course Team, 1981; Whitaker, 1983). Research into the role and behaviour of deputies is even less easy to find and much of what there is was conducted by questionnaire (eg. Coulson and Cox, 1975; Coulson, 1976). As far as I know, no study exists which looks ethnographically at the roles of the head and deputy in English primary schools or at the relationship between them. I have therefore made very little use of the available literature in this chapter.

In this chapter I have chosen for two reasons to focus on the part played by the deputy in this management partnership. There is now ample evidence (eg. DES, 1977; HMI, 1984) that the nature and quality of schools of all phases depends on the leadership of the head. Because this school is no exception the contribution of the head is described more fully in Nias (1987); I did not feel that it needed further emphasis here. Secondly, as I worked in the school I was increasingly struck by the extent to which the head was supported by her deputy and by the part which the latter played in the school as a whole. Yet the sparse published work on primary deputies tends to perceive them as powerless and ineffectual. The disparity between this picture and my experience called for further examination.

Data Collection

The school was a Group 4 4–7 nursery and infant school, with 210 pupils on roll, about a third of whom were of Asian origin. One teacher and two welfare assistants were funded by Section 11 payments. Altogether, apart from the head there were seven full-time teaching staff (plus a part-timer in the summer term) one full time nursery nurse and four part-time welfare helpers. In addition an Asian welfare helper visited the school two afternoons a week to do mother-tongue work with small groups. The school also had a part-time secretary and a full-time caretaker. The head had no timetabled teaching responsibility but was closely involved with all the children, individually and in assembly. Pupils came from a wide range of social backgrounds, from unemployed manual workers to well paid professionals. The school enjoyed a good reputation locally and within the authority and had much support from its parents. The building was an old one, adapted in the 1920s from community use and modernized in 1982. The offices of the head and secretary were fairly central but the deputy's classroom, at one end of the building and down two flights of stairs, was easily accessible only to the head and one of the other teachers.

I worked as a part-time staff member in the school from mid-October 1985 to the end of the summer term, 1986, and again during early September 1986. I spent the equivalent of one and a half days a week there, but in two or three week blocks spread evenly through the year. This arrangement enabled me to work at some point alongside all the teaching and non-teaching staff and I also undertook a one week 'shadow study' of the head. For one week in the spring term she and the deputy filled in 'time-task' sheets (15 minute intervals and a classification of task drawn from my observations of their activities). I also attended parents' evenings, open evenings and the summer fete.

I used the familiar methods of participant observation: jottings in a pocket notebook which I converted every night into lengthy, reflective, dictated fieldnotes, then, towards the end of the summer term, semi-structured interviews of all staff members, teaching and non-teaching. I also interviewed the head and the deputy in the spring term when it was known that the former was going into hospital for an unknown length of time, and again, informally, in the summer term. Interviews, usually lasting about one and a half hours and all but one on the school premises, were tape recorded, transcribed and copies given to interviewees for checking and clearance. This chapter has been cleared with participants.

I experienced all the often-rehearsed difficulties of the participant observer (see McCall and Simmons, 1969; Burgess, 1984), of the researcher-as-teacher and teacher-as-researcher (see eg. Pollard, 1984). However, the school is used to visitors, students and volunteers and I felt that by my second block of time at the school I was fully accepted by children and staff. Certainly, as I became more accustomed to working within a nursery-infant school (most of my previous experience had been in junior and middle schools) I had to fight hard against the well-known anthropological tendency to 'go native'.

As well as industrial action (which did not affect this school) the staff faced a number of anxieties during the year, the biggest of which were that in the spring term the head became ill with the possibility of long-term absence and that at the same time there was an unexpected confrontation with some parents, involving the parent governor. In addition, the deputy herself had major domestic worries and preoccupations throughout the year.

In this chapter I have used only my own recorded observations and the interviews with head and deputy. I have not attempted to triangulate their perceptions with the staff interviews (though this is done in Nias, 1987). Instead, I have tried to analyze the relationship as nearly as possible from their perspectives, to present, as it were, the insiders' view. It could be argued that my fieldnotes are in this sense no more illuminating than staff comments; however they do present, in a way that the latter do not, a nearly contemporary account of events.

Similarities and Differences

On first acquaintance, the head, Audrey Proctor, and her deputy, Julia Harris, appear somewhat similar — both are middle-aged, well built, smiling. Yet, as Julia said of the staff in general:

> Do you really think we're alike? We may look alike, but we're all different, because we have very different experiences of family life, education, marriage, background.

Miss Audrey Proctor, in her early 50s, has been twenty years in this headship. After a disrupted wartime schooling, she went as a boarder to a girls' public school and then trained as a teacher. She is widely known for her work in multi-cultural education and shortly before Julia's appointment completed a course of full time further study. Artistic and musical, she uses and enjoys these talents in her private life and in school. She is a committed Christian, closely involved with her local church and ensuring that school assemblies are overtly religious in tone and content.

Mrs Julia Harris is in her late 40s. She left her mixed grammar school at sixteen and after a brief spell of nursing, married at nineteen. The decision to train as a mature student for teaching was a joint family one and she enjoys a good deal of support from her husband. She had taught for four years in one school before coming to this school as deputy. Outside her work she is involved in community affairs in the village in which she and her family (husband, son, and disabled widowed mother) live.

Despite their different life experiences, both women share certain attitudes to their work. Both feel the school is vitally important to them, yet both have full lives outside it. Both care deeply about children, especially the unhappy and disadvantaged, and strive to help each pupil develop whatever talents he/she may have. Both are committed to 'standards', though they found it hard to define these. Similarly, both claimed all the staff (including themselves) shared certain values but could not easily articulate them. Audrey felt:

> They are concerned with the education of the whole child. They all have a common respect and concern for other people, which is expressed as courtesy and acceptance. There's a code of behaviour in little things, like standing up when a visitor comes into the room and shaking hands, certain standards of dress, accepting, for example, that if the phone rings they should leave the room while I am answering it. These little things. Also they'd all want the education we provide for their own children.

Julia saw them as being:

> A commitment to the job; caring about people; professional integrity; the desire to get the best for and give the best to children.

To a marked degree, these values are evident in the way they relate to children and to each other (see Nias, 1987).

Instrumental Functions: The Head

Both women were clear that the goals of the school would be best met if final authority were left with the head. In eight years of headship before Julia was appointed, Audrey had constantly been frustrated by deputies whom she perceived as challenging her right to run the school and by teachers who seemed to be making independent decisions on matters of school policy. Partly in consequence of this she felt the school made relatively slow progress towards the goals she had for it.

The partnership between Audrey and Julia is therefore built upon a shared understanding that Audrey is ultimately responsible for and in charge of the school, Audrey felt:

> From the start, she was so willing to support and help me ... there wasn't this awful feeling that perhaps the staff were saying things behind my back or anything like that. If they did, she would handle it so well, (four years ago) when I was ill for some weeks she said, 'But you know that it's your school and whatever I do I will always remember that it's your school'.

She contrasted this with her earlier experience of having a year's secondment and finding on her return that her position had been usurped:

> I was in the playground on my fourth day back and I said to a parent 'Can I help you?' and she said 'No thank you, I want to see the head'.

As she pointed out to me on my first day, the staff always addressed her as 'Miss Proctor'. Moreover I never heard any one refer to her by any other name, no matter how well they knew her out of school. For her part, Julia said:

> Miss Proctor likes to know everything that goes on. That's not because she doesn't trust us, as some people sometimes think, it's because it reduces the likelihood of errors and failings. She can have the overall picture, which we can't have, and that enables her to tie up loose ends. Ultimately, I think everyone feels, well she's the head, and that's fine. We've had our chance to have our say but it's her decision in the end. I'm not in competition with the head ...

Further, reacting to the news that Miss Proctor was to go into hospital during the spring term:

> I feel that it's Miss Proctor's school and while she's away I'm not going to turn it into my school. Therefore what decisions I make I will try to make as I think she would want them. If she's well enough I shall contact her over any big decision, because I do see that as my job: a caretaker, not to start making radical changes just to be able to say 'Well I've done this'.

Her actions in both formal and informal situations consistently bore out her acceptance of Miss Proctor's authority.

In short, the head was the obvious and undisputed leader of the school. In this capacity she decided upon the school's goals, communicated these to the staff and ensured their acceptance of them. To these ends, as her 'task-time' sheets confirm, she controlled the overall organization of the school. As Julia said:

> It's her plan, her decision, we do all meet together, but it's her ideas of how to organize the staff, the numbers and staffing ... Because she's around the school all the time she's able to pick out where we need to look at things and as head she then defines the path we're going to take.

She also controlled the formal curriculum (Julia felt 'Miss Proctor feels that it's her responsibility, though we all chip in with our ideas') stock and ordering, admissions, correspondence and, apart from the routine matters, all contacts with parents. She was able to do all this the more effectively because of the care and concern with which she kept in personal touch with staff, pupils and parents. Julia put it quite clearly:

> Miss Proctor is the leader ... she doesn't like people to tell her how she's going to run the school. She's very happy to hear your advice, your thoughts ... but she decides. And rightly so.

The deputy's conscious and unconscious acceptance of a subordinate role in the formal hierachy of the school conveyed to the staff and outsiders alike her total solidarity with the head. Commenting on a particular action taken by a parent in the absence of the head from school one day Julia said, with evident satisfaction:

> She's sussed out that she can't play one of us off against the other. Its finally dawned on her that Miss Proctor and I do tell each other what's going on.

For her part, the head was aware of her deputy's unshakeable loyalty and of the latter's personal and professional qualities and was quick to give her public recognition.

Instrumental Functions: The Deputy

By now it may appear that the deputy had little authority and few tasks of any significance to perform. Indeed, the head had difficulty in describing what her deputy did:

> Mrs Harris does all the rotas for playground duty, she does assembly once a week. She does so many things; anything that's not done, she does, really.

Julia concurred:

> If anyone asks me what I do, I tell them I change the toilet rolls, make sure there's soap in the loo, try and keep the staffroom carpet clean, try to keep the place as pleasant as I can.

One Finger and One Thumb

Reflecting on her participation in the local deputy heads' group she said:

> I always feel very conscious when people say, 'I'm a deputy head and I do all the ordering and I do all this and all that'. I can't classify any of the things that I do.

Later, in answer to the question 'what would a new deputy find difficult about coming into this school?', she replied:

> It would depend on her past experience and her expectations. She would probably find it very difficult that there are no concrete tasks or job specification. Audrey doesn't work that way. I had to find my own role and my own level. Even then, you've got to be prepared to change it as new needs develop in the school. Just like classroom teaching, you've got to adapt to the situation you find and not think that you've got the answer for ever.

Yet, as a participant observer, I rapidly became aware of how much she did, other than as a class teacher, a fact which was confirmed by her 'task-time' sheets. Overall, she had fewer interactions with parents and outside agencies than the head, but her daily contacts were more varied and lasted for less time. Every day I noted frequent incidents in which she intervened, acted, organized, facilitated. On several occasions I logged her activities during the day. This is a typical example in early March:

> Between her arrival and 8.50 am she had taken and dealt with phone calls from a parent, from Ruth about her absence and a message for Sarah. She had fielded Kath who was in a state because her windscreen had broken and arranged for her temporary absence to be covered — and done her usual round of the classrooms with a smile and a word for everybody. Being without Ruth she dealt singlehanded with the cloakroom and getting the children in, and then at assembly fed Miss Proctor a cue which enabled her to comment on care in the use of crayons. At the same time, she was alert to S's behaviour in assembly and my difficulties with him. On return to the classroom, she rearranged the morning's programme to cater for Ruth's absence and my presence. While I was in the classroom with her she addressed me two or three times and pulled me into what was going on, by saying 'Miss Nias, what would you do about so and so?' and encouraged me to participate in conversations that she was having with the children. At break, she sent messages for the children to go to a different exit because of the state of the playground, had a word with Kath who was on playground duty and was there at the door again ten minutes later, seeing the children in and intervening in a playground squabble. In the meantime, she had checked that no student was outside,

found her rosta for them and chivvied the recalcitrant one into the playground. In the staffroom she was on her feet at the two minute warning, with 'That was the warning, girls ...' After break she noticed that the cold water was not running and on her way to lunch she told the caretaker; also warned the dinner ladies about the ladder left by the maintenance men in the main thoroughfare. She was surrounded by laughter over lunch, a hilarious conversation about awful experiences in hospital led by Miss Proctor. As soon as she'd finished, Miss Proctor whisked her away with Sarah to discuss the forthcoming governors' meeting. At afternoon break she was introduced to the new Asian welfare helper, on her first visit to the school, and was called over to talk to her, I think to draw up some kind of schedule for her. After school, having organized Kath's group and the supply teacher who is to cover for her tomorrow, she remembered to introduce me to the latter and apologized for not having done so before. While we were talking two parents came in to hear their children read. Both were received in an open, friendly fashion and there was an individual word for them and their children. About 4 o'clock her husband appeared to fetch her, to collect her car which was being serviced. They were going to Cambridge to see her mother in hospital. After school, I asked her how she managed to stay on top of all the things that she does and thinks about. Answer: 'I don't always, I have to make lists, but at the start of every day I think about it all. I think about the people first and the jobs come later. For example, when I woke up this morning I thought "I know Kath's having her car serviced, I must find out if she's alright ..." That's what I often do. I decide what I'm going to do while I'm awake at night.' (Fieldnote)

As this extract suggests, her main instrumental role was as a communicator. This role was recognized by the head:

> She does her morning round, if there's a problem, if somebody's not feeling very well she'll let me know; making sure that all the staff do know dates; reminding people if anybody's coming; putting up notes in the staffroom to remind people; letting me know if stock is likely to run out.

and by the deputy:

> I do a lot of organizing and letting people know things — like visitors and dates for staff meetings.

However, though formally recognized, much of this communication took place informally. It was informal in two senses. First, it was apparently casual, even haphazard, its effectiveness depending on Julia's alertness and the goodwill and the good sense of individuals. For example:

> I asked Margaret: 'If you're on playground duty how do you know what's been decided in the staffroom?' Reply: 'Well somebody who was in there will make sure that you're told, usually Julia does, but someone will'. (Fieldnote)

> The nursery teacher said, 'We don't get up (to the staffroom) at break so we sometimes miss out on things that are going on. We have to be alert, though Julia is very good, especially on her morning round'. (Fieldnote)

Further extracts from fieldnotes show the informal way in which staff meetings were arranged:

> There was a staff meeting on Monday at lunchtime, which ran out of time, Miss Proctor said another meeting was needed; Julia quickly said, 'I can't manage Thursday, because I shan't be here', so it was settled that it was Friday. When I went in at break there was a sign on the mantelpiece saying 'Staff Meeting on Wednesday'. I asked Julia about this change. She said that when, as the meeting was breaking up, she suggested Friday, Miss Proctor had chipped in and said, 'That's too late, I think we need it earlier than that', so Julia had grabbed the staff as they left the room and checked that Wednesday was alright with them. Julia said 'The only one who may not know is Rosemary and I'll have to check individually with her'. I cross-checked with Kath about how the date of the meeting had been fixed and she thought it was still Friday. 'I only read the notice about the things we needed to talk about, because I thought we'd decided on Friday. I suppose I'd better go and read the other notice.' (Fieldnote)

> At the end of the afternoon break there was another *ad hoc* meeting suggested for tomorrow lunchtime, to finish up the details left from Tuesday's agenda. The way this was arranged was for Julia to go round each member of staff saying 'Is tomorrow alright? and then as she reached me she said 'Now its only Sarah' (who was on playground duty). (Fieldnote)

Even Julia's 'morning round' had grown up in response to circumstances rather than to a policy decision. As she explained:

> When I came I always made a point of going in to the classrooms — saying hello to everybody, to get to know people as much as anything ... My morning round really started when the change in traffic patterns meant Miss Proctor could no longer get in early to school and since I hoed locally we agreed that I'd get there first thing. Then we had some very unreliable members of staff who wouldn't turn up so I had to go and check whether they were in or

not and make arrangements for the children to be cared for. So then I began to see it more as a tour rather than just a sort of relationship ... I developed this way of trying to make sure people remembered because I know everybody isn't too good at remembering ... but I sometimes query whether I do it too much and they rely on me to the point that they don't bother to remember things themselves. And then I don't know whether that's good for them.

The deputy's role as communicator was also informal in the sense that it depended upon a sensitive capacity to pick up and interpret the casual remark or the unspoken response. She saw it this way:

I think that I probably have a bit more of an informal contact with the staff than Miss Proctor does, although I think that she has very good relationships with the staff ... and she does communicate well with them. Perhaps I have a broader knowledge. Simply because I probably spend more time with them ... It's picking up the hidden signals and hidden clues ... (that's one of the values of my rounds) it's easier to pick up a problem at the start of the day than it is at lunch-time, to see whether somebody is unhappy about something, has got some personal problem or a worry.

This perceptiveness was in evidence all day long, as one example from many in my fieldnotes suggests:

Today I was ticked off by the cook for taking yoghurt when I hadn't asked for it. I apologized and we parted good friends, but as I left the hatch (which is some distance from the staff dining table) Julia said 'Is everything alright?' (Fieldnote)

In fact Julia herself saw the deputy as a go-between, someone 'who will keep the head informed, make sure they're not missing out on any of the grass roots side'. She put it this way:

I do think that it's part of my brief, to be in the staffroom. I try not to spend my time in my room. It makes it harder in a lot of ways but I do think it's important. For the same reason I have dinner with the staff always ... I can also count on the fact that the staff will talk to me so that I can do my job as communicator. They'll often come and talk to me about something they would like to raise with Miss Proctor but they don't want to make a formal approach to her, like the cleaners, for example ... so I listen a lot and say things like 'Well I'll mention it to Miss Proctor', which is what people actually want me to do because they obviously think that I can cope without making a big scene. It's not that it's anonymous, people are quite happy for me to say 'So and so's worried about this'; 'Did you notice that so and so?' It's just that if it comes through me it's less formal.

Julia also had the opportunity to deputize for her head, a role in which she was encouraged by Miss Proctor who regretted that someone so competent should not have a headship. Referring to Julia's 'depth of sensitivity, warmth and clarity of thought', she said:

> To be truthful, it doesn't worry me that I may be away for two or three weeks (in hospital). I'm glad she will have a chance of running the school.

For her part Julia afterwards said that she had 'thoroughly enjoyed being acting head, on this occasion and on similar, longer ones, in the past'. When the head was absent, even for an afternoon, she made it obvious she was in charge. Early on I noted:

> In the staffroom at lunchtime Julia came in and said to everybody in general and me in particular 'Did you know Miss Proctor's out this afternoon at a headteacher's meeting? If you need anything come to me'. (Fieldnote)

I saw similar incidents on several occasions.

Without challenging the head's authority, she also had considerable influence on the staff, a fact of which she was aware. Recalling her arrival at the school, 'which was difficult because there were two camps, the ones that had approved of what the acting head was doing and the ones who were behind Miss Proctor', she felt that she had 'stopped the split developing further. Also because of my positive attitude that I adopted generally'. When she was sharing a teaching situation (eg. watching a video, taking children out) the other staff members always waited for her to take the lead or assume responsibility. She also influenced the formation of school policy. For example, though she took the role of interpreter at staff meetings her view often prevailed. Moreover, she encouraged people by example, encouragement and subtle intervention to think about the ways in which they carried these policies out. She knew that she affected 'standards of punctuality, for example' and after watching one incident, I noted:

> She seldom draws attention to things that people have done wrong, and never in a way that makes them feel ashamed, threatened or undervalued. But the message is clear. (Fieldnote)

She could, however, be forthright as well as oblique. I recorded one occasion on which she and another teacher had an outspoken, face-to-face argument and the head recalled that she had said to a visiting HMI 'I'm sorry but we don't smoke in this school'. In the spring term there was an incident involving parents and a parent governor which provoked great staff anxiety and anger. Observing Julia's reaction as the crisis rumbled on I noted:

> Once again, I am impressed by the extent to which she offers a very effective and important form of leadership within the school which is the more effective because it complements rather than competing with Miss Proctor's. (Fieldnote)

Reflecting on her failure to obtain a headship, she summed her position up:

> My father was the one who actually in the end helped me to come to terms with it. He was an ambitious man himself, he understood, and he sat there one day and asked me, 'Well, why do you want to be a head? Do you want to be a head just to say, I'm the head of the school? What can you do as head that you can't do as a deputy?' When I talked it through with him I realized that as deputy you can do an awful lot of influencing — it does not have to be seen — and the things that are of value are the things that you know that people do not see. You know your own worth, you know how you can change things, so you can get the satisfaction of that.

My observations confirmed that she did indeed wield a powerful influence over both pupils and staff.

Expressive Functions: Head and Deputy

Head and deputy both also saw themselves as playing an expressive role in relation to the staff, teaching and non-teaching. The head made her own daily visit to most of the classrooms before assembly and she visited the rest at some time during the day. Her morning contact with the staff was normally pastoral or related to a child. It was often brief, usually encouraging, always smiling. On several days I shadowed her and noted that by the end of each day she had had some personal contact with all but one or two of the teaching and non-teaching staff. Those she failed to speak to on one day were included in the next.

She talked freely of her out of school life saying on one occasion to me 'It's good to share these things with the staff and then they tend to share the same sorts of things with you too'. At the same time, she took an obvious but unintrusive interest in their activities, interests and domestic lives. The staff were as familiar with her friends and relatives as they were with one another's and she knew most members of their families, at least by name. She was swift to offer solace to teaching and non-teaching staff faced with, for example, unexpected family sickness or bereavement, did what she could to ease the burden of house-moving, family celebrations (such as weddings) or unpredicted breakdowns in childcare. Her gratitude to and appreciation of the staff was frequently and tangibly expressed (eg.

One Finger and One Thumb

'(After open evening) two cakes appeared in the staffroom "as a thank you for being there"'. (Fieldnote); (After someone had noticed her absence from the staffroom after dinner and had taken her some tea.) Every service however small or unobtrusive is recognized with appreciation, nothing is ever taken for granted. (Fieldnote)). I recorded many occasions on which, as one of the teachers, I was thanked, praised, treated with consideration, made welcome, treated as an individual who had a life outside school. I also always felt that help would have been instantly forthcoming, had I asked for or needed it. In short, the expressive dimension of the head's leadership was readily and constantly visible.

So too was that of the deputy. Little about the physical or emotional state of her colleagues escaped her, though she never gossiped. As she said:

> If you have a conversation, for instance, you may hear somebody's got a worry or somebody's trying to find out something, then if you pick the moment, you can use that to help them, which in a way is helping the school, because if the people are happy they're going to work better. And everybody needs to feel wanted and that people are interested in them, even the abrasive who at first push you off; very often that's even more of a reason that you should find out some way of getting to talk to them, to find out how they tick.

Though demanding a high professional standard of herself and others, she was (as I found myself) quick to offer help and to make allowances when others made mistakes. Because the assistance she offered and gave was unobtrusive, I can best quote a few from many personal examples in my notes:

> I had got half way home when I realized I'd left my handbag in Julia's cupboard. I found her still in conversation with Miss Proctor. 'You should have phoned' she said, 'I could have brought it over for you. It's not far (in fact 15 miles) from where I live' — and she would. (Fieldnote)

> In the hall at dinnertime Julia noticed I looked cold and went to fetch a spare sweater which she keeps in her room. I was extremely grateful for it. (Fieldnote)

> (In staff talk of weddings three weeks before) I had revealed I was going to two this summer. When we talked about clothes, I said I wasn't going to wear a hat. 'Did I have one?' 'No'. 'Then you can borrow mine. It's gorgeous. I wore it for my son's wedding last year and it'd be lovely to feel it was going to be used again'. I made appreciative noises and let the matter slip. (Later not so Julia who) remembered today and said I was welcome, but she

> didn't want to press it on me, if unwelcome etc. She offered to bring it in, so I could try it. Other teachers joined in — they too had wedding hats, but I must bring my dress. (Next day) after dinner I was prompted by the staff to put on my dress and tried the hat, we were like children dressing up. Much pirouetting, prancing and laughter, no one enjoyed it more than Julia. The 'two minute warning' came as a shock and there was a scramble to get away in time. (Fieldnotes)

This last incident brings together many of the elements of her expressive contribution — quick to see when help was needed, discreet in offering it, able to turn the simplest act into an occasion for conviviality and laughter. I noted laughter many times:

> I followed Julia on her rounds this morning and there was a good deal of laughter where ever she went. (Fieldnote)

> (In the week before she went into hospital I had noted that the head was being unusually sharp with the children and had been crisp with a teacher earlier in the day). At dinner time in the staffroom with all present, including Miss Proctor, a very lighthearted discussion broke out, led by Julia, about pierced ears 'while you wait', and threats to to 'do' Jane and myself with a cork and a needle. It was a warm matey discussion which included everyone including Miss Proctor. (Fieldnote)

Much of the laughter she induced had an earthy quality about it, eg:

> (The cook, anxious about a new recipe) asked Julia at lunch time, 'How do you like my Passion Cake?' Julia said it was excellent and then, 'I'll let you know on Monday if it was effective or not. (Fieldnote)

The usual effect of these and similar quips was to lower the emotional temperature of any gathering, a contribution which was especially important at those times when the teachers were under stress, This was very noticeable during the spring term in particular, which was, as Julia said to me on the last day, 'the most wearing term emotionally we have ever had'.

Head and Deputy: Mutuality

Head and deputy also both played instrumental and expressive roles in respect of each other. As a class teacher Julia depended like the other teachers upon the knowledge, forethought, experience and organizational ability of her head. Occasionally, this surfaced in a stark form, eg.:

> I bumped into Julia who said, 'I'm going to confess to Miss Proctor what I've done'. This appeared to be inadvertently having laid

violent hands upon S in her classroom. As she tried to stop him making mayhem among the paints he had tripped over the empty clay bucket and hurt himself and she thought, 'It's better to tell Miss Proctor and then it's out in the open'. (Next day) Miss Proctor went along to Julia's classroom and had a further quick word of reassurance with her about S's accident. (Fieldnote)

Further, the head encouraged and facilitated her performance of the deputy's role, actively supporting her participation in a local deputy head's group, making time for her to see the teachers without the head present during a period of tension with the parent governor, with overt confidence leaving her to run the school when she had herself to be away, sharing with her any information which could conceivably prove to be relevant to policy-making or internal developments and ensuring that she played a full part in all decisions relating to the school. Moreover, as Julia said,

> Because she has the ultimate responsibility, it gives me a lot of freedom — I can look more broadly at the educational scene.

Finally, the head was also quick to take on the deputy's responsibilities if the need arose (eg. doing the 'morning round' when she found that Julia had unexpectedly been detained).

For her part, the deputy head helped the head in the performance of her duties. Such assistance ranged from the seemingly trivial, eg.:

> During rehearsals for the nativity play, Mrs Proctor came into the staffroom and said 'Your head is in a panic, she's lost her glasses'. Julia put down her cup at once and went (successfully) to look for them. (Fieldnote)

to the more obviously important, eg.:

> I do try to keep her informed. If it's important, I write it down and put it on her desk, so she's certain to remember. (Interview with deputy)

> (Traffic changes began to prevent the head from getting to school early, so) We had this arrangement that one of Julia's responsibilities would be to check that everything was alright in the morning. And she used to get here at 8.15 am so she'd always be here for any early child. That was one of her major responsibilities. (Interview with head)

In addition, from time to time, the deputy also performed some of the head's tasks when the latter was in the school, but busy. As the head said:

> Julia and I work so well together ... If I can't do something, I ask her and usually if I can't manage it, she can, and vice versa ... You can't put what we do into little pigeonholes.

They worked well in tandem, as well as helping one another fulfil their individual responsibilities. They shared chores, such as arriving early for and locking up after open evenings and I recorded many examples of smooth teamwork which made them seem like actors in a long-running play. For example:

> Miss Proctor's birthday was celebrated in assembly today and Julia led a special ceremony because it comes in the holidays. As usual, both Miss Proctor and Julia gave the impression of playing well-rehearsed parts. The children were rapt and gleeful. (Fieldnote)

> (At an informal moment) Miss Proctor started to relate stories about the school's past. Julia swiftly made this into a highly effective double act, offering openings, supplying feed lines, prompting recollections. (Fieldnote)

They also shared information. The head said:

> I do put Julia in the picure ... (There are things) I don't generally tell the whole staff but I will make sure Julia knows.

Similarly, when the head was away, the deputy and the secretary kept a diary of every incident, no matter how small, so the head could, on her return, be fully informed. For her part, Julia knew she was the first person to be told any news:

> I know more about what is going on than other people ... Miss Proctor keeps me very well informed.

Sharing information was, moreover, a way of relieving stress. Head and deputy often telephoned one another at home to discuss school matters and almost every day they were to be seen in quick, private conversation in the passage or the cloakroom, outside the staffroom, on the stairs, at the end of lunch. On several occasions I noted examples such as the following:

> Miss Proctor was looking anxious for most of the day. I found it difficult to get hold of her because when she had a spare moment after lunch she said 'I must talk to Mrs Harris about something'. At the end of the day, after everyone else had gone, they were deep in conversation. (Fieldnote)

> At break I heard Miss Proctor tell Julia she'd just had a phone call she wanted to discuss, but 'There isn't anyone to take your class, is there?' I volunteered ... the conversation lasted for about 30 minutes ... (A week later) Miss Proctor and Julia in conversation again before school and at break ... (at a lunchtime staff meeting) Miss Proctor told the teachers what had happened, making it sound casual and unimportant. 'I haven't given this a great deal of thought', she said ... (Fieldnote)

'Miss Proctor called me into her room to tell me of an action she has taken. She then said, 'I went and fetched Julia because I said to (my visitor), 'Nobody else knows about this. Mrs Harris should know'. (Fieldnote)

This constant talking had, according to the deputy, made a significant contribution to the growth of their partnership:

> Our relationship developed slowly. It came about because she talked a lot to me and took me into her confidence. If you talk to someone it helps you to see the way they think and the reasoning behind what they're doing. So as she did this, it meant that, if there were occasions when she made a decision without telling me first, instead of thinking, 'What a silly thing to do' or 'Why on earth did she do that?' I became sure in my own mind that she would have thought it through, that her reasons would be good ones, even if at the time I didn't know why.

Another event which appears to have been crucial to the development of their relationship was the major disagreement which they had during Julia's first year. Both talked openly about it to me. They agreed upon the cause (it was fairly minor), but neither was explicit about the underlying reason. Be that as it may, Julia said:

> Afterwards we were able to talk it through and we both found we had misinterpreted the other ... As with all relationships, it's not having the row that counts but how you deal with it afterwards, whether you're able to build on it and go forward with the relationship.

More recently, they had had another heated argument when Julia felt she had been unjustly treated by the head, but, as before, they were able to talk it through.

In short, as both stressed on several occasions, as they came to understand one another's actions and modes of thought, the relationship between them came to be characterized by the high level of trust which is its hallmark today. The deputy claimed:

> It's a question of trust ... You know, if there's a problem, that she's behind you. It's absolutely sure knowledge and she gives you confidence to do things that you wouldn't normally do. Certainly when I started as a deputy and was very nervous and really thinking, 'What on earth did I take this job on for?', she very quickly made me have confidence in myself to cope with things;

while the head reflected:

> I would say that trust is the biggest factor, because if you trust somebody and they know that you trust them you haven't got to

put any defences up or anything and you feel free. And I knew I
could trust her, that she was willing to support and help me.

As they talked in the early years, the professional and private sides of
their lives became less separate, until after thirteen years neither found it
easy to make the distinction. Julia said, of her head:

She listens to me, she shares my problems. When my father was
dying I don't know what I would have done without her,

and reflected in her turn:

I soak up grumbles, so that she can face and cope with whatever is
worrying her. Sometimes after she's talked something through
with me ... she doesn't feel that she needs to take it any further.
Also I am a sounding board so that she can try ideas out and get
my reactions.

So far, for clarity, I have tried to maintain a distinction between
the instrumental and expressive dimensions of this partnership. Yet in
practice the two were often blurred. Indeed, it was essential to its
successful working that they should be. Early on I noticed that head and
deputy were often to be found, usually in the head's office but sometimes
in the latter's classroom, deep in conversation at the end of the day, for
periods ranging in length from twenty minutes to one and a half hours.
These meetings did not seem exclusive in nature — other teachers went
in and out and on several occasions I intruded on a routine errand and
myself stayed talking. Nor were they entirely devoted to serious discussion of the day's events or future policy. Conversation was sometimes
light-hearted, even flippant, punctuated by anecdotes and laughter. At
times it concerned the personal lives and interests of individual speakers,
at others matters of wider educational concern. Yet my fieldnotes constantly draw attention to the apparent importance of these meetings in
sustaining the partnership, something that each independently confirmed. Miss Proctor said:

We spend a lot of time after school chatting (Mrs Harris and I),
about anything and everything, just like two friends, 'Have you
had a good day? What's happened ...?' We never leave without
saying goodbye to each other and this happens really with the
majority of the staff. They nearly all say goodbye to me and I say
'Are you alright?' and they'll say if anything's happened, 'By the
way I forgot to say so-and-so'.

Int: If you're talking to Julia, would other people join in?

They'll come in and I'll say, 'We're just talking about so-an-so.' It's
not official; it's not like a head talking to a deputy head. It's like
two friends talking together. And I might be sitting on her desk

down in the classroom, with the cleaner sweeping round us, or we might be up here. Obviously if it's something we don't want the cleaner to know about, we'll move.

Mrs Harris presented a very similar picture.

The style and content of these after-school meetings exemplify the way in which task and personal concerns, instrumentality and affectivity, rationality and feeling were inextricably blended in the interactions between these two women. However, the blend was so subtle that I was able to identify it accurately only in the second half of the year. As I came to be fully accepted as a member of the school, I also began to be present at head-deputy encounters. Several times between March and July I made field-notes like these:

> I went in (to the head's office) and joined her and Julia. They seemed to be having three types of conversation, (1) Julia telling about her difficulties with particular children, especially S, (2) discussing jointly the necessity of adapting to a new kind of parental role in school government, and (3) Mrs Proctor talking to Julia about her problems. In short, they seem each to be supporting and counselling one another, but at the same time enabling one another to accommodate to new long-term educational demands. (Fieldnote)

Discussion

The evidence presented in this case study is relevant in a number of ways to the current debate on the management of primary schools, particularly as these relate to the role and status of the deputy head.

First, it supports many of the generalizations commonly made about the deputy's position in the staff hierarchy and her lack of role definition (see eg. Coulson and Cox, 1975; Coulson, 1976; Coulson, 1980; Management and the School Course Team, 1981; Whitaker, 1983). The head claimed both instrumental and expressive leadership of the school and the deputy accepted a subordinate position. The only role specifically assigned to the latter, other than deputizing for the head in her absence, was an administrative one, while her main negotiated roles in relation to the staff were supporting and encouraging them and acting as a channel of communication between them and the head. On the face of it, this partnership appears to have been characterized not by symmetry but by an acceptance by both parties of its asymmetry.

However, detailed examination of the way in which this deputy worked with her head suggests that this picture does little justice to the truth. Rather it reveals her as a person of very considerable influence within the school as a whole. Though largely unspecified, her roles complemented those of the head. She played a crucial role in the school's formal and informal communication systems. Her comprehensive and competent administration helped to keep staff morale high and kept her in touch with every member of the teaching and non-teaching staff, all of whom regarded her with liking and respect. Because of this and through her constant interaction with them, she was able to affect the way they thought and behaved, with consequent implications for school policy and the way in which it was carried out. Above all, she had influence with the head who used her as a confidante and sounding board in the formulation and prosecution of instrumental goals. She played a similar but rather more prominent role in respect of the school's expressive leadership, supporting the head in the latter's active concern for the wellbeing of the teaching and non-teaching staff and keeping her in touch with their feelings and problems. Through her warmth, humour and positive approach to problems she also made her own distinctive contribution to the tone and ethos of the school, particularly, in the context of this chapter, by promoting high morale and self-confidence among the staff during periods of stress and anxiety.

Now this conclusion is very different from the one drawn by the authors of the Open University *Management and the School Course (E323)* who, using Coulson's work and other unpublished evidence, draw a gloomy picture of the roles which deputy heads occupy in primary schools. They argue that deputy heads' lack of formal power and the vagueness and ambiguity which often characterize their job definitions (where these exist), necessitate a new look at the management structure of primary schools:

> The emerging system of departmental heads responsible for particular age groups offers a far sounder basis for primary school management than the continued existence of deputy heads ... the position of deputy head in primary schools has little substance or meaning. (Management and the School Course Team, 1981, p. 84)

I would suggest however that we so far lack the evidence on which to make such a judgment. Coulson's research asked respondents to indicate what they felt deputies *should* do. By contrast, this study, as far as I know the first of its kind, examines the day-to-day reality of one deputy head's management role. It shows that it would be a travesty to dismiss her as unimportant because she occupied a subordinate role in relation to the head and lacked a clear job specification. To argue that her post had neither substance nor meaning is to confuse power and influence, bureaucratic with personal authority. What is more, she knew this. When I asked her if she would be missed if she left the school, she replied without hesitation, 'Oh yes, I would, I can truthfully say I think I would'.

This study suggests another reason why deputies may be important. Head and deputy each played instrumental and expressive roles in relation to the rest of the staff. While these roles had become differentiated, by negotiation, accommodation and habit, they were still similar. So, for example, both the head and the deputy had a communication function, both undertook administration, both took assembly, both were alert to staff's personal and professional problems. Moreover, each could, and often did, temporarily take over the other's role. Small though the school was, as a system, it contained elements of what Landau (1969) has described as redundancy. Like a commercial airliner, its structure enabled every vital function to be carried out by more than one component, creating in its members (and its users) confidence in its security and strength.

The overlapping, duplication and substitution which resulted made the school's leadership relatively impervious to shock, absence, and disruption of routine. The fact that head and deputy could be nourished (one might say refuelled) not only within the organization but by each other, increased their confidence in the efficiency and effectiveness of the school. Their resulting sense of security and stability encouraged all the staff to be more relaxed and protected them all against an expenditure of nervous energy on unproductive ends. In other words, the head and deputy had evolved a system which gave them a degree of 'slack', a term used by management theorists (eg. Cyert and March, 1963) to describe spare resources which can be used to cushion an organization against uncertainty. At a time when many primary schools face considerable uncertainty, induced, for example, by financial cuts, falling rolls, amalgamations, redeployment, accountability pressures, curriculum debate, the deputy may, by effectively doubling the school's leadership potential, play a crucial role in helping a school to adapt productively to a changing environment.

Next, the fact that head and deputy helped one another in both instrumental and expressive terms led to a high degree of interdependence in their relationship. As La Porte (1975) has suggested is the case in complex organizations, this in turn increased the strength and resilience of each of them. Like finger and thumb, they were similar but different, capable of independent operation but adapted to coordination, functional when alone but additionally powerful when acting together.

In the development of this partnership, communication was important. First, it helped to establish trust between the actors. In a study of school accountability in secondary schools, I argued that predictability and shared goals were the necessary conditions for the growth of trust between individuals or groups (Nias, 1981). It was by talking to one another, in the course of day to day affairs and after differences of opinion that this head and deputy came to understand and find each other predictable and to negotiate aims which they both shared, in short to trust each other. Secondly, constant, informal interaction supplemented by regular, but equally informal after-school meetings, ensured that the communication channels between them remained open. This fact enabled them to build constructively upon their rare disagreements. Thirdly, frequent contact and communication enabled the instrumental and expressive dimensions of their relationship to be blurred and intermingled, thus ensuring that business was transacted in a friendly, supportive context in which both felt comfortable. It was, it may be argued, a particularly efficient way of managing the organization because it suited the culture of a nursery/infant school (See Nias *et al*, forthcoming). Lastly, no study which looked only at the formal communication system of this school would have thrown a great deal of light upon the effectiveness of the interaction between its two formal leaders, since most of their contact was informal and much of it could be understood only by having access to their shared meanings, built up over time.

It is, of course, risky to draw general implications for the management of primary schools from a study of two people in one school. Nevertheless, on the basis of the evidence presented here, a number of points may be made. The first concerns role definition. Too tight a job specification, for either head or deputy, especially if it is drawn up before the deputy is in post, may result in reducing the interdependence of a school's two designated leaders and, as a consequence, the capacity of both to help each other and the school. By contrast, a degree of ambiguity may allow the management structure to develop a healthy degree of redundancy and slack. However such ambiguity is likely to result in growth rather than frustration only if the head makes it clear that he/she welcomes the development by the deputy of both instrumental and expressive activities and if the deputy is sensitive enough to respond flexibly and perceptively to such an invitation — whether tacit or open.

The second point follows from the first: the development of such partnerships requires tolerance on the part of both participants. Heads who encourage their deputies to take on important expressive or instrumental functions must accept that, as a consequence, their power as well as their responsibilities will be shared. Deputies who play a vital role in their schools must know how to stop short of usurpation. It follows that the emphasis of management training for either post must be upon the development of personal and interpersonal qualities and skills such as sensitivity, empathy, flexibility and the capacity to see a situation from another's viewpoint.

Thirdly, to stress the importance of communication is to argue that learning to talk and to listen in informal as well as formal contexts is a crucial part of management training. Business cannot be transacted independently of the culture in which it is rooted; in primary schools this means accepting the blurring of the personal and the professional, the expressive and the instrumental. Heads and deputies need to listen to one another, to share and negotiate, to find regular times to talk, to keep open the option of talking about their out-of-school lives as well as their jobs and to learn that this can never be a quick or easy process, wholly free of tension.

Finally, I would like to raise the issue of gender. When I asked these two people whether they thought that the nature of their co-operation and the extent of their interdependence were related to the fact that they were women, they both said 'No', arguing that a successful partnership was a question of personalities rather than gender. This flies in the face of feminist orthodoxy; it would be interesting to know whether other primary teachers, male and female, think that the kind of relationship described in this study also develops between two men or a man and a woman.

Reference

BURGESS, R. (Ed.) (1984) *Field Methods in the Study of Education*, Lewes, Falmer Press.
BURNHAM, P. (1968) 'The deputy head' in ALLEN, B. (Ed.) *Headship in the 1970s*, Oxford Blackwell, pp. 169–96.
COULSON, A. and COX, M. (1975) 'What do deputies do?', *Education 3–13*, 3, 100–3.
COULSON, A. (1976), 'Leadership functions in primary schools, *Educational Administration*, 5.1, 37–48.
COULSON, A. (1980) 'The role of the primary head', in BUSH *et al.* (Eds.) *Approaches to School Management*, London, Harper Row.
CYERT, R. and MARCH, S. (1963) *A Behavioural Theory of the Firm*, Englewood Cliffs NJ, Prentice Hall.
DEPARTMENT OF EDUCATION AND SCIENCE (1977) *Matters for Discussion: Ten Good Schools*, London, HMSO.
DES (1984) *9–13 Middle Schools, A Survey by HMI*, London, HMSO.
ETZIONI, A. (1964) *Modern Organizations*, Englewood Cliffs, Prentice Hall.
LANDAU, M. (1969), 'Redundancy, rationality and the problems of duplication and overlap', *Public Administration Review* 29, 346–58
LA PORTE, T. (1975) 'Organized social complexity: Explication of a concept.' *in* LA PORTE, T. *Organized Social Complexity*, Princeton, Princeton University Press.
MANAGEMENT AND THE SCHOOL COURSE TEAM, (1981) *Policy Making, Organization and Leadership in Schools, Block 4*, Milton Keynes, Open University Press.
MCCALL, G. and SIMMONDS, J. (1969) *Issues in Participant Observation*, London, Addison Wesley.
NIAS, J. (1981) 'The nature of trust' in ELLIOTT, J. *et al, School Accountability*, London, Grant McIntyre.
NIAS, J. (1987) 'Lowmeadow Nursery and Infant School: A case study of cooperation', Cambridge Institute of Education.
NIAS, J., SOUTHWORTH, G. and YEOMANS, R. (forthcoming) *Understanding the Primary School as an Organization*, London, Cassell.
POLLARD, A. (1984) 'Opportunities and difficulties of a teacher-ethnographer: A personal account', in BURGESS, R. (Ed.) *Field Methods in the Study of Education*, Lewes, Falmer Press.
WHITAKER, P. (1983) *The Primary Head*, London, Heinemann

The Role of the Curriculum Postholder

Jim Campbell

Over the past fifteen years or so, significant changes have been made in conceptions of the role of the curriculum postholder in primary schools. In the first place, what has been expected of the postholder has been more clearly articulated; the duties of the job have been specified in greater detail. A second change is that the significance of the post has been increased, because the postholder's role has been moved from a position of marginality in the curriculum, to one of centrality. A minor and relatively insignificant role prescription mainly concerned with helping headteachers write schemes of work, has been transformed into the substantial expectation that the postholder will provide the main, and possibly the only, impetus for maintaining and raising standards in the curriculum of the schools.

In order to consider the content of this role, it is useful to summarize the activities currently expected of curriculum postholders by constructing a broad two-fold classification of them, with five sub-divisions. The two broad categories are:

1. *Curricular Skills*: that is those skills and qualities involved in knowledge about the curriculum area for which the postholder has responsibility.
2. *Inter-personal Skills*: that is those skills and qualities arising from postholder's relationships with colleagues and other adults.

The sub-divisions are:

1. *Curricular Skills*
   A. *Knowledge of subject:* the postholder must keep up-to-date in her subject, must know its conceptual structure and methods etc.
   B. *Professional skills:* the postholder must draw up a programme of work, manage its implementation, maintain it and assess its effectiveness.

C. *Professional judgement:* the postholder must know about, and discriminate between various materials and approaches in her subject, must relate them to children's developmental stages, manage the school's resources and achieve and a match between the curriculum and the pupils' abilities.
2 *Inter-personal Skills*
D. *Social skills:* the postholder must work with colleagues, lead discussion groups, teach alongside colleagues, help develop their confidence in her subject, advise probationers etc.
E. *External representation:* the postholder must represent her subject to outsiders (other teachers, advisers, governors, parents etc).

The categories are not offered as discrete ones; a postholder engaged in developing a new scheme of work in science, which involves her leading workshops for staff, will obviously be using both curricular and inter-personal skills. The classification is offered merely as a descriptive summary of the range and nature of the demands upon postholders that have emerged in the literature.

Two brief comments on this role prescription need to be made. Firstly, it has not arisen haphazardly or spontaneously; it has been promoted from the central authorities as part of the shift to school-based curriculum development at a time when national curriculum projects have been seen as both ineffective and expensive. it has also been seen by Hargreaves (1980) as providing a kind of surrogate promotion for postholders in a period of educational contraction. Secondly, it is clear that if Keddie's (1971) distinction between the 'teacher-as-teacher' (that is instructing children in the classroom) and 'the teacher as educationist' (that is, in her role outside the classroom engaging in educational discourse with colleagues, parents and others) is adopted, the new role is mainly as 'educationist', since it requires the postholder to lead groups of teachers, give an account of the school's approach to her subject, understand aspects of child development, analyze the conceptual framework of her subject and so on.

An attempt was made by Campbell (1982) to record empirically the role performance of postholders in ten school-based curriculum development programmes. He reported upon the wide ranging nature of the postholder's role in school-based curriculum development, and drew attention to four features, summarized below:

1 *Complexity of School-Based Curriculum Development* Using the five categories outlined earlier, Campbell analyzed the skills exercised by postholders and presented them in table 1. It immediately becomes clear that the postholders were involved in very complex and demanding roles. In all ten developments skills

in at least four dimensions, and in six developments, skills in all five dimensions, were exercised.

2 *Other Role Responsibilities* School-based curriculum development was typically only one of the responsibilities of postholders. Except where postholders were used as specialist teachers (cases 9 and 10), they had other major responsibilities as can be seen from the table 2.

Perhaps the extreme case (case study 2) was the postholder who shared responsibility for a class, was in charge of two curriculum areas, including remedial work throughout the school, was fourth year coordinator and as deputy head, had in addition, some managerial duties. Thus not only was school-based curriculum development in itself an extremely demanding aspect of the postholder's role but the school contexts were such that it was only one of a number of equally legitimate role obligations laid upon postholders.

3 *Achievement of Postholders* Despite the complexity of their role, postholders appeared to be making significant achievements in respect of curriculum development. Although there were variations from school to school in the extent of achievement, improvements were perceived in respect of the following five criteria
  i) increase in curricular continuity through the school;
  ii) increase in respect for the postholder's expertise in her subject;
  iii) effective performance by the postholder of the 'teacher as educationist' role in staff discussion groups;
  iv) increase in confidence/morale of the postholder's colleagues;
  v) the adoption of collaborative procedures for curriculum decision making.

These improvements were not 'curriculum innovations' in the sense of dramatic or substantial change to the schools' existing curricula. On the contrary the postholders were helping slowly and haltingly to engage their colleagues in the processes of renewing, or perhaps revitalizing, the kind of work that was already established in their schools. For that reason 'development' is a more appropriate term than 'innovation' or 'change' for the kind of improvement the postholders were achieving.

4 *Role Conflict* The achievements outlined above were not realized easily, for in moving towards them, the postholder's role appears to have built into it sources of tension and ambiguity. Three may be mentioned here:
  i) The mismatch between power and authority in curricular

The Role of the Curriculum Postholder

Table 1 Range of Skills Exercised by Curriculum Postholders in Ten School-Based Curriculum Developments

SKILLS INVOLVED IN SCHOOL-BASED CURRICULUM DEVELOPMENT	CASE STUDY										TOTAL (b)
	1	2	3	4	5	6	7	8	9	10	
I CURRICULAR SKILLS											
A SUBJECT KNOWLEDGE											
1 updating subject knowledge	✓	✓		✓		✓	✓	✓		✓	7
2 identifying conceptual structure of subject(s)	✓		✓			✓	✓	✓			5
3 identifying skills in subject(s)	✓		✓	✓		✓	✓	✓	✓		8
B PROFESSIONAL SKILLS											
4 reviewing existing practice	✓	✓	✓	✓	✓	✓	✓	✓	✓	✓	10
5 constructing scheme/programme	✓	✓	✓	✓	✓	✓	✓	✓	✓	✓	10
6 implementing scheme/programme		✓	✓	✓	✓	✓	✓	✓	✓	✓	9
7 assessing scheme/programme		✓	✓			✓	✓	✓	✓	✓	6
C PROFESSIONAL JUDGMENT											
8 deciding between available resources	✓	✓	✓	✓	✓	✓	✓	✓	✓	✓	10
9 deciding about methods	✓	✓	✓	✓	✓	✓	✓	✓	✓	✓	10
10 identifying links between subjects	✓	✓	✓			✓	✓	✓	✓		7
11 ordering, maintaining resources	✓	✓	✓		✓	✓	✓	✓	✓	✓	9
12 relating subject to its form in other schools			✓	✓		✓	✓				5
II INTER-PERSONAL SKILLS											
D WORKING WITH COLLEAGUES											
13 leading workshops/discussions	✓	✓	✓	✓	✓	✓	✓	✓			8
14 translating material into comprehensible form	✓	✓	✓	✓	✓	✓	✓				7
15 liaising with head and/or senior staff	✓	✓	✓	✓	✓	✓	✓	✓	✓	✓	10
16 advising colleagues informally		✓	✓	✓	✓	✓	✓	✓	✓	✓	10
17 teaching alongside colleagues		✓			✓		✓	✓			5
18 visiting colleagues classes to see work in progress		✓	✓			✓					3
19 maintaining colleagues morale, reducing anxiety etc.		✓	✓	✓		✓		✓	✓		4
20 dealing with professional disagreement	✓	✓		✓		✓	✓				5
E EXTERNAL REPRESENTATION											
21 consulting advisers, university staff etc.	✓	✓		✓	✓	✓				✓	6
22 consulting teachers in other schools	✓			✓		✓				✓	4
TOTAL (a)	17	18	17	17	13	21	16	15	12	12	158

Table 2 Other Major Responsibilities of Ten Curriculum Postholders with Scale Level Held

	CASE STUDY									
	1	2	3	4	5	6	7	8	9	10
1 RESPONSIBILITY										
a) Class teaching	√	√	√	√		√	√	√		
b) Year co-ordination		√	√	√				√		
c) A second subject	√					√			√	
d) Management	√			√	√					
2 LEVEL	2	d.h	3	3	h	2	3	3	3	2(0.5)

matters, especially in respect of the postholder's responsibility for school wide curriculum development and the perceived autonomy of the class teacher.

ii) the high degree of 'visibility' in the 'teacher-as-educationalist' role, whereby the postholder carried out curriculum development activities, often of a novel and complex kind, under the fairly constant scrutiny of her professional peers and occasionally of outsiders perceived as 'experts'.

iii) the expectation that the postholder should assess work in her subject throughout the school, which leads to her being placed in the difficult position of appearing to 'inspect' her colleagues' work.

Conclusions

A number of conclusions about current role expectations for the postholder in primary schools may be made.

Firstly, official role prescriptions have substantially underestimated the complexity and challenge of school-based curriculum development — or, at worst, have ignored it. This is to be regretted not merely because it thereby has undervalued achievements made by postholders, but mainly because it is likely that if the complexity of the role demands is not understood by teachers, in advance of school-based development, disaffection and disillusionment with it, will arise as the complexity is experienced ... Skilbeck (1972) had indicated something of the combination of expertise and social skills required: 'The task is complex and difficult for all concerned. It requires cognitive skills, strong motivation, and postponement of immediate satisfaction, constructive interactions in planning group, and emotional maturity.'

Secondly, in some aspects of their role, the postholders are currently underpowered to achieve all that is expected of them. This is particularly true of expectations concerned with assessing the quality of work in their colleagues' classes, but also in respect of those teachers who remain uninvolved in school-wide policies. A further difficulty derives from the fact that postholders have obligations other than school-based curriculum development. These may mean that if a particularly strong commitment of time and energy is necessary to initiate a development, the equally important but less dramatic business of *maintaining* it, may be adversely affected. Although therefore it is true, as HMI argue (DES, 1978), that the status of the postholder is a 'product of the way they regard themselves and also of the attitudes that other teachers have towards them' there is still the need for increasing both the formal power attached to their status, and for increasing time attached to their within-school duties.

It would however be wrong to leave an impression of curriculum postholders as permanently and unmitigatedly angst-ridden teachers, poised ambivalently and ineffectually between the demands of curriculum renewal, class teaching and collegial goodwill. For by their activity in curriculum development the postholders may be helping to revise the curricular ideology that has dominated thinking about the primary school curriculum since Plowden. In their schools two characteristic assumptions about the curriculum were emerging. The first of these is *enhanced respect for subject knowledge;* the second is the acceptance of *collective or collegial responsibility* for the school's curriculum. Staff participating in SBCD acknowledged the superior expertise of the postholder as the basis for her leadership of the development, accepting so to speak the legitimacy of her holding the responsibility post, and thus of influencing work in their classes. At the same time they were clear about the procedures they thought should be observed. They expected to be consulted, and to participate in the process of revising and reforming the curricular policies that they would have to implement. The underlying assumptions of this shift, if it becomes more strongly established, raise questions not merely about the potential of school-based curriculum development in primary schools, but also about role relationships in them, most clearly relationships of authority, responsibility and control in curricular matters.

References

CAMPBELL, R.J. (1982) 'School based curriculum development in middle schools', Mimeo, University of Warwick, Department of Education.
CENTRAL ADVISORY COUNCIL FOR EDUCATION (England) (1967) *Children and Their Primary Schools* (The Plowden Report), London, HMSO.
HARGREAVES, A. (1980) 'Teachers, hegemony and the educationist context', paper

delivered at 4th Annual Sociology of Education Conference, Westhill College, Birmingham.

HMI (1978) *Primary Education in England*, London, HMSO.

KEDDIE, N. (1971) 'Classroom knowledge', in YOUNG, M.F.D. (Ed.), *Knowledge and Control*, London, Collier-Macmillan.

SKILBECK, M. (1972) 'School based curriculum development', in WALTON, J. and WELTON, J. (Eds.), *Rational Curriculum Planning*, Ward Lock.

Primary School Headteachers and Collegiality

Geoff Southworth

Introduction

Those who work in primary schools are currently receiving many messages about how they should operate. This chapter will look at two of these messages: those to do with leadership and those to do with collegiality. On the one hand there is a persistent acceptance of schools as being hierarchical organizations requiring top-down management and leadership (DES, 1977). On the other hand the value of involving teachers in the decision-making process is being promoted (DES Welsh Office, 1985). It is also common to see both being advertised at the same time:

> The head is always, in law as well as in fact, responsible for the situations in his or her school. Successful heads have interpreted these considerable powers and duties wisely. They have not been authoritarian, consultative, or participative as a matter of principle; they have been all three at different times as the conditions seemed to warrant, though most often participative. Their success has often come from choosing well, from knowing when to take the lead and when to confirm the leadership offered by their colleagues. (ILEA, 1985 para. 3.25)

This quote suggests that the two can be synthesized, that there is little conflict between leadership and collegiality, and that they are compatible. I think this assumes rather too much. Leadership and collegiality warrant examination, in their own right and because of the tensions which are created by their coexistence. This chapter will review such research data as exists, look at some of the perspectives in the literature, and embody observations based on work with headteachers on management courses and my personal experience of primary headship.

Geoff Southworth

Perceptions of Headteachers in Primary Schools

Headteachers cannot be understood seperately from their contexts, the most important aspect of which is the school. Yet even this apparently simple term has different meanings in different countries. King (1983) shows that in England we regard the school as a *community*, unlike the USA where schools are seen as part of the community. In England the school is a unique collection of people (Oldroyd, 1984) a fact which has two implications for headship. First, the head is not just head of a school but the leader of a community. Headteachers often act as leaders of their particular school community. For example, at school ceremonies the head who welcomes parents to a special assembly, or concert, or event, and who thanks the staff and children and parents for their participation is signalling their leadership role since the fact that s/he is making these remarks to everyone present is part of the message (King, 1983). Second, because each school is unique the head has a degree of autonomy. For the head the context of the school creates a leadership role in relation to his/her colleagues and some freedom from others outside the school so that s/he can lead the community of the school in his/her own way, since only s/he as head will know what the conditions warrant. Small's (1984) investigation into five headteachers illustrates how the role of each is affected by the circumstances of the school s/he is in and how these differences also make them independent. The title of the study is significant: 'A Scandal of Particularity? Headship in the mid-1980's'.

One effect of this sense of separateness is that the head's boundary and filtering roles are emphasized. Richardson (1975) identified a boundary role for the headteacher. Those 'outside' the school customarily approach those in the school via the headteacher (eg. parents, LEA advisers, welfare and support agencies). Frequently those communications coming out of the school require the headteacher's acknowledgement, if not approval (eg. pupil reports, INSET course attendance requiring day release, letters to parents). Although his/her consent may be given in an informal, non-bureaucratic manner, the fact that it is deemed necessary emphasizes the head's boundary role. Coulson (1980) suggests that the head also acts as a 'filter', for example in relation to school governors. The 1980 Education Act makes schools accountable to their governors. Yet if materials intended for school governor training (NAGM, 1981; and Sallis, 1982) and personal experience are valid indicators, a headteacher's ability to 'filter' information by means of their reports to governors is not significantly diminished.

Another effect of this idea of heads leading a community is that heads develop a sense of attachment to the school. Coulson (1980) provides evidence that heads and the schools they lead become so closely identified that he calls it 'ego-identification'. Heads talk about 'their' school and refer also to 'my' staff, and 'my' deputy. However this identification is more than a sense of placement, it is frequently a feeling state. The majority of heads I have worked with genuinely *feel* a strong sense of responsibility for much, if not all, that happens in 'their' school.

This feeling of personal attachment and involvement suggests that we should be trying to understand not just the sociological and organizational aspects of headship but also its 'psychology'. We need to examine the roles of headteachers in terms of their feelings, motives, perceptions and judgments. At present we can say only that primary heads *are* closely attached to 'their' schools, and that by a sense of boundary they are identified with that particular school. There is, however, a great deal more we need to know about what this means for the individual head.

However, there is also a need to highlight some other features which affect the headteacher. The first of these can be labelled school ethos. Heads appear to feel that they have the responsibility for determining 'their' school's 'ethos'. The underlying philosophy of the school should be the heads' (see Coulson, 1980). This seems to arise from their sense of example. Primary heads are typically promoted straight from the classroom. It is their practical abilities as a classteacher which has kudos with the selectors (King, 1983). They are therefore expected by the selectors to exert an influence. The very title is significant — HEAD-teacher. The process of promotion effectively approves the individual's professional values. Moreover on becoming a head the person may feel that their teaching is of such an order that it is worthy of emulation by others. Whitaker (1983) speaks of a 'sense of mission' accompanying a person's entry into a new headship. An issue then is that the head, as an individual, arrives at a level of influence feeling a sense of professional self belief and example and accepting a responsibility to project these values onto the school. The head is not just the leader of the school, s/he is now the leading exemplar for the school.

As leading exemplar the head's values become the significant benchmarks for the school. Dearden (1968) has argued that there are no aims of primary education, only aims of education. This implies that there are no terminal points for primary education; there is no time or stage at which teachers can say they have achieved the aims. Primary teachers often feel that there is always more they could be doing. Alternatively, many argue that primary education should be viewed in terms of its processes and evaluated by reference to the kinds of experiences and activities that constitute it rather than to the anticipated outcomes (Blenkin and Kelly, 1981). In the face of a lack of consensus as to what primary education should be achieving and how to evaluate this it may mean that, on a day-to-day basis, the headteacher's values became the adopted ones, since they are more tangible than any other indicators.

Given this set of features the challenge for heads is to generate commitment to 'their' values. Whatever the exact nature of a headteacher's roles and responsibilities in a particular school most heads attempt to exercise a unifying influence on the school. Coulson (1980) describes how heads 'generate commitment' and foster loyalty not so much to the abstract idea of the school but to themselves as individuals. Certainly this personal relationship exists between heads and 'their' deputies. The role relations of head and deputy frequently operate on the basis of a code of conduct whereby heads and deputies do not disagree on matters of school policy in 'public', that is in front of other staff. Disagreements are only allowed to surface in 'private'. Given other features of the deputy head's role, which will be mentioned later, this pact tends to work most often to the benefit of the head. Deputies seldom question the head's ruling or decision in formal situations such as staff meetings, and are expected to actively support decisions at such times. It is my experience that at times of deputy head selection acceptance of this code of conduct by candidates is examined by the headteacher. Certainly, many heads and deputy heads subscribe to this view of 'loyalty' believing it to be an acceptable arrangement.

However, 'loyalty' is only one way of creating unity in the school. The recruitment and selection of staff to vacant posts is a tactic of considerable significance. The strong feelings expressed by groups of heads when discussing how much, or how little opportunity they have had to recruit staff is an indicator of how central this aspect of management is to them. When a head talks about 'his/her' school to another and describes the situation, responsibilities of staff, curriculum developments, rates of change, staff relations and so on the listening head will very quickly seek to discover how many of the staff the head has appointed. And often heads will say 'I appointed' this teacher when in fact it was the appointment of the school governors. Indeed, amongst heads there is a belief that the ideal state of school leadership is when the head has selected all of his or her 'own' staff. If that cannot be achieved then the next best thing is to have appointed 'one's own' deputy.

Another tactic for creating unity is through job descriptions. Such descriptions do a number of things. First they frequently make it quite clear to teachers that they are directly responsible to the headteacher (Lancashire LEA, 1980). Second, teachers often have job descriptions but the headteacher does not, which suggests that whilst teachers each have a framed and clearly delineated set of tasks or functions the head has an over-arching, omnipotent role. Thirdly, job descriptions also seek to direct teachers into areas of activity which, broadly, are congruent with the head's philosophy and long term aspirations for the school.

Teacher appraisal systems may also be used to unify a school. Although the specific proposals are only now emerging (Suffolk, 1985) appraisal looks to be taking place within the existing hierarchies and conventions. What is likely is that headteachers will articulate a set of views on the teachers' competences according to some agreed schedule. However, whilst a schedule of teacher appraisal may structure much of the context and some of the content, it is obvious that a headteacher's adoption and interpretation of these schedules will also incorporate their senses of example and loyalty. In other words, quite properly, their professional values will pervade the whole enterprise. Given the points already made about the head's role one can clearly see appraisal as a device whereby the head consciously and unconsciously can apply pressure to unify the school.

Of course what is not being suggested is a mirror-like correspondence between the teachers and the head. Heads cannot clone. Yet this idea of unity is intended to bring out the opportunities that a headteacher has to affect the parameters of divergence. It looks as if the head becomes the norm to whom the staff refer.

Another way to determine the headteacher's influence on the school is to consider not his/her role but that of the deputy head. In a primary school the deputy head is typically in an ambiguous position. The scant literature on the deputy head's role shows that there is no common agreement as to the nature of the role. Bush (1981) is unequivocal saying that the position of deputy has little substance or meaning because the leadership of the primary school is overwhelmingly the function of the head. In addition primary deputies are seldom released from their class teaching duties and as Coulson (1976) noted it is rare that the deputy's job, on a day-to-day basis, differs from that of other teachers. The ILEA report 'Improving Primary Schools' (ILEA, 1985) says that the deputy should be regarded as a trainee head. This implies that there is no intrinsic need for deputies in the school. The meaning of the role is cast into the future, not the present.

In reality what deputies do rests almost entirely upon what the head allows them to do. Some small scale research into headteachers' conceptions of the deputy head's role (Southworth, 1985(a)) revealed that high priority is given to the deputy being a 'good' teacher. Discussions with groups of primary headteachers suggests that heads ideally see deputies as 'disciples'. The deputy should be appointed by the head-in-post, selected on the basis of a close match to the head's image of a 'successful' teacher. The deputy would then spend most of their time working in the classroom providing a good example for other teachers to follow. Deputies, therefore, are classroom surrogates of the headteacher. This is also useful because heads in large and medium sized primary schools will have been 'promoted out' of the classroom which has been the basis of their exemplary activity. Heads thus need to find a substitute. Deputies, therefore, are not there to help the head unload some of his/her duties. Ideally deputies are regarded as putting into operation, in the classroom, a set of values on behalf of their sponsor, the head. If this is achieved then the head will have doubled the forces of influence (Whitaker, 1983). The head will have influence over the whole school *and* a classroom disciple providing a direct example for teachers to follow.

The influence of heads upon 'their' school is also revealed during periods of headteacher succession. When heads talk about 'taking over' from another head it is unusual, in my experience, that the succeeding head is full of conviction for their predecessor's regime. Often there are doubts expressed about certain ways of doing things, or of procedures strangely absent. It is common that the in-coming head is critical of aspects of the school.

There are two things to focus on here. First, it suggests that there is some discontinuity at the time of headteacher succession. This is consistent with the picture drawn here. If heads are autonomous, able to set the ethos for the school and 'unify' the staff within a framework of values compatible with the head's beliefs, then one would expect that there would be discontinuity. Second, when these differences relate to the curriculum, and teaching and learning issues, then such discontinuity is potentially disruptive and even damaging. When a change of head occurs what could be happening is a change in the school's value system.

At this point it is useful to look at some of the implications of the perspective which has been outlined. It is widely accepted that primary heads have a formidable concentration of power (Alexander, 1984). However, that is not to say that all heads are autocratic or paternalistic. Heads can choose to exercise their power in different ways. A great deal of what is described here is *latent*. How an individual activates these patterns of control, if at all, will be a matter of individual practice. Nevertheless, the analysis offered does support the idea of heads having considerable scope for influence. The analysis, moreover, does not rely solely on an organizational perspective to do with role, position or function. The viewpoint presented here also substantially relies upon subjective states such as personal beliefs, values and felt perceptions. This raises some important issues concerning the current views on leadership.

First, primary heads now have greater opportunities to acquire management skills (DES, 3/83; 3/85). These skills may help them with many aspects of their job but how useful will these skills be unless primary management courses also analyze the headteacher's role? If so much power resides with the head then management courses should focus on this. Heads need to understand the nuances of their position and power since heads are as likely to be the obstacles to development as the creators of change. Unfortunately the programmes of many primary management courses tend to mean that primary heads consider many other roles and managerial functions but seldom focus on *their* role in 'their' school.

Second, how helpful is it for heads to be told that the single most important factor in a successful school is a good head (DES, 1977, DES Weish Office, 1985). The notion that a good head equates with a good school is far too simplistic (see Winkley, 1984). For one thing it only adds to the headteacher's heavy sense of responsibility — if the school's success is also the head's success, its failure is also the head's failure (King, 1983).

Such a crude equation is likely to be stressful to many headteachers. It is also a negation of the role of many, many teachers. It certainly does not help to develop a sense of collegiality.

Third, this analysis has important implications for heads as individuals. Elsewhere (Southworth, 1985 (b)) I have advocated the need for support mechanisms for headteachers because they find their responsibilities a heavy burden. They also find the role often isolates them from others in the school. Work with cohorts of headteachers who have attended management courses suggests that whilst these heads hold views which support this analysis they also demonstrate associated pressures and strains. They need to talk about 'their' schools, about the challenges, changes and developments which face or confront them: headteachers are people too (also, see Coulson, 1985). A problem with role theory, and some of those who use it to describe headship, is that role theory assumes that individuals are persons rather than illuminates it. If the primary head's leadership role is to continue or change then greater support will be needed for them.

Fourth, it follows from much of this that it is the *person* of the head, his/her perceptions and values, which are of fundamental concern (Coulson, 1985). If leadership is to alter in the primary school then some serious attempts are going to be needed to the personal growth needs of the individual head.

Lastly, primary heads evidently have influence and power and feel the strains of these responsibilities, but this accummulation of power is at odds with the model of primary school development which is currently being promoted and which I label as collegiality.

Collegiality

Collegiality has become a popular notion and is advocated by a number of sources. One can be identified as 'professional accountability' (Elliott *et al.*, 1981; Campbell, 1985), where all members of the school, regardless of role or status, see themselves as mutually accountable. Another source is that of certainly organizational theorists (McGregor, 1960; Herzberg, 1966) who have encouraged participation. Thirdly, there are those who offer collegiality as an alternative to the headteachers concentration of power (Hargreaves, 1973; Coulson 1980), since as Handy (1984) says, in a democratic society schools can look strangely feudal to the outsider.

The idealized 'collegial school' has small working groups of teachers feeding back suggestions for school-wide change to the collectivity of the whole staff meeting for decision-making. These working groups are usually led by curriculum 'leaders' or 'consultants' who might also work alongside teacher-colleagues. This collaboration is supported by heads who have committed themselves to devolving responsibilities to the staff group and

Geoff Southworth

to servicing such activity (Campbell, 1985). Campbell's distillation of collegiality is supported by official policies from several sources, some of which are given verbatim below:

(i) Where teachers with responsibilities for a particular area of the curriculum were effective in influencing the work of the school this was apparent in a number of ways: in the case of English language and mathematics there was evidence of teachers planning programmes of work in consultation with the head, advising other teachers and helping to encourage a consistent approach to the work in these subjects.

> DES (1978) *Primary Education in England: A Survey by HM Inspectors of Schools*; para 4.5

(ii) Few teachers are expert in all parts of the curriculum. It becomes increasingly difficult for an individual teacher to provide the width and depth of all the work required to be taught ... The necessary help, support and advice may in part be given by heads and local advisers. It may also be provided by other teachers on the staff who have a special interest, enthusiasm and responsibility for a part of the curriculum and who act as consultants. Such teachers may give support in a variety of ways: by producing guidelines and schemes of work; by leading discussions and organizing study groups; by disseminating work done on in-service courses; by working alongside class teachers, by assembling and organizing resources; and occasionally by teaching classes other than their own.

> DES (1982) *Education 5 to 9: An Illustrative Survey of 80 First Schools in England*; para 3.19

(iii) Usually the whole staff were involved in the process throughout and were all members of the specific review and development teams. This was possible because of their comparatively small staff size and it did facilitate a good, if informal, exchange of information about the review and development process.

> McMahon et al. (1984) *Guidelines for Review and International Development in Schools: Primary School Handbook* (GRIDS) Schools Council Programme 1, p. 56

(iv) The professionalism of the teacher also involves playing a part in the corporate development of the school. HMI reports frequently refer to the importance of professional team work, where the teachers within a school agree together on the overall goals of the school, on the policies for the curriculum in the widest sense, including policies for the standard of behaviour expected of pupils and for the relationship expected between teacher and pupils. The pupils' own ability to co-operate and work well with each other is enhanced by the experience of members of staff working productively together in a professional relationship. HMI reports also draw attention to the value of agreed policies for marking and assessment within a school

> DES (1985) *Better Schools*, (Cmnd. 9469) para 143

(v) We believe that many primary schools would benefit from increased delegation of responsibilities to members of staff ... It is a matter of high priority that each school should have a sense of wholeness. That can be achieved only through clear and sensitive leadership ... It is important to be sure that the various aspects of the curriculum cohere for the school as a whole.

> ILEA (1985) *Improving Primary Schools*, paras 3.27, 3.28 and 3.43.

(vi) A key issue in extending the influence of teachers with posts of special responsibility is the willingness of heads to delegate and to give scale post teachers the necessary support and authority. This has been achieved in one junior school where all posts of responsibility are for curriculum development. Each scale post teacher was asked to produce detailed schemes of work and all have done so. These have commendable depth in terms of aims, objectives, approaches and content, although to date only the language scheme has a built-in assessment schedule. Considerable whole school discussion accompanied the production of the schemes, and all teachers have a clear understanding of the aims and all share a common purpose in implementing them. Curriculum leaders call at least one meeting a term to discuss their specialism, to evaluate the schemes in practice and to invite ideas for future development. A recent initiative has been the involvement of curriculum leaders in teaching alongside colleagues and subsequently discussing the work. The discussion occurs when a peripatetic teacher takes the class. A rota of team teaching has been drawn up and according to staff all are enjoying the experience and feel they are gaining from it. A sense of corporate team work has been established within which scale post teachers have made a substantial mark upon the work of the school as a whole. This is a model worthy of wider emulation.

> DES Welsh Office (1985) *Leadership in Primary Schools: Primary Education in Wales*.

Two things emerge from these statements. First, one can see the key components of collegiality: consultation, communication, continuity, co-ordination and coherence. All have been part of the vocabulary of curriculum planning and organization for some time (see Blythe and Derricott, 1977), but have now been adopted as school management strategies. In one sense this is encouraging since it maintains the connection between school and curriculum management structures, between curriculum development and school development. However, school management involves rather more than curriculum management. External communications and internal relations will only partially be accommodated by such curriculum strategies. Moreover, each of these key components deserves detailed scrutiny. For example, continuity is now being given careful attention (Derricott, 1985) and can be seen to have two distinguishable meanings — communicational and structural (Southworth, 1985c). Continuity as communication describes teachers reporting what they have covered in curriculum content. Continuity as structure is to do with how teachers conceive 'development', and 'knowledge'. Nor is the meaning of consultation clear. Some DES documents (DES, 1984) use the term consultation within a top-down framework. What is not being offered is a partnership of equals (Southworth, 1985(c)). Schools are probably more consultative now but it does not follow that they are more democratic. Much of the language of curriculum management is couched in terms of staff meetings, working parties and in-service course dissemination. A lot of this may simply be the exchange of information and have little bearing on decision-making. Indeed, it can be argued that the model of curriculum management seemingly offered by HMI provides heads with greater opportunities to unify 'their' schools since whole-school co-ordination and coherence lend themselves as much to that interpretation as to colleagues working collaboratively and democratically. The key words of collegiality require careful study. At the moment they are used far too loosely, are ambiguous and may be misleading.

The second thing to emerge is that collegiality will change the existing role relations in school. Collegiality is likely to reduce the predominance of the headteacher and the autonomy of the classteacher. The former will occur through increased delegation and participation. The latter because classteachers are now being encouraged to take on a dual role: the responsibility within general school policies for the coherence of the programme of work of their class; and an advisory/consultancy role in some aspect of the curriculum throughout the school (ILEA, 1985 para 3.37). Both of these role changes will be major changes.

I can find no acknowledgement in the writings of those who advocate collegiality that it will involve major change. Indeed, the documents which promote collegiality seem to ignore how collegiality will be implemented and developed. The absence of any discussion as to the challenges this change will create tends to leave one with the impression that collegiality is easy to adopt. The foregoing discussion of the head's role obviously presents many barriers. Packwood's case study (1984) reveals that introducing a collegial approach will be far from easy. Packwood describes how a junior school changed its responsibility structure so that subject responsibilities could be delegated to teachers. There are three things which should be highlighted from this study. First, the idea of 'subject specialists' needs considerable clarification. Secondly, Packwood shows how even within this particular school's staff there were differences as to how a specialist should proceed, and what the job involved. Thirdly, the case study points towards the fact that collegiality will not just affect formal role relations, but the nature of all relationships.

Focusing on the third point one can anticipate that collegiality would alter adult interactions both individually and in groups. Collegiality would affect the whole nature of school discourse, decision-making and evaluation. It would test the whole professional culture of primary education and the power structure of individual schools (Alexander, 1984). Moreover, collegiality would intrude into areas often seen as 'private'. Handy (1984) notes that because schools are faced with blurred aims, conflicting functions and no simple way of measuring success every judgment is subjective and personal. To encourage teachers to come together to discuss plans, practice and evaluation is to ask teachers to examine their different approaches, methods, values and beliefs. This will undoubtedly create tensions, competitions and sometimes conflicts. It turns the practical into the political and the interpersonal.

Change usually brings with it uncertainties, but a switch to collegiality would bring uncertainty *and* some risks. Differences in practice and philosophy have in many schools been avoided because the individuals are convinced that they cannot (or would not) cope with the turbulence created by facing them and talking about them. To ask that teachers now do this is to underestimate the nature and structures of feeling which any individual and all organizations embody. Collegiality *will* affect the adults in the school because collegiality will disturb both formal and informal group processes. In addition there is a lack of published work to help guide schools towards a collegial approach. Those who try will be working in the dark.

There are other problems too. First the rate of change is problematical. The time taken to switch to a collegial approach, and the time collegial processes take in school are both likely to be slower than autocratically announced changes. Oldroyd (1984) in his account of how a Canadian school moved towards group cohesion and collegiality, says that sufficient trust emerged only after a two year process of incremental development. Is this a pace which is in harmony with the rates of change implied in the current rash of curriculum policy documents? Reports emanating from the DES and HMI (see Southworth 1985 (d)) who are designating and redesignating the areas of the curriculum, stimulating interest in CDT and technology, science education, and home economics imply a faster rate of change than Oldroyd's case study depicts. A second problem is that the call for collegiality has occurred during a time when primary schools have been adversely affected by falling pupil rolls. The problems this has created have not been conducive to headteachers attempting to re-model their leadership patterns. Issues of redeployment, early-retirement, or whether a school will be amalgamated or closed are too fraught to provide the stability needed for a change to collegiality. In any case the idea of heads delegating more tasks has come when the head may well have fewer staff to delegate to. These turbulent conditions have probably inhibited interest in collegiality whilst the barrage of curriculum documentation has further hindered the adoption of a collegial approach.

Conclusion

It would appear from this examination that leadership and collegiality are not necessarily compatible. Collegiality is aimed at reducing the head's load through increasing their scale of delegation. In this way it is hoped that the excesses of monopolistic headship will be avoided and that staff will be more participative. In the first instance this fails to take sufficient account of the headteachers' perceptions of their role and their strong feelings of responsibility for the school.

A second issue is that collegiality has enormous implications for staff development. If collegiality is to be encouraged then we need to look very carefully at how headteachers are to be developed and might need to change. The kinds of management courses which primary heads need are not so much ones of systems theory, instrumental rationality and industrial production as of curriculum awareness, social understanding and interpersonal skills. The head will probably need to act more as a facilitator (Southworth, 1984). As a facilitator the head needs a particular order of insights and skills. To quote Shaw (1983) s/he must be able to make complex, synthetic judgements of the type needed in ethics, politics or diplomacy, not like those needed in engineering or economics.

It was noted that this is a major role change for headteachers. Therefore, before collegiality can become a viable option heads need to be able to examine and understand the dynamics and consequences of their present leadership role. It needs to be recognized that in offering heads a collegial approach they are being asked to do something which is both complex and uncertain. Few of us will go out of our way to do that. Heads are being asked to change their role and become more active in curricular leadership in the school. This role change is a far more important innovation for the head than any other specific curriculum innovation. Role changes for heads and teachers will create ambivalence even among those willing to try (Fullan, 1982). As there is already a need for support for headteachers (Southworth, 1985 (b)) further support facilities are likely to be needed.

Then there is the matter of management training for heads. It has been suggested that a feature of these courses should be that heads devote attention to their role in 'their' school. However, one needs to ask more fundamental questions of the way management training is being conceived. How helpful is it at a time when collegiality is being promoted for only heads to be given management training? Surely, if collegiality is to be taken seriously we need to be looking at courses for the whole staff group.

Another aspect of the staff development implications is the consideration which teachers will also need. They too will need considerable help. Some of this could take place as part of school-based staff development, but there are also reasons why some of this should take place away from the school site and the staff group. Initial work on leadership and communication in the staff group is possibly best done with teachers from other schools and under the tutelage of those proficient in group processes, communication and counselling. Teachers who accept a curricular responsibility will also need to enhance their knowledge both of the chosen area and of change processes and evaluation.

All of these staff development programmes will require rather more than a short course taken after school. The existing low levels of funding for in-service, the lack of day release in many LEAs and the frequent absence of these kinds of course in some areas, suggests that collegiality will suffer because of impoverished resourcing.

The third issue to raise is that if collegiality is to be more widely accepted and adopted then it needs to be more thoroughly discussed. Before we rush into collegial ways a more sophisticated understanding needs to be developed. At present we only have the advocates' word that it works well. Surely we need further research data and case studies, since only then can we examine in detail the tensions between headship, leadership and collegiality. At present we need to regard both leadership and collegiality as invitations to enquiry, not as a rhetoric of conclusion (Eisner, 1985).

References

ALEXANDER, R.J. (1984) *Primary Teaching*, London, Holt, Rinehart and Winston.
BLENKIN, G.M. and KELLEY, A.V. (1981) *The Primary Curriculum*, London, Harper and Row.
BLYTH, W.A.L. and DERRICOT, R. (1977) *The Social Significance of Middle Schools*, London, Batsford.

Bush, T., (1981) 'Key roles in school management', in Open University *Policy-making Organization and Leadership in School*, E323, Block 4, Part 3, Open University Press, Milton Keynes, p. 84.
Campbell, R. (1985) *Developing the Primary School Curriculum*, London, Holt, Rinehart and Winston.
Coulson, A.A. (1976) Leadership function in primary schools in *Educational Administration*, 5(1) pp. 37–48.
Coulson, A.A. (1980) 'The role of the primary head' in Bush, T. *et al* (Eds.) *Approaches to School Management*, London, Harper and Row.
Coulson, A.A. (1985) 'Recruitment and management development for primary headship', *School Organization*, Vol. 5, No. 2, pp. 111–23.
Dearden, R. (1968) *Philosophy of Primary Education: An Introduction*, London, Routledge and Kegan Paul.
Department of Education and Science (1985) *Better Schools*, Cmd. 9469, London, HMSO.
Department of Education and Science (1978) *Primary Education in England: A survey by HM Inspectors of Schools*, London, HMSO.
Department of Education and Science (1982) *Education 5 to 9: An Illustrative Survey of 80 First Schools in England*, London, HMSO.
Department of Education and Science (1983) Circular 3/83
Department of Education and Science (1984) *Parental Influence at School*, Cmd 9242, London, HMSO.
Department of Education and Science (1985) *Better Schools*, Cmd. 9469, London, HMSO.
Department of Education and Science Welsh Office (1985) *Leadership in Primary Schools: HMI (Wales) Occasional Paper*, Cardiff, HMSO.
Department of Education and Science (1985) Circular 3/85
Derricott, R. (1985) *Curriculum Continuity: Primary to Secondary*, Windsor, NFER-Nelson.
Eisner, E.W. (1985) 'Emerging models for educational evaluation' in Eisner, E.W. *The Art of Educational Evaluation: A Personal View*, Lewes, Falmer Press, p. 71
Fullan, M. (1982) *The Meaning of Educational Change*, Columbia Univ., New York, Teachers College Press.
Handy, C.B. (1984) *Taken for Granted? Understanding Schools and Organizations*, Schools Council Programme 1, York, Longmans/School Council.
Hargreaves, D. (1973) 'Do we need headteachers?' in *Education 3–13*
Herzberg, F. (1966) *Work and the Nature of Man*, New York, World Publishing Co.
ILEA (1985) *Improving Primary Schools*, Report of the committee on Primary Education, London, ILEA.
King, R., (1983) *The Sociology of School Organisation*, London, Methuen,
Lancashire Education Authority (1980) Job Description for Scale Post Holder, Lancashire Mimeo
McGregor, D. (1960) *The Human Side of Enterprise*, New York, McGraw-Hill.
McMahon, A. et al. (1984) *Guidelines for Review and Internal Development in Schools: primary school handbook (GRIDS)*, Schools Council Programme 1, York, Longmans/Schools Council.
NAGM (National Assoc. of Governors and Managers) 1981, *The Role of the Chairman*, Paper No. 17, NAGM Secretary, Sheffield
Oldroyd, D. (1984) 'School-based staff development: Lessons from Canada in *School Organisation*, Vol. 4, No. 1, pp. 35–40.
Packwood, T. (1984) 'The introduction of staff responsibility for subject development in a junior school', in Goulding, S., et al. (1984) *Case Studies in Educational Management*, London, Harper and Row, pp. 85–98.

RICHARDSON, T.E. (1975) *The Teacher, the School and the Task of Management*, London, Heinemann, p. 36

SALLIS, J., (1982) *The Effective School Governor:* a guide to the practice of school Government, London, Advisory Centre for Education, 2nd ed.

SHAW, K.E. (1983) 'Rationality, experience and theory' in *Educational Management and Administration*, 11, pp. 167–72

SMALL, N. (1984) 'A Scandal of the Particularity? Headship in the 1980s' conference paper BEMAS conference, Cambridge.

SOUTHWORTH, G.W. (1984) 'Development of staff in primary schools: some ideas and implications' in *British Journal of In-Service Education*, Vol. 10, No. 3, pp. 6–15

SOUTHWORTH, G.W. (1985a) The role of the primary deputy head — unpublished data collection of 50 headteachers' views: 1983–1985

SOUTHWORTH, G.W. (1985b) 'Primary heads' reflection on training' in *Education* Vol. 165, No. 25, p. 560

SOUTHWORTH, G.W. (1985c) 'Perspectives on the primary curriculum', in *Cambridge Journal of Education*, Vol. 15, No. 1, pp. 41–49.

SOUTHWORTH, G.W. (1985d) 'Further perspectives on the primary curriculum' in *Cambridge Journal of Education*, Vol. 15, No. 3

SUFFOLK EDUCATION AUTHORITY (1985) 'Those Having Torches ... Teacher Appraisal: A Study'

WHITAKER, P. (1983) *The Primary Head*, London, Heinemann.

WINKLEY, D. (1984) 'Educational Management and School Leadership: An Evolutionary Perspective' in HARLING, P., (Ed.) *New Directions in Educational Leadership*, Lewes, Falmer Press, pp. 205–22

Section Two
Roles and Relationships

Introduction

At the end of Section one the notion of collegiality was discussed. Essentially, collegiality is about teachers working together, it is one way of teachers working collaboratively. This section looks at a number of issues associated with how teachers collaborate. The chapters in this section build on the ideas raised in the last chapter in section one and develop and elaborate them.

Robin Yeomans' first chapter takes up the idea that teachers are both professionals and persons, and that rather than seeing them as distinguishable the two are often blurred. As both a professional and a person teacher's have needs which can be met if the staff operate as a *group*. Indeed, Yeomans suggests that a staff can be developed into an effective *task* group and *support* group.

Jennifer Nias' chapter in this section presents a different perspective. First, the chapter begins to show how teachers, early in their careers, learn the job. Much of the evidence here is consistent with Yeomans' views: namely that teachers can learn from one another and support each other. Nias presents some valuable data on staffrooms, professional parents, role models and exemplars. However, later in the chapter the argument develops to show how teachers also preserve their sense of personal identity. The implications of this for teacher development are clear. Teacher development is both a professional and personal matter. This is consistent with Alan Coulson's and my chapter in Section one. Moreover, we need to start with where the teachers-as-learners are; we need to consider their values and philosophies. Finally, asking teachers to work together is more complex than some would believe. Working collaboratively may energize the exchange of information about classroom matters but it may have no impact on teacher development unless the depth of each teacher's individuality is appreciated.

Both Yeomans' and Nias' work, as well as the chapters in Section one, demonstrate why teacher selection is such a crucial concern. Yet in recognizing the centrality of selection, particularly at a time when col-

Introduction

laboration is prized, there is a need to ask whether the appointment of a teacher to a school is determined solely by the head (and/or governors) or with the help and involvement of staff? My chapter tries to look at the kinds of staff involvements which took place at a time of teacher selection. What emerges is how the selection was both informal and subtle, how the staff were concerned with the candidate-as-person as well as a teacher and that in a staff which valued collaboration the candidate's ability to 'fit in' was paramount.

Robin Yeomans' second chapter develops some of his ideas in the first chapter and also considers issues raised in section one. If teachers are now operating as curricular postholders, having greater leadership and playing a more active co-ordinating role, what does this mean for teacher collaboration? Yeomans' suggests that leadership and membership become more ambivalent, and he shows that a team and a group are not necessarily the same thing. The chapter adds another layer to the concept of collaboration and shows how asking teachers to work together is far from being straightforward.

Indeed, all the chapters in this section suggest that collaboration is problematical and challenging. Although no writer dissents from the view that collaboration may be a 'good thing' no one suggests that collaboration and collegiality are 'easy things'.

Are Primary Teachers Primarily People?

Robin Yeomans

Introduction

For some time, I have been preoccupied by the perception that the problems of schools are as much those of the teachers as of the taught, that meeting the needs of the children is interdependent with, if not dependent on, meeting those of the staff, and that influential thinking about education has long ignored this.

Many problems arise from the area of teachers' interpersonal needs. They have restricted opportunities for developing adult interaction skills, since they spend most of their time with children and much of their non-teaching time with other teachers, who have similarly restricted opportunities. This restriction is particularly great in primary schools because of the children's age. Paradoxically, the small group size of primary school staffs places a premium on interaction skills, since smallness increases the sense of personal interdependence. This is paralleled by an increasing need for professional interdependence, since all primary school full-time teachers normally teach the full curriculum. However, most primary teachers are isolated within separate classrooms, and are uneasy about exposing themselves professionally. They have inadequate encouragement to develop professional trust within their colleague group. Thus talk about educational issues can be anathema in many primary staffrooms.

The potential group pressure from small staffs makes many primary heads ambivalent about their position. It is not easy to stand aloof, and probably impossible if the head wishes to lead successfully. However, instinct and tradition may tell heads some aloofness is obligatory.

This chapter suggests one key to successful primary school leadership is an understanding of the processes which operate in small groups, and of the part such groups play in meeting personal needs as well as schools' organizational needs. Present circumstances make the need for such an understanding particularly acute, but there are few signs of it developing.

The chapter also discusses hindrances in developing effective staff groups, and makes suggestions for attaining greater understanding and appropriate new skills.

The Changing Context

The socio-economic background of the 1980s conspires to prevent primary staffs becoming effective task groups. One instance is the demand that schools become more responsive to the needs of society at a time when there is no consensus as to what these are. There is no clear view on how to prepare people for the fundamental psychological re-orientation of a society in which labour-intensive industry is being replaced by robot technology, permanent unemployment, and increased leisure. Thus the distress and confusion of a society where harmony and work have been replaced by strife and unemployment is mirrored in schools.

Another instance arises from the falling rolls and financial restriction of primary schools which have reduced promotion prospects and mobility, producing aging, static teacher population which frequently has thwarted aspirations. Wragg (1984) noted that 'by the end of the decade three in every five teachers will be over 40'. This development has been accelerated by the pattern of women returning to and staying in teaching after having families.

Research indicates a major area of teacher job satisfaction is within the classroom in the identification and solution of children's problems (Nias, 1980). With lengthened experience, this situation may change. Resolved problems may lose their satisfying quality as they become new routine activities. Although every new solution may suggest a fresh problem, it is increasingly likely to be an intractable one, which teachers perceive as beyond their control or present financial resources. Thus a source of job dissatisfaction emerges. Twin dangers arise of a personal failure and its projection onto the children for their inadequacy. Great insight and maturity are demanded in accepting some problems do not have solutions currently available, but this does not imply fault or failure — a maturity very difficult to develop in isolation. A sense of being of decreasing value can arise from the inevitable feeling of inadequacy experienced by many who take teaching seriously. On the one hand teachers feel threatened by those politicians and employers who tell the nation that they, the teachers, are to blame for national moral, social and economic decline. On the other they face the daily inevitability of failure to teach some child something, however much they and the child tries. Teaching can feel like trying to collect water with a sieve.

Because of the changing age profile, instances of life crises increase. I can recall staffs which have counselled worried members whose children are about to leave school with no hope of a job; those where some members have reached the age when they no longer see teaching or the prospect of promotion as a source of self-esteem and where disillusionment taints the staffroom air. There are staffs which have shared the loss felt by a widow and supported the need for fellowship; staffs which empathize with colleagues meeting the needs of aging and ailing parents and facing eventual bereavement. Divorce; adolescent offspring leaving home; menopausal effects on relationships for some women in their late 40s and 50s; the identity crisis of the psychological male menopause occurring earlier than ever in a profession where the promotion peak is early at the best of times; each can be an event of both individual and group significance resonating in the echo chamber of a primary staff. Recognizing where life has taken us and what it has excluded us from may increase a sense of imprisonment. Belated attempts to control personal destinies are increasingly likely to fail, and this failure to lead to apathy — or escape — if escape can be found. There may be no one under 30 on the staff, the threat of disillusionment becomes a group experience, and a head, having stayed beyond expectations, who is in the grip of the same forces as the rest of the staff.

Does It Matter?

In jobs which have obvious outputs, there exist alternative ways of gaining a sense of achievement. But primary teaching has few deadlines or production targets. Moreover, it offers few opportunities to work out personal needs through adult relationships. Short bursts of adult interaction punctuating days spent overwhelmingly in interaction with children, can be flawed by the projections and overtones of the dominant child-adult relationship. A teacher whose day is spent interpreting the nuances of children's lavatory requests and pencil-breaking frequency, trying to decide whether they hide work avoidance or a challenge to authority, may become conditioned to believing that things are seldom what they seem, even in the staffroom. The need to play God in the classroom can lead to staffroom disaster if fiercely defended infallibility is questioned. When classroom survival depends on being convincing, we can come to believe our own performance. It is not surprising if staff meetings become arenas where unsophisticated gladiators (heads included), indulge in the range of game-like personal combats identified by Berne (1968) — rather than places where skilled communicators engage in rational professional discussion and decision-making.

A sustained performance for a child audience demands considerable acting skills. Success requires that the actor thinks, speaks, looks and even moves in the ways s/he perceives a child would expect of an effective teacher. For the purposes of effective performance, it is deemed necessary to suppress or at least to make subordinate the teacher's needs as a person. An authoritarian teacher style will probably seem appropriate to a person who has a need to dominate, but will be presented as a view that children need discipline. A person with strong affilation needs may adopt a more egalitarian style seeing it as recognizing and preserving children's identities as people. Neither is likely to recognize the real basis of choice or see it as other than a rational one based on children's needs.

The staffroom and colleague group offer the best chance to allow personal needs to achieve legitimate status. There is a conscious feeling that closing the staffroom door excludes the pupil-oriented teacher role — though it may be illusion that the role can be shed so easily. The teacher is allowed to see him/herself as a person. Personal needs (eg. for affiliation, dominance, dependency, approval) become a stronger influence on behaviour. Through the group the individual may express a sense of self, and in the primary school size may dictate that that group is the whole school staff. However, the staffroom is also the place where the individual is asked to operate a professional consultative and decision-making role as a group member, in which effectiveness and interdependence are inextricable. Difficulties which any teacher has in shedding the pupil-oriented role when operating within the staff group are likely to limit both the social and professional potential of that group.

Thus, the success of contemporary primary schools is dependent on the teacher's interaction skills as much in the staffroom as in the classroom. This situation is underlined by the HMI (DES, 1985) and ILEA (ILEA, 1985) vision of a future primary school staffed entirely by subject consultants. We must all learn the skills of leading and of belonging. I have considered elsewhere in this volume the implications of this view of staff leadership and membership (Yeomans, 1987).

Creating effective curricula and achieving learning continuity for the seven years of a child's primary school life depends on the ability of the staff group to negotiate effectively through rational appraisal of educational needs, undistorted by the intrusion of personal need fulfilment and considerations. The staff which is not a group of secure adults is less likely to overcome those fundamental barriers to successful interaction — the absence of shared meanings and shared intentions, and therefore the presence of shared misunderstandings.

Differences of age, education, personal experience and professional training may mean that a staff group does not even share the basic coinage of interpersonal transactions, namely the very vocabulary which is used. You may wish to add to this list some of the more obvious linguistic obstacles that divide staffs ... 'basics', 'integrated', 'structured', 'knowledge', (remembering? knowing how to? understanding?) 'curriculum' (process? product?). Even the language of interaction itself invites misunderstanding ...'consultation', 'participation', 'leadership' ... 'School?' Without a process of continuing discussion, the staff group may not realize their common language divides them. Proceeding to counterfeit agreement based on shaky conceptual foundations, the head may discover that each member has implemented policies based on individual misconceptions of what has been decided. Often the dialogue peters out before spurious agreement is reached. The effect is broadly the same — the staff fails to function as a unit.

Which Way is Forward?

A positive step could be to recognize the importance of a primary staff being effective as a group in which the head has membership. Such staff groups are not yet extinct. However an over-eagerness to apply line-management assumptions to primary schools may make these 'collegial' (Coulson, 1976) schools an endangered species, if it is assumed that a system appropriate to the management of production is equally appropriate for managing professionals.

Even when the importance of group effectiveness is acknowledged there is no clear understanding of how to achieve it. It is not clear what constitutes a 'good' primary staff group in the sense of understanding what makes individuals blend as an effective educational group. Must consensus always mean agreeing with the head, or can its impetus come from the members? Are divergence and individuality allowed? Does the group shatter if it disagrees, is an individual inevitably ostracized if s/he dissents? Are the qualities of effective colleague relationships those of effective friendship? Is becoming a friendship group an essential ingredient or an inevitable by-product of success as a task group? Or does success in interactive decision-making demand an objective detachment which is enfeebled by the cohesion of friendship?

Who Leads the Way?

We usually assume the head should lead anywhere that is worth going. But in terms of group relationships today's primary heads send their colleagues conflicting messages. The stance which advises, invites consultation, discussion, involvement and mutually trusting exploration clashes with the role of implementer of cuts or freezes in resources, redeployer, agent of reduced staff hours, and reporter on colleagues' industrial behaviour. The head's own behaviour becomes one of the major problems to which their colleague group has to accommodate. Yet the head's involvement as an accepted leader and member of the staff group is essential if there is to be a match between a school's public intentions and the day to day realities of classroom life.

However successfully the head clarifies head/staff relationships, harmony between staff may be difficult to achieve. Members do not always agree on the definitions of each others' functions. Sometimes caretakers complain about teachers' untidiness and teachers complain about caretakers' failure to understand what teaching involves. Secretaries bridle at the untidy state of a teacher's dinner register, teachers object to a secretary's officious attitudes. Teachers express resentment at the excessive interference from a curriculum consultant who demands the right to do the job. The effectiveness of the head's interventions is less likely to depend on Solomon-like qualities than on the rational maturity of the participants. Such disputes are an indication that points at issue can acquire personal overtones. They can become so ego-involving that the combatants demand a referee to adjudicate in terms of victory and defeat. Under such circumstances, the head as arbiter makes an unenviable choice between sectional alienation and muddy compromise.

You may ask how so many heads have achieved the balancing of these roles for so long? Often they have not and a price has been paid. The continuum may stretch from sterile authoritarian aloofness to abdication in favour of an anarchical level of participation, exemplified by William Tyndale. But there are equally dangerous versions. One involves resolving the role conflict by redefining the role. Frequently this becomes role avoidance rather than role resolution. Another, carrying the slogan 'follow me and work all hours', is subtitled 'learn to be 99 per cent teacher and 1 per cent person'. This successfully inflates the head's ego, but distorts the staff's long-term personal and professional development. A third involves diverting attention from thorny educational problems by emphasis on packaging the classroom and the school, with the growth of a collusion in which the heads are sales managers and the staff their representatives. Selling the school is the predominant strategy, but selling of self is the prime aim. This approach may be successful in developing the cohesion of a common purpose, but is irrelevant to the long-term needs of the children.

In the search for an ideal model heads may allow their perception of self to dominate the role. However if a situation develops which demands a different self (as it will) the head has to adapt without damage to the group's view of the head and to the head's own self-image. S/he may turn to leadership research findings and decide that salvation is in being 'transactional' (Getzels and Guba, 1957) 'initiating structure' and showing 'consideration' (Halpin, 1966), or in operating a 'contingency' approach (Fielder, 1967). But no real clues are offered which reveal the mechanism for operating the chosen model. Where the head's relations with other staff are concerned, the primary school context is dominated by the daily role conflict between the competing demands of being colleague, co-professional, friend, group leader, chairman, manager, administrator, two-way channel of communication, decision source, authority figure, and responsible person. It may be necessary to operate some roles concurrently and consecutively, with the result that conflicting behaviour may produce bewilderment in the staff group. A frequent response to this situation is collusion between staff, consciously and unconsciously, to seek to impose on the head a role which the staff find coherent. The head may be conscious of this group pressure, but feel unable to respond. If the head continues to resist, group pressure may increase to the point where continued resistance threatens the relationship between staff and head, and communication is affected. Staff may disagree about what they expect of the head. But agreement between staff, children, parents, governors and LEA is even more unlikely.

Some heads do not see inter-personal relationships as an area to dabble in — 'I leave all that to the deputy', said one well-regarded head. She may well be right. The implication is that one method of performing the headship role is to maintain strict separation of personal and professional spheres. The difficulty is that the compartments are seldom watertight.

Who Follows the Lead?

The individual teacher has problems too. To behave in a mature, adult and professional manner may involve recognizing and subordinating one's personal needs. Among other things this may mean empathizing with a head who is behaving as s/he perceives the role demands though the teacher finds the head's behaviour personally threatening. Yet when affiliation needs are being rejected it may be difficult to recognize that there is 'nothing personal' and that the head is only 'doing the job'. It may require only one member to feel personally affronted by the head's actions or by the 'interference' of a co-ordinator for fragile group relationships to shatter.

The group can intimidate an individual too. It has the power to reward egos and meet affiliation needs as mentioned earlier. Group pressure on the individual to conform to group norms may be experienced as a pressure to give priority to satisfying personal needs and group needs before professional obligations. A head's rational but unpopular decision may make him/her staff room enemy number one and provoke opposition-by-inertia. In some groups voicing support for the head in such circumstances is interpreted as disloyalty to the group and invites alienation from ones peers. It is even harder to express an honest doubt when you are the single voice dissenting from head/staff agreement. Thus a scale of values is proposed which rates group cohesion above task effectiveness. In such a situation the individual who values professional integrity above group loyalty, and will no longer consider duplicity, may be forced into the position of bystander, incapable of influencing the group. Often s/he finds refuge in concentrating energies on the classroom role.

Alternatively the group can become a mirror in which members examine themselves and their own values. Collaboration may have the purpose of ensuring effective curriculum meshing as children move from teacher to teacher. But it may lead to the evolution of that task — generated cohesion which can be a most potent source of continuing task motivation. Heads have to be empathizing members of their staff groups if they are to lead in any sense. Then they can discover where the group is prepared to be led. The group in turn must endow heads with the status of influential insiders rather than perceive them as irrelevant outsiders.

The self-exposure to adult interaction can be threatening, especially to teachers, who have less experience of this than have many other kinds of workers (by the nature of their job interactions) and who can be especially short on exposure to non-teacher adult interaction. Perhaps this means that teachers who are involved with non-teachers away from school are most effective in staff group interaction. This would depend on using reflection on experiences of non-teaching groups to gain insight into their performance in the school staff group.

Planning Ahead

There can be no rational strategies or solutions for developing effective primary staff task groups without some testable hypothesis suggesting how successful primary staff groups operate. No such hypothesis seems to exist, but it can be developed. It would be derived from close and extended observation of such groups at work, coupled with the distilled perceptions of insiders in those same groups, in a series of case studies. The ethnographic movement in educational research is growing in importance, but most of its effort has been centred on secondary schools (eg. Woods, 1979). The size of staffs in such schools means these studies make a limited contribution to understanding how primary staffs operate. It is time for the participant observer to set foot inside the primary staffroom.

LEA enthusiasm for a management approach to the running of schools seems to have undervalued the influence of social psychologists on decision-making organizations. Their concepts and methodologies may offer pointers to other possible ways forward. Elsewhere, uncovering informal role-networks through extended questionnaire has proved a valuable way of helping organizations to understand their own functioning (Faris, 1981).

The purpose of understanding how primary staffs function is to help key individuals and individual schools understand themselves. The crucial interpersonal skills operating within staff groups are an important focus for courses on leadership and membership. The growth of support groups for heads, deputy heads and curriculum consultants is similarly encouraging in helping the individual thrive, cope or accommodate. However, they are not an adequate substitute for helping the interacting group-as-a-whole to recognize, meet or modify its needs. There is a need to develop skills of seeing situations from the viewpoints of others, and of seeing ourselves as others see us. The staff group may only be able to deal with its difficulties and recognize its needs when all its members are involved. There may be a way forward through self-evaluation techniques such as the 'critical friend'. A primary head may find exchange of observations with a trusted fellow-head is personally valuable. However, expanding that trust to a whole staff group is problematic. The LEA adviser/inspector role conflict generates ambivalent responses from staffs which hampers them in any supportive role. Pairing of schools might be the kind of answer which would allow exchange and trust at all levels to develop long-term.

Initial teacher education focuses on the understandings and skills required for classrooms but largely ignores the understandings and skills required for schools. The distinction is principally between working as an individual in isolation within an organization and working as a member of a task group. Adult group membership requires capacities such as interactive skills, the ability to distinguish the rational from the emotional, flexibility, objectivity and the self-awareness to understand one's effect on others. Given that the child-oriented climate in schools is counter-productive to learning these skills on the job, college is the only continuous period when teachers participate in sustained adult interaction over a sufficiently long period to develop and practice inter-adult skills.

Conclusion

This chapter has suggested why primary schools are particularly vulnerable to intra-group difficulties. It offers the hypothesis that inter-personal staff group dynamics are an important influence on a primary school's success as an organization. The staff group is important as a setting in which members can develop rewarding relationships and achieve personal and professional growth. The nature of relationships may influence the effectiveness of the task group and thus affect group decision-making and curriculum continuity. Furthermore staff relation-ships provide an important model for children who are particularly suscep-tible to teacher influence at the primary stage.

Understanding how primary staffs operate will help teachers, including heads achieve the difficult task of reconciling their personal needs with role demands. Self awareness can lead to an understanding of the motivations of others. Through interaction mutual understanding may develop, leading to inter-personal reward and a growth in professional effectiveness. We need to understand what happens when the staffroom door closes on the staff group and how this influences what happens when the classroom door closes on the individual teacher. This means less emphasis on line management concepts derived from industrial models and more on understanding the needs responses and interactions of people working in groups.

References

BERNE, E. (1968) *Games People Play*, Penguin.
COULSON, A.A. (1976) 'The role of the primary head', in PETERS, R.S. *The Role of the Head*, Routledge and Kegan Paul.
DES (1985) *Better Schools*, London, HMSO.
FARIS, G.F. (1981) 'Groups and the informal organization, in PAYNE, R. and COOPER, C. (Eds.) *Groups at Work*, John Wiley.
FIELDER, F.E. (1967) *A Theory of Effective Leadership*, McGraw-Hill.
GETZELS, J.W. and GUBA, E.G., (1957) 'Social behaviour and the administrative process', *School Review*, Vol. 65, pp. 423–41.
HALPIN, A.W. (1966) *Theory and Research in Administration*, Macmillan.
ILEA (1985) *Improving Primary Schools*, London, ILEA.
NIAS, J. (1980) 'Leadership styles and job satisfaction', in *Approaches to School Management*, Harper and Row.
WOODS, P. (1979) *The Divided School*, Routledge and Kegan Paul.
WRAGG, E.C. (1944) 'Retreating the downtrodden', *Times Education Supplement*, 26. October.
YEOMANS, R.M. (1987) 'Leading the team, belonging to the group?.' In this volume.

Learning the Job while Playing a Part: Staff Development in the Early Years of Teaching

Jennifer Nias

Fashions change, in education as in cars. In the 1960s our concern was with innovation; in the 1980s educational writers are busy explaining why these innovations have made so little difference either to teachers or to schools. Yet with the exception of Fullan (1982) most of these accounts ignore the facts that change in schools is brought about by teachers and that teachers are people. In this chapter, I conclude that there will be little alteration in the practice of a teacher, in or out of the classroom, unless the person who is that teacher also changes.

In the tradition of symbolic interactionism (Cooley, 1902; Mead, 1934), that person (or 'self') is both a social product, shaped by the response of others and an independent actor capable of innovating, initiating actions and reflecting upon them. The self has an individual identity, and an individual capacity to reflect not only upon the actions of others but also upon its own behaviour and the response it invokes from others. In short, mature actors are self-conscious, even though they can know themselves only through their social identities.

The contexts which determine these social identities change with time, place and the part which is being played. Symbolic interactionists have therefore evolved the notion of 'multiple selves' which reflect individuals' perceptions of themselves in relation to the different groups in which they participate. These 'multiple selves' encompass individuals' 'ideal' and 'real' selves, as well as taking account of the way they seem to themselves ('self-as-ego') and how they think others see them ('self-as-alter').

Yet few social psychologists would wish to defend a totally situational view of the self. Katz (1960), for example, suggested that each individual develops, through contact with significant others, an inner self or core. Ball (1972) developed this notion, distinguishing a person's 'situational selves' from his/her 'substantial self'. The latter comprises an individual's most salient values and highly prized views of and attitudes to self. It is persistently defended and is highly resistant to change.

If we adopt this perspective, teachers' 'selves' can be seen as both situational and substantial. However, as Lortie (1975) has argued, as a professional group teachers are notably free from collegial influence or restraint. Pupils, of course, play a crucial part in defining the individual's sense of occupational identity and competence, but in other respects teachers are generally protected by the nature and traditions of their work from much direct situational influence. Teaching is still perceived as an individual art, one in which 'personal predispositions are not only relevant but, in fact, stand at the core of becoming a teacher' (Lortie, 1975, p. 79).

An exception to this state of affairs, it might be argued, occurs in the early years of teaching. Although new teachers are often left alone to learn by their mistakes, they are, for two reasons, more open at this time to the influence of their colleagues than they are later on. First, in order to survive, they are ready to learn the conservative tricks of the trade, the time-honoured techniques of control, instruction and classroom organization. Secondly, as beginners they appreciate, and often rely heavily upon, the sympathy and reassurance of their headteachers and other staff members; their vulnerability makes them open to persuasion.

This chapter sets out to examine whether there is any evidence that a group of primary teachers, interviewed in the first decade of their careers, changed their 'substantial selves' in response to these kinds of situational influence. It concludes that little change occurred; that, as teachers, they relied heavily upon support and help from their colleagues while preserving their own aims, values and concerns, and that they masked the contradictory aspects of this behaviour by adopting a number of self-protective strategies.

Data Collection

Full details of the methodology used in this enquiry are available in Nias (1984). This chapter draws upon the personal accounts of ninety-nine graduates who trained in one-year Post Graduate Certificate in Education (PGCE) courses for work in infant and junior schools and who, at the time of interview, had taught for between two and nine years. Just over two-thirds had attended, over five years, a course of which I was tutor. The remainder were a random sample who between them had attended similar courses at seven universities, polytechnics or colleges of education. Altogether there were thirty men and sixty-nine women, the balance of sexes in each group being roughly the same.

I knew all the members of the first group very well, and three-quarters of them had been in touch with me between the time that their course ended and my enquiry began. Few of the second group knew me previously. I found that members of both groups were not only equally keen to talk to a neutral but interested outsider about their professional experience, but that all of them were free (sometimes to the point of indiscretion) in their comments. Twenty-two members drawn from both groups also kept a diary for one day a week for one term, and the perspectives revealed in these accounts were very similar across groups. The interpretation of the experiences reported in diaries and interviews is, however, that of an outsider rather than an insider. Although they were tested in conversation with teachers as they evolved, the generalizations presented here are mine.

I contacted all the members of each group by telephone or letter. Six of the first group did not wish to be included in the project. With their prior consent, I visited in their schools (in many different parts of England) thirty-three of the remainder and all the second group. I spent roughly half a day with each of them in their classes, making unstructured observations which I subsequently noted down before each interview. I also visited in their own homes twenty of the first group who had left teaching. I had long telephone conversations with a further eight from the first group (six were at home, two teaching outside England).

The purpose of the school visit was to provide a background against which I could interpret subsequent interview data and not to undertake any formal observations. Afterwards I conducted semi-structured interviews, taking rapid notes in a personal shorthand and using a very loose interview schedule, framed in terms of broad key questions. Respondents were encouraged to give long and, if they wished, discursive replies and I often used supplementary questions. The shortest of the interviews took one and a half hours, the longest five hours. Most took about three hours. The diaries were chiefly used to triangulate individual accounts of perspective and practice.

Many interviews of those in the first group were completed in the pub or in members' homes. All of those in the second group took place at school. Respondents talked equally freely both inside and outside their places of work. The data used here are drawn from responses to questions such as: What sort of help did you feel you needed in your first (and subsequent) jobs? Did you get as much help as you wanted? From whom? How did you feel about your colleagues? What plans do you have for the future?

I also contacted by letter, telephone or visits about 70 per cent of the headteachers of any school in which any of my interviewees had taught during the previous ten years. The purpose of these interviews was to cross-check factual information and sometimes statements of opinion, and to provide an institutional context for teacher replies. They have not been a primary source of evidence for this chapter.

Learning the Job while Playing a Part

Learning the Ropes

These teachers entered school after a nine month training, anxious to do the job well (Nias, 1981) and aware that they still had much to learn. They turned to other adults in their schools for two main types of assistance with their work.

First, lacking experience, and often therefore confidence, they needed reassurance that they were behaving in professionally acceptable ways. They therefore tried to copy the behaviour of specific teachers whom they wanted to resemble in one or more respects. Yet this was not easy; in primary schools teachers are seldom visible to one another. To be sure, all teachers have themselves been pupils and, as Lortie (1975, p. 64) reminds us, 'many are influenced by their own teachers in ways they do not even perceive'. However, as a pupil, one sees one's teacher in contact only with oneself and other learners; one has little idea of what goes on behind the scenes. By contrast, as a teacher one has access to one's colleagues' 'backstage' and public behaviour but, except in open-plan schools or in team-teaching situations, their interaction with pupils is hidden by classroom walls. So, since my interviewees' saw or remembered only a limited range of teacher behaviours, they relied on inference, extrapolation and imagination in constructing their picture of 'what real teachers do'.

One third recalled a teacher, and a few a headteacher, in their first or second school who, they claimed, had had a lasting influence on the way they wanted to teach. If one includes those who remembered such a person from teaching practice or a period of unqualified teaching, the figure rises to nearly half. Apart from the small number of 'outstanding' headteachers (who are remembered as wise, charismatic figures with unlimited time for the individual teacher, a well-articulated philosophy, a keen grasp of practicalities and a 'genuine commitment' to education (Nias, 1980)), these models had one main characteristic. Time after time they turn out to have had the classroom across the corridor from or next to the interviewee and/or to have taught the parallel class, or to have shared an open-plan unit with him/her. It was possible for my interviewees to 'pop in and out' of their models' classrooms during the school day, occasionally to hear (if not see) them teaching, to borrow or copy materials, to gather ideas, plan joint ventures, discuss problems and possibilities. In short, the teachers whom they copied were visible or, at the least, accessible.

In the absence of models in school, a further tenth of my respondents recalled drawing on what they remembered as the behaviour of teachers whose pupils they had been. These came from all sectors of education from primary schools to college and university, and appear to have shared no common characteristics. In addition, one or two teachers had idealized memories of teachers whose classrooms they had visited during their

PGCE courses. The tendency to draw on personal experience as pupils persisted even after many years of experience, particularly when individuals took on roles or responsibilities for which they felt unprepared. One of them wrote, 'I have been asked to take over the science ... I find myself drawing on 'A' level biology and 'O' level geology and memories of physics and chemistry which go further back than that ... It gives me some idea of what I ought to be doing'. Lortie (1975, p. 65) draws attention to this phenomenon (of 'modelling the mentor') arguing that it reduces the status of the profession by reinforcing the notion that 'those who have been pupils are equipped to be teachers'.

A further fifth of the total number felt that at some point they had used one or more of their colleagues as negative role models, that is, examples of attitudes or practices which they wished to eschew. However, since much of the conduct that they did not wish to emulate either took place in public parts of the school or was inferred from staffroom behaviour or from glimpses of teaching, classrooms or materials, their sense of 'the sort of teacher I don't want to be' was also based on partial knowledge.

Many teachers were critical of this aspect of their professional education, remarking sadly on their colleagues' lack of visibility or inaccessibility. 'It's incredibly difficult to discover what other teachers do', was a typical claim. 'I'd love a chance to observe others, to sort out what I want to do.' One teacher voiced the view of many others when she said 'I don't know how successful teachers behave'. The general opinion of teachers of all lengths of experience was 'You never see another teacher except at assembly or in the playground or sometimes if they're telling someone off in the corridor'. So they all tended to create their own pictures of 'what successful teachers do' and then copied 'whatever I see someone else doing that I think I could use/would suit my style/seems a good idea to me'.

Elsewhere (Nias, 1980; 1985(b)) I have argued that the absence in schools of opportunities for open discussion prevents teachers from working out their aims in a collegial context. When this lack of professional discourse is coupled with inadequate opportunities for role-modelling, teachers are thrown completely back upon their own resources. Their main support then comes from individually constructed reference groups which are often outside the school or include only a few people from within it. For schools, the result is divisive.

Professional Parents

A second source of help available to some of these teachers as they learnt the occupational behaviour appropriate to their schools was practical assistance from one or more of their experienced colleagues. Whatever teachers' values and attitudes, they have to acquire craft knowledge, as my interviewees are all too aware. They spoke of their felt need for apprenticeship in their early years of teaching. Naming familiar areas in which they would have welcomed help they listed problems with discipline, classroom organization, teaching of the three Rs, art, science and PE and of difficulties in relating to parents. While some blamed their training and others its length (nine months) or the narrowness of their teaching practice experience, most felt that this kind of knowledge could only be learned 'on the job'. Overwhelmingly, they wanted more opportunity than they had been given to 'sit by Nellie' so that they could benefit from the technical expertise of those with more practical experience than they had.

Yet few received all the help they felt they had needed and some recalled that their technical problems had been ignored or overlooked by their colleagues. They said, for example, 'I didn't know what I was doing and no one offered to show me'; 'My main problem was being entirely on my own, entirely without help'; 'If someone had been there to help me, I might not have made such a mess of my first year'; 'If only I could have sat down once a month and discussed what I was doing'. One teacher went straight to an infant school, despite training for work with older children. She left her job after two years with a deep sense of failure and, reflecting on this experience, said 'I'd go back tomorrow if I could find a head who'd train me on the job. But there aren't many like that, are there?'

However, not all the probationers who struggled to achieve technical competence felt that they did so alone. Some found within their first appointments the practical help which they craved. Notably, they were given assistance with the technology of teaching (eg. classroom organization, display, worksheets, apparatus) and with control. Indeed, nearly half my sample attributed their survival in their first posts to help from one or more specific individuals, speaking with profound gratitude of the headteachers or colleagues who, as one said 'taught me the job: I didn't want to be like him...but I couldn't have survived without him'. They said: 'She spent hours with me after school sorting out my reading materials, helping me get the room organized and showing me what to do for display'; 'There was one teacher in particular I leant on very heavily; she showed me all her materials, lent me things, was always ready to help with the difficult children. I couldn't have coped without her'.

Sometimes, rescue was available during the school day (eg. 'One day when the head said he wanted reading tests administered by Friday and my class was in its usual uproar, another teacher suggested I send my children across to him in twos and threes and he'd administer the test. And without that sort of help I'd have gone under'). More frequently, help was given in individual classrooms at lunchtime, early in the morning or after school, and was facilitated if the two teachers lived in the same neighbourhood or travelled to school together.

The main 'rescuers' were senior teachers. In a few schools (mostly infant or primary) it was the head. More frequently, it was the deputy, senior mistress, year or team leader, although sometimes it was simply an older teacher without formal responsibilities for new recruits. Moreover, in the absence of help from other teachers, some of my interviewees gratefully accepted the support of untrained personnel, such as the secretary ('Without saying anything, she used to do my register and all that ghastly dinner money... she was always ready to help with materials and sometimes, when the head was out, I even used to send a child I couldn't cope with to sit in her office'); the caretaker ('If it hadn't been for him, I'd have been there till nine every night'; and, 'He really helped me to understand the children'); and non-teaching assistants (eg. 'She was much better at a lot of the practical things than I was and she showed me how to avoid confrontations with the kids').

Some teachers needed help so badly that if it was not seen to be available within the school, they would search for it in other places. For example, 'I used to save my problems up and go on courses run by that particular adviser'; 'There was a college lecturer who had a student in the school and she was ready to help but the head wouldn't let her'; 'There was a terrific row when I went to the adviser and said I couldn't go on without help from someone, so could he please come in and see me'; 'There was a teacher from another school living in the same street and she was more use than anyone'; 'Fortunately we had a good teachers' centre and I used to go there and talk to the warden'. Interviewees also recalled turning to visiting remedial teachers, educational psychologists and social workers.

Whatever their formal status, these 'rescuers' tended to be perceived as 'middle-aged', 'experienced', 'capable' and were sometimes explicitly described as 'motherly' or 'fatherly' (eg. 'There was a group of older men in that school, willing to give up plenty of time to younger teachers. I still go back and see them... They were marvellous. One was almost like a father to me'). The secret of their success seemed to lie in their ability to anticipate when help would be needed and to provide it quietly and sympathetically. In short, their role appears to have been that of 'professional parents'. Years later they were remembered with an almost filial affection, for their kindness, interest, readiness to listen, to offer sympathy and practical help, and for their generosity with time, materials and ideas. They helped many young teachers to survive their early experiences of the classroom without despair, disaster or excessive disillusion. Without them, the drop-out rate in the first two or so years of teaching would probably have been very heavy.

The function of these 'professional parents' is one which, it has been envisaged, would be included in the role of the professional tutor. Four of my interviewees were part of pilot schemes for professional tutors. They could all identify men or women who played the part for them of 'professional parents'; none of these was the officially designated professional tutor. Accessibility, experience and kindness were more important to the probationer than a formal role in a support system.

Staffrooms

These teachers were conscious of their colleagues for reasons other than simply classroom survival. Teachers work in schools not classrooms. Few can remain completely immune from the pressures of the staff group or from the dominant ethos of their schools. As Sherif and Sherif (1967) report, membership groups often exert a strong influence on the attitudes and actions of participants, however unwillingly they at first belong to them.

So, my interviewees reported relying on their colleagues in several ways. They expected guidance in entering and becoming part of the school as a social system, appreciated support when they received it and resented its absence (eg. 'Nobody even told me where the toilets were'; 'No one would tell me anything about how the place worked, not even what the rules were'). Many spoke with appreciation of schools where their colleagues had appeared 'friendly', 'helpful', or 'supportive'. They seemed particularly aware that the job of social facilitator (ie. the person who helped 'me to become part of the school' or 'to get familiar with the things no one writes down') was normally undertaken by colleagues of the same sex as they were, though when several newcomers arrived together, the latter tended to form a group which bridged gender differences. Either way, as DES (1982, para. 5.8) reports, 'a general background of support and encouragement from the staff as a whole' was of crucial importance in promoting the new teacher's sense of acceptance into the group.

Once accepted, they wanted reassurance, sympathy and the attention of people who would share the highs and lows of their classroom lives. Some seemed to share Waller's belief, stated over fifty years ago that since the relationship between teachers and pupils is inescapably one of conflict, self-interest prescribes the maintenance of staff solidarity *vis-à-vis* pupils. Others, as Lortie (1975) suggests, used staffrooms as places in which they could share their sense of guilt and worthlessness (eg. 'I had a permanent sense of failure because I wasn't meeting the needs of individuals and it was a help to know other people felt that way, too'). Both views were summed up in this comment:

> We've got to preserve the staffroom as a place where we can all come and tear our hair and laugh and collapse. If we didn't, we'd none of us survive. It doesn't matter whether you like them or not. When you're dealing all day with the sort of problems we are, you have to get along with other adults in the place. So we get on

together ... we have to. You can't stand the classroom stress for long if the staffroom's full of tensions as well. We need each other's support, to keep us going, let alone the school ... Here, we're all failing all the time — you can't carry that on your own for long.

The need for social approval, reassurance and friendly listeners persisted beyond the individual's first appointment; several people recalled finding their second school as daunting as their first. Typically they looked in the first instance to the head (and sometimes the deputy) (Nias, 1980; DES, 1982). Later, they became more aware of the whole staff group (Nias, forthcoming). A teacher with several years' experience said 'Even now I couldn't do what I do if I didn't get on with the staff ... you do need the support of your colleagues'. Typical comments from other established teachers emphasized this feeling of mutual dependence: 'I've learnt to shut up in the staffroom and not antagonize others. You can't exist solely in the classroom'; 'I've bent my ideals a bit in order to get the support of my colleagues ... support from other teachers is very important'.

Personal Identity

It is clear then that beginning teachers use their colleagues in several ways: as exemplars (of both good and bad practice), for guidance, practical assistance and moral support. This is not surprising; the literature of teacher development and innovation is full of examples which have been used to substantiate the claim that when probationers join schools they forget their training and, chameleon-like, merge with their colleagues.

Yet further evidence from my interviewees challenges this conclusion. It suggests instead that, whereas new teachers undoubtedly value the assistance and support of their headteachers and fellow staff members, they also wish to be able to choose how much and what kind of help to accept. In the first place, there appears to be widespread acceptance of the notion that entry into the status of qualified teacher is marked by *rites de passage*, and that if initiation is made too easy, individuals will not feel themselves to be 'real teachers'. This view was most cogently put by one of my interviewees who had taken a post near her home in a physically handicapped school, where she taught a group of six children. She said 'I don't feel a real teacher yet. I haven't been through the fire of having total responsibility for a large class. I shan't feel a real teacher till I've suffered a bit'. Several more recalled that 'some of the teachers (in my first school) wouldn't help. They said I'd got to go through it by myself if I really wanted to be a teacher'. Many others argued, 'I would think I was failing if I had to ask for help'.

Secondly, alone among the professions, teaching does not ac-

Learning the Job while Playing a Part

knowledge a 'learner' role. Probationers count, for staffing purposes, as fully qualified members of staff. This forces upon them the need to assume the identity of 'teacher' as soon as their employment begins. Publicly to confess their inadequacies is to deny this identity in their own eyes and those of their colleagues. However sympathetic the latter may be, new teachers are unlikely to ask for much help until the role of probationer is formally recognized to be a transitional one between student and full-qualified teacher (as many, most recently the HMI Report (DES, 1982), have urged).

Finally, as I have argued in detail in Nias (1984), people often choose primary teaching as a career because they feel that, as teachers, they can live consistently with the values which form a central part of their sense of personal identity. When they enter the profession they have, as adults, a 'substantial self' which incorporates a well defined core of beliefs, assumptions and attitudes. The defence of this is of paramount importance to them, and offers a key to understanding the patterns of an individual's development throughout his/her teaching career. (Nias, 1985 (a), (b); forthcoming.) Indeed, these probationers were very conscious of their sense of personal identity, and as a result often found it hard to distinguish help from interference. They talked about some of those who offered assistance in terms such as: 'They pushed their ideas on me even when I didn't want to hear what they said'; 'She really was a terrible busy-body ... I had difficulty keeping her out'; 'I wish I had had the courage to keep him out. He was a completely different sort of teacher to the one I wanted to be. I think the help he insisted on giving me probably delayed my own development'. They also described in detail incidents which seemed to them to illustrate their capacity to act autonomously, even as beginners.

Psychotherapists (eg. Winnicott, 1955) have long agreed that in forming an idea of ego, as distinct from alter, children have to learn to draw a self-defining boundary around themselves. As adolescents, they may defend this boundary (which is not, however, static) with particular ferocity, feeling 'usurped' (Burn, 1956) when parents and significant others pre-empt, for example, their ability to make moral judgments or decisions about their own lifestyles. It is not unreasonable to suggest that when people begin a job, especially one which relies heavily on the infusion of their own personalities, values and attitudes, they will feel a similar need to draw boundaries around their professional selves and to defend these from intruders.

A further explanation may be found in the notion of cognitive dissonance. Festinger (1957) argued that it is psychologically uncomfortable for us to hold views which are mutually incompatible or to act in ways which are inconsistent with one or more of them. This discomfort he described as 'cognitive dissonance'. He suggested that we resolve such dissonance by changing our views so as to bring them into line with one another. Katz (1960), building on Festinger's work, argued that it is attitudes that allow us to express our values in a consistent fashion. Rokeach (1973) extended this idea with the claim that the dissonances most likely to cause an individual to change his/her views arise at the level of beliefs and values and, by implication, that it is against dissonance in values or between values and actions that we most strongly protect ourselves. If we accept the resulting conclusion, that we most protect from exposure to possible inconsistencies those attitudes which are expressive of values, then we have an explanation for why some teachers rejected help even when they felt in need of it: the psychological costs were too high, in terms of likely value-dissonance. There is evidence in my study that this was indeed the case. When help was spurned, it often seems to have been because it threatened to challenge the deeply held values or beliefs of individual teachers. For example, 'She offered to "deal with" my worst children herself, but I knew what that meant and I couldn't have gone on teaching if I'd felt I was treating children like that'; 'He gave me some of his worksheets, but they went against everything I believed in and I couldn't bring myself to use them'; 'The advice I did get, I didn't want ... I didn't want to be like them'; 'Of course you make some compromises, but if I never thought I'd follow his example, I'd give up teaching tomorrow'.

It seems, however, that it is not simply any values which we defend, but those values which form part of the self-image. Katz argues that attitudes which defend the ego are the least subject to dissonance and the most resistant to change. Rokeach makes a similar suggestion, that dissonance is experienced only when the referent for inconsistent attitudes (or actions and attitudes) is the self. Now values appear to play an important part in the aims of many teachers (Ashton, 1975; King, 1978; Nias, 1981; Woods, 1981; Sikes *et al*, 1985). Indeed, in Nias (1985 (a)) I have shown that teachers often leave their jobs or even the profession when they are faced with prolonged and continued dissonance between the values which form a central part of their self-image and their occupational lives. In addition, some teachers make an early decision to teach so that 'teacher' becomes an integral part of their self-images (Lortie, 1975; Nias, 1981 and 1984) So the more deeply committed to teaching individuals are, either because teaching enables them to translate values into actions or because they have a long-standing and powerful picture of themselves as 'teachers', the more likely they are to refuse help, if in so doing they can protect themselves from actions which are dissonant with their idea of themselves as teachers. Moreover, with experience they become 'more confident in my own decisions'; 'more relaxed about what other people think', more ready to claim, as many did, that 'I do what I think most of all. When it comes down to it, you have to rely on yourself'. In other words they become even less open, as time goes on, to challenge from the opinions and actions of others.

The Defence of Self

So, teachers, especially new ones, face a difficult problem: how can they learn from their colleagues, gain and take advantage of their support and work harmoniously with them, while at the same time preserving a feeling of individuality and the values which lie at the heart of their own sense of personal identity?

The answer, I suggest, lies in their adoption of two main sets of strategies. The first I have dealt with in greater detail in Nias (1985 (a); forthcoming): after their initial, testing period of survival teachers tended to move between schools and phases of schooling or into other occupations, looking for a context in which they felt they could 'be themselves'. If they did not find one, they reduced their commitment to their work until it became a confined and relatively insignificant part of their daily lives.

A related form of self-protection was avoiding contact with one's colleagues. Typical descriptions of their own behaviour from those who acted in this way were: 'I didn't get on with any of them because I spent all the time with the kids or in my classroom'; 'I never made any attempt to make any relationship with them; 'I shut myself up and got on with the job; getting to know them wasn't important to me'. One man said 'You've got to be prepared for conflicting pressures from the staff ... you've got to be prepared not to be liked', and a woman who left teaching after three years summed it up: 'I never had a personal relationship with any of the teachers I worked with. It takes time and effort to create a common language, especially when all my previous experience was so different from theirs. I wasn't ready to give that amount of effort to it'.

However, for many people a period varying between a few months and four years tended to elapse before they felt ready to use these strategies. Up to this point they continued to rely to some degree upon their headteachers and colleagues. They therefore fell back, when it seemed necessary, upon another set of strategies similar to those described by Shipman (1967) as impression management and by Lacey (1977) as strategic compliance. Membership groups always impose a certain level of behavioural conformity. Schools, in particular, require their members to show (eg. through dress, language, appearance) many signs of social orthodoxy; primary schools are sometimes markedly restrictive in these respects. So, my interviewees wore suitable clothes ('my school uniform'), adopted appropriate school behaviour (eg. in assembly, on playground duty), fell in with staffroom conversational norms (eg. 'I don't disagree for the sake of peace'; 'They're my mates, so I try to behave as they want me to'), used 'teacher language' when speaking to children in front of colleagues. In short, they bought social approval by consciously maintaining a double standard. As one said, 'You do the visible, conforming things ... not because you believe in them but because that's what you see everyone doing. But in your classroom, you do what you think is best'. Studies which show that probationers move in their opinions towards those of their established colleagues (eg. Finlayson and Cohen, 1967; Morrison and McIntyre, 1969) ignore the possibility of impression management. My evidence suggests that it is widespread among teachers in primary schools, especially in the early years of teaching.

Both sets of strategies depended for their success upon individuals' ability to obtain reinforcement from some other source for their definition of themselves. They achieved this by using other teachers in their schools as negative reference groups (Newcomb, 1943) and by drawing on the referential support of pupils and of those who shared similar perspectives to their own (Shibutani, 1955). Sometimes they found the latter group in a school; indeed it apparently needed only one other like-minded person for the resulting pair to become relatively impervious to the opinions of the rest of the staff. Often, however, the teachers' reference groups were outside school — spouses, family, teachers on courses, university tutors, friends from church, political parties, other schools and sectors of the education service. I have described and discussed them in further detail in Nias (1985 (b)).

Conclusion

If these primary teachers are typical, many of the profession seem to receive little systematic assistance in their early working years. Although they lack experience and would be glad to extend it by observing others, they seldom have the opportunity to do so. Instead, they fall back on partial role models, constructing their own models of teacher behaviour from chance encounters, inference and imagination. At the same time they learn appropriate public actions and attitudes by observing their colleagues in assembly, the playground and the staffroom. In addition, they master the technical aspects of teaching by trial and error, assisted by the curriculum materials, classroom walls and pragmatic advice of a more experienced colleague. However, the latter is not normally chosen for his/her occupational competence or skill, but falls into the role of 'professional parent' through accessibility or kindness. Outside the classroom, as members of a social group, they need the day-to-day support and encouragement of their colleagues, especially in the staffroom. Whether they receive this appears to depend a good deal on the presence or absence of interpersonal tensions among the staff as a whole.

The potential impact of colleagues on new teachers is however reduced by the latter's tendency to preserve their own attitudes and values from what they perceive as the intrusive influence of others. Even as probationers, they reject the help they crave, if they see it as inconsistent with the values which form the core of their self-images as teachers. When the norms of the staff group conflict with their own beliefs and attitudes, they reconcile the two through the use of strategies such as impression management. In the process they learn how to present an acceptable public appearance in their classrooms and their schools without letting the need for social orthodoxy seriously affect their aims or values. They acquire the behaviour of 'teachers' without necessarily learning more about education.

Overall, then, the evidence presented here suggests that teachers' first experiences of learning in school, and thus the bases of their future professional development, are selective and individualistic. They borrow as they can and as they think fit from the accumulated craft knowledge of kindly senior colleagues, masking disagreement and reserving the right to reject ideas, materials or practices which they find alien or inappropriate. Few of them appear to have been exposed in their early years of teaching to the notions that professional learning involves the modification of deeply held values and assumptions and that this is best achieved through open debate among equals. Changes in the structure and administration of schools might reduce the isolating nature of classroom teaching and facilitate the exchange of technical expertise. They will not necessarily affect the rooted individualism of teachers. Initiatives in staff development need to take account of the latter, of the tenacity with which teachers, as people, defend their sense of personal identity and the way in which it is expressed through their work.

Ten years ago Stenhouse reminded us that 'curriculum development must rest on teacher development' (1975, p. 24). The next step is to realize that teacher development rests on personal development, that the management of change in schools can proceed no faster nor further than the individual's sense of personal identity allows. Since individual teachers are the only people who know how they see themselves, anyone interested in staff development should start by listening to them.

References

ASHTON, P. et al. (1975) *The Aims of Primary Education: A Study of Teachers' Opinions*, London, Macmillan.
BALL, D. (1972) 'Self and identity in the context of deviance: The case of criminal abortion', in SCOTT, R. AND DOUGLAS, J. (Eds.), *Theoretical Perspectives on Deviance*, New York, Basic Books.
BURN, M. (1956) *Mr Lyward's Answer*, London, Hamish Hamilton.
COOLEY, C. (1902) *Human Nature and the Social Order*, New Brunswick, N.J. Transaction Books.
DES (1982) *The New Teacher in School*, (Matters for Discussion 15) London, HMSO.
FESTINGER, L. (1957) *A Theory of Cognitive Dissonance*, Stanford, Stanford University Press.

FINLAYSON, D. and COHEN, L. (1967) 'The teacher's role: a comparative study of the conceptions of college of education students and headteachers'; *British Journal of Educational Psychology*, 37, pp. 22–31.

FULLAN, M. (1982), *The Meaning of Educational Change*, New York, Teachers College Press.

KATZ, D. (1960) 'The functional approach to the study of attitude change', *Public Opinion Quarterly*, 24, pp. 163–204.

KING, R. (1978) *All Things Bright and Beautiful*, London, Wiley.

LACEY C. (1977) *The Socialization of Teachers*, London, Methuen.

LORTIE, D. (1975) *Schoolteacher: A Sociological Study*, Chicago, University of Chicago Press.

MEAD, M. (1934), *Mind, Self and Society*, Chicago, University of Chicago Press.

MORRISON, D. and MCINTYRE, D. (Eds.) (1969) *Teachers and Teaching*, Harmondsworth, Penguin.

NEWCOMB, T. (1943), 'Attitude development as a function of reference groups: The Bennington Study' in MACCOBY, E., NEWCOMB, T., HARTLEY, E. (Eds.) (1966), *Readings in Social Psychology*, London, Methuen.

NIAS, J. (1980) 'Leadership styles and job satisfaction in primary schools', in BUSH, T. et al. (Eds.) *Approaches to School Management*, London, Harper and Row.

NIAS, J. (1981) 'Commitment and motivation in primary school teachers', *Educational Review*, 33, pp. 181–190.

NIAS, J. (1984) 'The definition and maintenance of self in primary teaching', *British Journal of Sociology of Education*, 5, pp. 267–80.

NIAS, J. (1985a) 'A more distant drummer: Teacher development as the development of self' in BARTON, L. and WALKER, S. (Eds.), *Education and Social Change*, London, Croom Helm.

NIAS, J. (1985b), 'Reference groups in primary teaching: Talking, listening and identity' in BALL, S. and GOODSON, I. (Eds.) *Teachers' Lives and Careers*, Lewes, Falmer Press.

NIAS, J. (forthcoming) *Becoming and Being a Teacher*, London, Methuen (forthcoming).

ROKEACH, M. (1973) *The Nature of Human Values*, New York, Free Press.

SHERIF, C. and SHERIF, M. (Eds.), (1967), *Attitudes, Ego-Involvement and Change*, New York, Wiley.

SHIBUTANI, T. (1955), 'Reference groups as perspectives', in MANIS, J. and MELTZER, B. (Eds.) (1972), *Symbolic Interaction: A Reader in Social Psychology*, 2nd edn., Boston, Allyn and Bacon.

SHIPMAN, M. (1967) 'Theory and practice in the education of teachers', *Educational Research*, 9, pp. 208–212.

SIEGEL, A. and SIEGEL, S. (1957) 'Reference groups, membership groups and attitude change', in WARREN, M. and JAHODA, M. (Eds.) (1973) *Attitudes*, Harmondsworth, Penguin.

SIKES, P.J., MEASOR, L. and WOODS, P. (1985), *Teacher Careers: Crises and Continuities*, Lewes, Falmer Press.

WALLER, W. (1932), (1961 new edn.) *Sociology of Teaching*, New York, Wiley.

STENHOUSE, L. (1975), *Introduction to Curriculum Research and Development*, London, Heinemann.

WINNICOTT, D. (1955) *The Family and Individual Development*, London, Tavistock.

WOODS, P. (1981) 'Strategies, commitment and identity: Making and breaking the teacher role', in BARTON, L. and WALKER, S. (Eds.) *Schools, Teachers and Teacher*, Lewes, Falmer Press.

Staff Selection or By Appointment? A Case Study of the Appointment of a Teacher to a Primary School

Geoff Southworth

Introduction

The appointment of teaching staff to a school is commonly regarded as a key management task. The significance of appointments has been further increased with the encouragement of teachers to work collaboratively to implement whole school policies. Teachers now must work not only with children but also with their adult colleagues. Consequently, there is some need to examine a candidate's abilities in both these areas. Given the need to examine a candidate's fitness with regard to collaboration there is a further issue of whether this examination is a task for the school's management or should the candidate's future colleagues be involved?

This chapter will consider these issues utilizing data from the Primary School Staff Relationships (PSSR) project. This is an ESRC funded project based at the Cambridge Institute of Education. The chapter will consider teacher selection in a school which places value on teachers working collaboratively. The data is derived from a single school's approach and experience.

Some Issues from the Literature

The burgeoning literature on school management has generated a corresponding growth in the attention given to the selection of teaching staff in schools. However, whilst in quantitative terms there is now rather more written about selection, the scope of the literature is still far from comprehensive. Within the literature there are many gaps. There are also particular features and issues which are emphasized.

Generally the literature provides a critical review of practice in schools, often noting shortcomings (eg. Barry and Tye, 1972; Poster, 1976;

Ferguson, 1979; Morgan, 1981; Samuel, 1986). Yet in so doing a number of the writers base their views on personal experience as selectors, or as candidates, or both. Whilst there is a degree of consistency between their collected criticisms, individually their arguments may not, in terms of evidence, be very substantial.

More substantial and investigative studies have been carried out by Hilsum and Start (1974), and Morgan, Hall and Mackay (1983). Hilsum and Start focus on promotion and careers in teaching to an extent that reduces attention paid to selection. Morgan, Hall and Mackay have produced a major piece of research under the aegis of The Project on the Selection of Secondary Headteachers (POST). The very title demonstrates the particular emphasis so that although the investigation is methodologically more sound than those writers who work solely from personal experience, the scope of POST is limited and partial, and its recommendations may not always be transferable to primary school appointments. Nevertheless, POST represents a careful and critical review of staff selection approaches and the project team identified one very significant issue, that of 'amateurism' which they attribute to two features:

> ... first to the culture of education which tends to see practice outside education as inapplicable to education, stresses the importance of personality and rejects notions of management; and second, to the skills and attitudes of education officers, which indicate a lack of professional expertise in this area and a reliance on intuition or 'feel' as a basis for judgments about the suitability of candidates. (Morgan, Hall and Mackay, 1983, p. 144)

Further recognition of this kind of 'amateurism' has possibly manifested itself in these and other writers advocating a more formalized and rational approach. Selection is now presented as a process which requires all the constituent parts being thought out, planned and organized (Morgan, 1981; Morgan, Hall and Mackay, 1984). Moreover these constituent parts should also interrelate and interlock (Day, Johnson and Whitaker, 1985). It is also interesting to note that these writers cited above (and below) tend to consider staff selection not only as a formal and rational process itself, but also in the context of organizations which are similarly formal and rational. Writers on staff selection do not only prefer the formal mode of organization, they also give little attention to the democratic, political, subjective and ambiguous modes of organization (see Bush, 1986).

It is not surprising then that the formal and rational approach to staff selection has turned the discussion in the direction of skills and techniques. Quite a lot of the literature is pre-occupied with *what* selectors should do and *how* they should proceed (eg. Day, Johnson and Whitaker,

1985; Whitaker, 1983; Morgan, Hall and Mackay, 1984; Phipson, 1986). Examples of practice are offered and the writers become more prescriptive than analytical. Nor is it surprising that many writers devote space to interviewing skills. The value of interviewing remains largely undiminished in the selection process for jobs in school, and there are many skills to acquire. Only Riches (1984) and Mackay (1981) appear to avoid a singular focus on interview techniques since they critically discuss the validity, purposes and weaknesses of interviewing. From a review of the literature one is left with the impression that the interview is a main, if not *the* main event in selection. Information gained informally from IN-SET management courses, discussions with heads and deputies and from job particulars for primary school posts around the country reveal a persistent and enduring belief in the formal, panel interview, frequently only supported by a brief visit to the appointing school, and written data on the candidate (curriculum vitae/application form/letter of application/reference).

Although skills figure prominently there is another issue which occurs simultaneously, that of ethics. What is permissible in law obviously is mentioned but the notion of ethics can be identified across the literature as a theme since the authors often refer to what is 'fair', particularly for candidates (see Morgan, Hall and Mackay, 1984; Ferguson, 1979). With this regard for candidates one can also note that generally only two perspectives are offered. The first perspective is that of the selectors who are, in formal, hierarchical organizations, exclusively taken to be heads, governors and LEA officers. The second perspective is that of the candidate. Discussing selection strictly in terms of selectors and candidates tends to overlook any potential role which staff from the appointing school, other than the head, might play.

To summarize it is possible to list six issues arising from the literature:

1. there is no individually comprehensive piece of research, nor does the accumulated literature comprise a comprehensive overview;
2. staff selection in schools is regarded as amateur;
3. staff selection is currently being presented as needing to be formally and rationally planned;
4. the acquisition of skills and techniques will enhance the process;
5. the panel interview, with or without a school visit, represents the major face-to-face selection event;
6. only two perspectives are considered, those of the selectors and those of the candidates.

Collaboration

Having noted the partial and limited coverage of the literature, this is thrown into greater relief by recent trends in primary education. From a number of sources teachers are being urged to participate in decision-making, collaborate, and strive for cohesive schools (eg. Coulson, 1980; DES, 1985; Campbell, 1985; ILEA, 1985; Southworth, 1985 and 1987). It is no longer sufficient for primary school teachers to be competent with children, there is now an expectation that they should also be able to work with their adult colleagues. This means then that in schools which work collaboratively (or want to) at times of staff appointments at least two sets of qualities need to be examined: classroom competences and skills with colleagues. These two areas may already be being scrutinized.

Discussions with heads and teachers and data from my own 'dipstick' surveys of job particulars, show how schools are now referring to the successful candidate as needing to be capable classroom practitioners and willing to contribute to the staff's 'teamwork'. Teamwork is an interesting concept since it is rather imprecise — there are, after all, different kinds of teams (eg. hockey and athletics). For the purposes of this chapter I have rather simply taken teamwork to mean the willingness of school staffs to work together and to collaborate.

There is, though, something of an assumption in all of this, chiefly that 'appointment' guarantees team *membership.* Yeoman's (1986) suggests that working at a school is not the same thing as being a member of that school's staff group. Those who have experience of joining a school's staff may recall the *rites de passage* they endured. Such rites may signal not just a 'getting to know you' phase, but, perhaps, a series of 'tests' of the newcomer's ability of fit in. These 'tests' are likely to vary from school to school, as will the criteria employed to make judgments but whatever the tests are they constitute the staff group's conditions of membership. Such an induction process is therefore important, especially where incoming teachers are appointed to work with colleagues, since induction becomes a second stage selection process and every bit as important as the first stage. In these circumstances it is likely to be desirable that the selectors find candidates who will satisfy the staff group's conditions of membership. To do this selectors will probably need to recognize the staff group's values and, perhaps, utilize these values in the selection process.

However, the discussion has noted three possible obstacles to this:

(a) the absence of a recognized role for staff at times of selection;
(b) the assumption that appointment automatically ensures membership;
(c) the emphasis placed on a formal and rational approach which

may obscure the kinds of subjective 'tests' which candidates will also face.

Therefore a key question emerges; how do schools which work collaboratively select teachers who will continue and contribute to that school's collaborative traditions and ways of operating? It was in pursuit of data which begins to respond to this question that led to this research.

The Research

The main method of collecting data was by using structured and semi-structured interviews. Since I was already a participant observer of the staff group because of the PSSR project* I was well placed to pursue this issue. However, because my role in the school was that of a part-time teacher (nominally one day a week) I decided to focus my attention on the main actors: the head, Graham, deputy head, Jim, scale 2 teachers Vera and Victoria and scale 1 infant teacher, Carol. By using interviews I hoped to gather in each actor's individual perspective of what happened, namely how this school selected a new teacher.

I did not observe any of the formal aspects of selection (interview, short listing, governors' meeting) but was able to observe informal discussion within the staff group. The case study took place during a period of teacher action. It is likely that this reduced the level of informal discussion and consultation between staff.

The School

Greenfields C.P. School, as I shall call it, is situated in a village which is both a rural community and a dormitory settlement for the professional classes who mostly work in the nearby town. Parents' occupations vary: lawyers, doctors, academics, commercial managers, business representatives, farmers, and farm labourers. The majority appear to be professional and business people living in owner-occupied homes, and the village is affluent. The school serves Greenfields and another village with the children 'bussed' in. The school is a group 3, 5 to 11 primary school. Children are arranged into five classes so that each class is a mixed-age group. The building is a composite of three phases. Two classrooms are housed in the original nineteenth century school. Two more classrooms (plus library and toilets etc.) are housed in an extension added onto the old school. Finally the fifth classroom is in a completely separate block along with the hall, and kitchens, built in the late 1960s.

*PSSR project is the Primary School Staff Relationship project based at Cambridge Institute of Education funded by ESRC, 1985–87: Director D.J. Nias.

Details of the staff are set out below:

Name	Role and responsibility post	Teaching load	Age of class
Graham	Headteacher	0.3	6–7+
Jim	Deputy	0.5*	8–9+
Victoria	Scale 2 Maths	full	9–10+
Mary	Scale 1	0.7	6–7+
Carol	Scale 1	full	5–6+
Vera	Scale 2 i/c Infants & Language	full	5+
Joan	Scale 1	full	9–10+

*The deputy, being engaged on Union and Education Committee duties was nominally present for 0.5 of the week. His class were taught full-time by Joan who was in the school on temporary annual contract basis. Thus the school had enhanced staffing.

Additionally, I was present in the school for one day each week, working as a part-time teacher. This meant I worked as a class teacher, or with small groups of pupils, or alongside the class teacher, or with individual pupils. The age of the staff is such that no one is younger than 30 or older than 50, the oldest being the head. The school has a 'secretary', Norma, who comes in for three mornings and an ancillary assistant, Maggie, who is in every day. Everyone refers to everyone else by christian names.

The claim that the staff works together is based on a number of perceptions. Firstly, the conditions of entry for the PSSR project required someone in the LEA to nominate schools whose staff worked together. Then all the staff needed to approve the presence of a researcher and the researcher had to be satisfied that the school was a suitable setting. So both 'insiders' and 'outsiders' had to be in agreement that the school was appropriate. As the research progressed this was validated and certainly it is my view that Greenfields is a school where teachers relate to one another frequently, productively and closely. It is a school which does exhibit collaborative ways of working:

> *Carol:* 'I think this staff ... is a very strong staff. Graham allows his staff to say what they think and to be what they are and that works well with the people we've had ... it's a very giving staff, we pour things in on people when they're new, we're always available with time and ideas and everything ...'
>
> *Jim:* 'There are four or five of us and I suppose we have been together for six years now and we know our ways and we've moulded our personalities accordingly.'
>
> *Graham:* 'I think the staff feel very special themselves, as a staff. They feel they have a special relationship with each other which other people don't understand and they don't want other people to understand because they want it to be special ... There's a great deal of warmth between them ... So there's that form of emotionalism. It's not any deeper than that, but they do feel that there's a special relationship.'

Staff Selection or By Appointment

The Situation

In early March, 1986, Vera, Scale 2 (i/c Infants and Language) the Infant reception class teacher was appointed to a similar post in another local school. Vera applied for this post because she was already involved with her 'new' school's community since her husband was the minister at the church there: 'I just want to become more involved with that community, that's really the reason'. Also having been at Greenfields for six and a half years she felt it was time for a change: 'I certainly wouldn't want to stay anywhere longer than ten years. I have moved around a fair bit and I think its a good idea'. Vera was leaving for positive rather than negative reasons. The school governors agreed to Vera leaving at the end of the term in order to start her new job immediately after Easter. This left Greenfields with the need to quickly find a replacement.

What Happened

The head, Graham, was initially busy with a number of decisions. He now had a scale post to award and responsibilities to determine. How did he assess the situation?

> Graham: 'My first reaction is regret, because Vera is an excellent teacher, particularly in her language work and in fact in our top class we've now got thirty children who have gone right through the school having been with Vera and there isn't one of them who isn't a good reader, not just a reader, but a good reader. So obviously there is a feeling of regret there.
>
> Not unmixed, though, because we're an experienced staff, and it's probably not a bad thing at this point to have an injection perhaps of a young teacher with lots of enthusiasm and perhaps some different ideas. So what I'll be looking for is a scale 1 reception class teacher from September. From Easter we need to appoint a temporary teacher and what I'm going to try and do is to persuade somebody that I know ... I've got two or three ideas. I haven't got one person, but two or three ideas of people I might just contact and suggest that they apply for the temporary post. People who have done supply work and so on for us and have fitted in very well.
>
> The day before Vera was appointed, the County changed the rules so that we can't actually advertize for a scale 1 teacher next September. The idea, I think, is that they appoint a number of probationary teachers to the County and then those probationary teachers are in some way apportioned out to the

various schools. Now it may be that none of those are reception teachers, but there will obviously be re-deployments so that exercise has got to be gone through before we can even start looking anywhere else. So provided we can get somebody young and enthusiastic, then it's not a disaster, although obviously we shall miss Vera. As for the language coordination which she's doing, I shall ask Jim to do that. Obviously he'll make an excellent job of coordinating language throughout the school and I shall be asking the governors to give the scale 2 post to Carol. It's ridiculous that she hasn't got one anyway, so the idea is that Carol will become scale 2 coordinator for infants and Special Needs and then Vera's position as coordinator for language will be passed on to Jim.'

Up to this point Graham had closely followed the school management 'manuals' on staff selection. He had assessed the situation, was treating the vacant post as a new post rather than as the post was when Vera was appointed, and he was redistributing responsibilities and tasks (see Morgan, Hall and Mackay, 1984; Morgan, 1981; Phipson, 1986).

The fact that this appointment was for a temporary post of one term is relevant and does not detract from this case study's significance. Within the school there is a history of teachers coming on either temporary contracts and then being made permanent, or of part-time staff being made full time. Two of the present staff, Carol and Victoria, are examples of this whilst Mary was likely to be made full time as soon as possible, although not in this instance, because this post was for reception class infants, a specialism Mary could not offer. This pattern of teachers coming on a limited basis and then being admitted more comprehensively is found in another of the PSSR project schools. It perhaps points to the distinction between appointment and membership being recognized by the schools since membership is 'suspended' or 'with held' until certain criteria are satisfied through actions observed in the 'trial period' of temporary or part time employment.

Values

In speaking of 'certain criteria' I am acknowledging that the teachers have certain values concerning what constitutes a 'good teacher'. These values are of central importance. Staff selection can be described as a search for someone to fill a vacancy. In order to search for this person you need to know what you are looking for and what a 'good teacher' looks like to you. Barry and Tye's (1972) question expresses this succinctly: Do you know what you want? I tried to gather some answers to this and in so doing discovered some of the teachers' values in terms of what a 'good teacher' looks like.

Staff Selection or By Appointment

(i)

GS: 'What will you be looking for with regard to how somebody would fit in here? You've talked of a young, enthusiastic person but what kind of social skills do you think they need?'

Graham: 'I think probably that's a very important question for me to answer and think about. We've got to be looking for someone who will, again just to use the phrase 'fit in' with the rest of the staff. They (the staff) don't actually take kindly to anybody who is too shy. They don't mind somebody taking a little while to settle down, but once they've settled down the rest of the staff here are the kind of people who are delighted to help and give help, they like to be asked for it and they like a fairly outgoing sort of person. Even somebody relatively quiet like Mary was when she first came, she soon fitted in because she had confidence in her own ability, so we need somebody confident, not arrogant, but reasonably outgoing and prepared just to talk to the others and, to use a much over-used word, to be professional. I see the reception class as very crucial, it's a very important position. It's got to be somebody very strong, they've got to be really good in knowing about teaching reading and knowing how reading is taught and really getting down and doing a good job there, because it's vital to the rest of the school.'

(ii)

GS: 'What, generally speaking, do you think a teacher needs to be a Greenfields teacher? What are the kinds of things you know your colleagues look out for?'

Carol: 'I think actually to say it's Greenfields is terribly wrong. It's what I think all teachers in all schools should be like, I'm going to generalize in that respect. I'm not going to say what I think they look out for. I look for somebody who uses initiative, now this is not in any order of priority, is resourceful, takes on board responsibility without taking over anything, because I think when you've got a strong staff that can bring about dreadful repercussions, is thoughtful, thinks outside the school, beyond the bounds of the school — it may be in interests or it may just be not limiting themselves to school, but certainly thinking outside the bounds of the school.'

GS: 'Is that both educationally and in general life?'

Carol: Yes, I think so. I'm not saying that we're scuba-diving or anything like that, or hot-air ballooning, it's an attitude I think I'm talking about, rather than a type. Interested in what they are doing, to the point of being fascinated, inventive and imaginative, I don't mean just in pictures, arty-crafty inventive, I mean in everything. A confident person, and yet Victoria and I have both commented that we have grown in confidence since being here, so I don't know how confident we were when we arrived. I think Graham has given us the confidence, we've both said that. He's given us something, space in which to become confident in our jobs and that is important, that is something which may be particularly important here, because you are expected to deal with a lot of people. In other schools I've taught in, if anything happens or comes in from the outside you say 'I'll go and see the Headteacher' or point out his room, but here you are expected to deal with people yourself and I think that it's important to have that confidence. I take it as read in all this, when I'm talking about personal qualities, that they are good teachers. Thoughtful, I don't know whether I've said that, two others: (a) A concern for others, a concern for this community. (b) A sense of humour. They are very determined people here, with principles, not necessarily all the same. There's also a respect of privacy; people as personalities and as individuals, although they are very close, they respect each other's privacy and I think that sometimes can get confused in a small staff.

GS: 'You spoke of two supply teachers who fitted in well, there were qualities about them that you clearly liked and found attractive. Do you know what the qualities were that appealed?'

Carol: 'They were both very competent. They came in, and they were starting things off all the time, they weren't just hanging on my every word, they were asking how many children there were and absorbing, there was a calmness about them that goes with the competence. It's odd that I say that, actually, because I'm not the calmest person there is in the world, but there was an air of competence — calmness is the wrong word. Both of them were thoughtful teachers, and even though they'd been here a short space of time they were remarking on things the children were doing, they didn't see themselves as just filling in for a couple of days. They did interesting things with the children. One of them in particular was very bright and thought in terms of education rather that teaching and the terror of my life I think would be to have a Joyce Grenfell reception class teacher, who does what infant teachers sometimes do, they limit themselves to an age group in their minds and their thinking, instead of seeing education, and one of them was very thoughtful about education ... '

(iii)
GS: Given all you've described about the cohesion of four or five

people, the person 'coming in' will have to work with that group, what do you think they need to be able to fit in, what will you be looking for?'

Jim: 'Well, socially I think a sense of humour and receptiveness to new ideas, which I think all the staff, including Vera share. A certain attitude towards the children which I don't think necessarily Vera does share ... she's a reception teacher, but there's a ... well no, having seen her in action it's not so marked as I thought it was, but I think she still has a 'mother hen' feeling towards children, which isn't shared by anyone else on the staff. I'd like to see someone treating the children in reception as Carol treats her children. I'll be looking for that sort of approach to education, because I think one's attitude towards children does colour one's educational outlook so I'll certainly be looking for that. What other qualities? Sensitivity, certainly, I think we are a fairly sensitive staff, I mean sensitive in picking up signals and reacting in certain ways. Somebody who is good at the job and I'd be the first to acknowledge that Vera is, she's an expert at her job.'

(iv)
GS: 'What kinds of qualities would you like to see in the new teachers?'

Victoria: 'Well, I'd like to see somebody lively. That's because I like lively people, enthusiastic people. Someone who would be fairly open minded about the kind of ideas that would be around. Obviously people have to develop their own style of teaching, but if they are enthusiastic and imaginative then I think that's the sort of person I would like to see, given that we get a probationary teacher, that is. I suppose if it's an older person then that's different. You're going to ask me how it's different. I don't think it's impossible to find somebody who's prepared to soak up the ideas in a primary school. That's what I did when I went to Greenfields. There were lots of things that I did before that I've gradually changed since. It isn't impossible. But how you choose somebody at an interview I don't know.'

The teachers use some key words which other discussions throughout the year validate. The key words are: competence, confidence, enthusiastic, sensitive, open minded and concerned. They are hardly precise, and certainly do not match up to the degree of specificity suggested by many writers on staff selection who advocate carefully framed job and person descriptions. One interesting feature is how the teachers are interested in both the newcomer as a professional and as a person. There is quite a measure of overlap between the professional skills of the newcomer and their personal qualities. Furthermore there is a marked emphasis on personal qualities rather than professional functions. It matters far more that the newcomer is confident and sensitive than that they are an integrated day operator or can use the school's particular reading scheme or approach to maths:

Victoria 'I think the feel of the school has a lot more to do with the personalities in it than the actual roles that people play'.

One other feature implied in what the teachers say is the scope of the individual's perspective. In mentioning the avoidance of a narrow focus on one's own class the teachers are, I believe, indicating that the individual should have a sense of the school as a community as well as a sense of 'my' class. Other comments alluded to the need for all staff to come into the staffroom, for newcomers to ask all staff for help and advice, and to be concerned with the school's reputation.

Involvement

There appears to be some shared understanding about what a teacher needs to work at Greenfields, and there is some consistency about what a 'good teacher looks like'. The fact that it is shared probably helps involvement. Indeed, there is likely to be a relationship between involvement and shared understandings. The school has a tradition of open discussion and communication. Very little is written down, almost all communication is verbal. There is also little private communication. Rarely does the head talk alone with someone in his office. Typically the head talks in front of others about day to day matters, policies, events, plans and staffing issues. Staff respond by talking in the same way amongst themselves and to Graham. It was also usual for professional matters, such as who has applied for the job and what that person's application looks like, to be discussed in front of the secretary and ancillary staff. The feeling is that they too are 'staff'.

There was one major constraint on involvement, namely teacher action. This particularly affected Jim, the deputy, who was not on the premises at lunchtime. It also prevented any formal meetings taking place between Graham and the staff.

I wanted to find out whether there was a tradition of formal involvement such as whether teachers were members of the interview panel or if senior staff were included in the short listing of candidates. The fact that the answers emphasize the informal suggests that there would have been little formalized involvement regardless of teacher action.

(i)
GS: 'Who is likely to be involved?'
Graham: 'All of them. we all have an input, whether I want to be involved with them or not, they'll all be involved, they'll all be saying something. They've already made suggestions as to who might possibly be the temporary teacher for next term —

people that they've seen coming in as supply teachers. There's a quality about certain people, they're accepted. I think it's efficiency and effectiveness, more than anything else, that's recognized by the rest of the staff.'

(ii)

GS: 'What level of involvement would you like in the appointment of what we might call your partner?'

Carol: 'I would like to be involved. Always, anyway, when we have new appointments, the person comes to the school, they come to the school in ones, rather than a batch on the day of the interview, and this staff always says what they think about people who come for new jobs anyway, that is what Graham wants because he wants people to work together. I would like to spend time with the person ... I work very instinctively with people, terribly instinctively, but I would like to be involved. Somebody new will come in, a supply will come in for the summer term and then somebody will be appointed permanently ... Things seem to be moving fast ... there was the problem of Vera giving her notice, whether it would be accepted, and who we would have across there (in Vera's class), we've had two very good supplies, one I thought was a very attractive person ... '

It was Carol who had mentioned the supply teachers to Graham.

(iii)

Victoria had also offered a suggestion:

Victoria: 'I said Mrs 'Z' would be suitable last week. I said somebody like Mrs 'Z' because she was the first person who came into my mind as an example of a professional supply teacher.'

GS: 'Graham has obviously heard, if not asked for, people's views on a short term replacement. How much do you think the staff will be involved, people like yourself, in helping to choose this person?'

Victoria: 'I find it very difficult to know how much I am consulted about these things and how much I just tell Graham what I think.'

GS: 'That's a nice distinction.'

Victoria: 'You've noticed that I don't hang back if I've got something to say. But then I don't believe in letting things happen and then carping about them because you don't like them. If I tell Graham what I think — I mean I didn't suggest a probationary teacher, but I did suggest somebody like Mrs 'Z' as a temporary replacement and obviously he absorbed that idea and to a certain extent acted on it, if he mentioned it to the Adviser — but having said that I think I wouldn't then expect him to take notice of what I'd said. I wouldn't be offended if he didn't, but I would think it was a bit stupid to just sit back and let something happen and then afterwards say why on earth did you get somebody like that.'

(iv)
GS: 'How much do you think you'll be involved in the selection of Vera's replacement?'
Jim: 'The actual formal process? I'm not really a teacher-governor, so I don't know whether I'll be involved in that at all, which is a shame I think. In the informal process — yes, I think I shall be fairly heavily involved. Graham is the type of Head who will consult me and the type of person who will probably let me see the application forms and such like, and he'll take note of what I advise. So from that point of view yes, perhaps that's even more valuable than being involved in the formal procedure. Graham's view at the interview will be the main one, because he does have a lot of influence over the governors, which isn't the case in every school.'
GS: 'His influence works in a very quiet way, doesn't it?'
Jim: 'Yes. It's a sort of pervasive influence. I've talked about him making hard managerial decisions, but in fact I think, like myself, he is generally loath to make hard managerial decisions and that doesn't imply that he fudges, but I think his style of management is very much the one that I would adopt, of full consultation, consultation meaning actually listening to what people say and acting upon it.'

These comments indicate both a willingness to be involved by the teachers and a feeling that Graham will involve them and be influenced by them. Other data supports this. The openness of communication and discussion has created a climate where teachers offer ideas and solutions to each other, and since Graham is a member of the staff group that naturally includes him, and he includes them. As a result staff feel involved and that their views are recognized. They also feel that Graham represents their views to the governors. One other fact to mention is that governors on the selection panel also ask the staff for their views about candidates.

What Took Place

An advert was published in the LEA staffing lists for a scale 1 teacher for the summer term. Then I talked to Graham:

Graham: 'I've only had three applicants. Of course, it's very short notice. What I've done is to arrange with the governing body's staffing sub-committee of three, a chairman and two others, all very experienced interviewers in their own field, to interview next Monday afternoon. I've photocopied all the documents and given them to the three governors. Today I'm intending to invite all three to interview and we're (Graham and governors) meeting tomorrow evening to discuss the application forms and during the day I hope I get telephone references from Heads and I'll invite them (the candidates) to come into the school all day Monday if they want to, if they want to come in during the morning and stay to lunch or whatever, they'd be welcome to do that. Then everybody (ie. the staff) gets a look at them. Two of them we have actually met; one of them we know quite well, she's been doing supply work for us for some years. Another one came into the school to have a look around last week and everybody was quite impressed with her. The other one Vera knows, and reading between the lines, with Vera's very kind way of talking about people, I doubt whether she'd be suitable, her form is very wishy-washy.'

GS: 'So you know a fair bit about these three.'

Graham: 'That's right, although they have met the second, but not for more than a few minutes.'

GS: 'To what extent will the staff comments about the candidate weigh with your decision?'

Graham: 'One of the criteria is that there must be a possibility at the very least, of their fitting into the staffroom. I don't think I've actually ever said this, but it's probably been obvious from some of the things I've said, but I do believe that the atmosphere in the school actually moves outwards from the staffroom or wherever the staff meet, like ripples on a pond. If you've got a happy school you've almost certainly got a staff who work together well, who can relate well to each other and you've got a reasonably happy staffroom and that leads straight out to the rest of the school and affects the children and the parents and everything else. So it is to my mind fairly important that whoever we appoint is acceptable to the staff.'

GS: 'So Monday you interview and decide which of these three. How do you see that day going? You're inviting them to come for the day?'

Graham: 'I hope that they'll all come in the morning, sometime during the morning.'

So three candidates were called. Not only did they come on the day of the interview, but some visited before then. Alex was one who did.

> GS: 'Did you, during the course of yesterday (the day of the interview) pass on to Graham who you thought was the best candidate from your viewpoint?'
>
> Vera: 'Yes, I'd done so in fact the other day when Alex came to visit. She came into this room and said "This feels like home" and as soon as she came in I thought "Well, you look as if you are at home" and I could see she was an infant teacher and I immediately felt that she was the right person. I do know the other two who were interviewed but it just seemed to click.'
>
> GS: 'Has Alex been here before? She's not done any supply work?'
>
> Vera: 'No. I've never met her before.'
>
> GS: 'So this was the first time you'd met her. Who did you tell that you felt very positive about her?'
>
> Vera: 'I told Graham and some of the staff who were in the staffroom at the time. In this school when a new teacher's being appointed it's very much a family affair and people do make their own observations and tell Graham what they're feeling, and so it's quite normal to go and say to the rest of the staff if a person seems very suitable.'

Even though Vera was the teacher who was leaving her views still influenced others. The three candidates visited the school, interviews were held on a Monday and Alex got the job for the Summer term.

> Carol: 'Alex came and looked round the school ... It was at that very busy time in the term, Graham and I talked about it almost in passing ... We were all very impressed with her. Vera was particularly impressed with her, and we had information on other candidates. One person we did know, that we shortlisted and this person wasn't really considered, wasn't in the running at all. The third person was somebody who had been in the school on supply and proved to be very, very disappointing and in fact Alex interviewed extremely well apparently, there was no competition at all, so Alex was appointed.'
>
> GS: 'What was your involvement in each of those phases?'
>
> Carol: 'I didn't see a great deal of Alex. I listened to what Vera said, read her (Alex's) application form, her letter of application, which was extremely satisfactory. I listened to the information that we had on the other people. Graham told me all the conversations that he'd had and the phone calls, so, yes, I suppose there was an involvement all along the line.'
>
> GS: 'What about other staff, were they involved?'
>
> Carol: 'Yes, I think we tend to be involved because of the

Staff Selection or By Appointment

people coming into the school. So the staff saw all the personalities, they saw the people.'

GS: 'What happened then?'

Carol: 'We discuss them, and not just the person, but their situation. I'm trying to give it in some sort of order. Graham would tell everybody, Graham would tell us of the conversations he had had about them. So that would have a great bearing on how we felt about the person. The application forms, I saw them and I presume Jim did. And then her impact on Vera, as I say, in the classroom and then her impact on us. There's no doubt about it one looks at people and says "Am I going to be able to work with her" or "What type of personality is this? Am I going to like this person, not necessarily work with them, but like", because you don't necessarily have intimate dealings with everybody on the staff, so therefore possibly, for somebody who isn't going to have any immediate relationship with the person from the curriculum or child point of view, they may look at the person and say "It's more important that I like them than anything else", that they can talk to them and be with them.'

GS: 'Given all this discussion going on and this level of involvement you've talked of Graham sharing it with staff, what about the other direction, of staff sharing things with Graham?'

Carol: 'Oh yes, that certainly went on, with people pointing out things or asking things or saying how they saw the situation, that always happens whatever the appointment, really. Again, because of this teamwork, it's something that Graham encourages. He's not going to be the only person they will be working with and in fact I think it's more important to him that we get on as a team, he will select people who fit into the team working together, so it's probably very important that he knows how we feel about a person. So yes, we feel very free to say what we think about it.'

Carol went on to talk about influencing and she did believe that this exchange of information influenced Graham's decision. For Graham, the decision of who is appointed rests in one sense with the governors:

Graham: Well, strictly speaking the position is that it's the governors who recommend to the Authority, that's the legal position. In practice, of course the governors and I work together. I would start by telling the governors just what we're looking for so that would be their starting point. Then I would be present at any interviews and discussions about potential candidates and what I said would carry a lot of weight, not 100 per cent but, I think I said once before, usually what happens is

121

that it comes down to a couple of people that we would all be quite happy to work with, and then the governors have got an opportunity to make a decision. If it came down to one that they wanted and one that I wanted, then if I really stuck to it I would have to get the one I wanted, because at the end of the day I've got to work with that person. But it's very rarely ever come to that, I can't remember it ever coming to that ... I'm not prepared to have somebody pushed onto me that I don't feel I can work with, or I don't feel the rest of the staff can work with.'

GS: 'That last bit is interesting. "Who the rest of the staff can work with", as well as yourself. How do you gauge whether the rest of the staff can work with that person?'

Graham: 'They always have an opportunity of meeting the candidates beforehand ... they talk to the candidates and before the interview they will have spoken to them and conveyed some sort of opinion. They've usually said something like, "Well, those two seem alright, or that one is the best." In Alex's case, I don't think there was ever any doubt that she was going to get the job, because the staff all took to her straight away. There's this indefinable personality thing which I find very interesting but almost impossible to actually put my finger on and say "That's the reason why that person is acceptable." She was cheerful, she was open, she was — to coin a phrase — "quietly confident" about doing the job and she's proved to be just that. The other people, some of them come across as overbearing, or pushy. It's very interesting, what it is that makes the staff take to a person, but it's usually the same thing that makes me take to that person, or the governors.'

GS: 'So you take in the views of others. What about Jim. As Deputy, what's his role?'

Graham: 'We discuss the candidates: in this case I discussed them with Carol as well for two reasons, one, because she was newly appointed coordinator of infants and two, because of Jim's 'coming and going' role. So I talked to Carol perhaps more than Jim, but I do talk to Jim and gave him an opportunity to give an opinion, which he gave, which was positive in the case of Alex, and which was positive in the case of this other lady who had been on supply. So I was left with the governors, knowing that either of those two would be fine. The other one had really not been sensible about the way she applied, her application form was a mess and she didn't know enough about the reception class, in particular, for the interview.'

GS: 'The visit is obviously an important aspect.'

Graham: 'Yes, even if the visit is only the morning of the actual interview, I always invite candidates to spend a whole day in

Staff Selection or By Appointment

the school and if they don't come, of course that tells us at least something.'

GS: 'Looking at it from the staff's point of view, what do you think they are looking for?'

Graham: 'They'll always talk about the job, in fact every conversation is a form of mini interview. They'll talk about the job, they'll ask pertinent questions about experience and they'll discuss the kind of set up we have here with someone, who will then presumably express an opinion and say "I would like to work to that", or "I've worked in similar ways before", or "That's the way I like to work", that kind of positive response would impress. I think they would probe fairly deeply ... What it comes down to really is personality and effectiveness in the job.

There's a lot of intuition involved, I think perhaps there ought not to be, but it seems to work. When you've been doing a job for a long time you have a feel for somebody else who will do the job quite well. Obviously a lot of what is said is taken in and processed almost unconsciously. But a teacher has a particular kind of personality, which shows. It's not by any means a uniform personality, but I've often said of someone "That person would make a good teacher", even it it's someone who isn't a teacher, without really analyzing it. There is something which comes across to someone who has been at the job a long time, it says "This is a teacher".'

Graham, Jim, Vera and Carol, found of the three candidates, that Alex was the most suitable and closest match to their criteria. Alex interviewed well and satisfied the governors' requirements and was offered the post of reception teacher for the summer term.

Conclusions

On the basis of this single case study it would be unwise to present any firm conclusions. However, the case study raises a number of issues which I shall now list.

1. The tradition in the school is that the staff give freely of their views. Exchanges are open and sometimes frank. This is further enhanced by the recognition that the headteacher not only encourages discussion but also actively listens to everyone's views. There was the added ingredient that governors also consult with the teachers, seeking their opinions on candidates. Taken together this creates a climate of open consultation. There is nothing new in this discovery but it is necessary to note first this climate exists

generally, and secondly that it also operates during the process of teacher appointments. At present there is much talk of consultation and collaboration and of whole school policies, but no specific mention of whether this extends to teacher appointments. This case study reveals that in Greenfields it does include teacher selection and suggests that consultation is an activity which operates consistently rather than selectively.

2 The staff feel, because of the consultation, that their views are both recognized and legitimate. In turn, this seems to help them trust the head, Graham. Graham is seen as a member of the staff group. Consequently, not only does he listen to the staff's views, he is a constituent of those views and thus able to know, intimately, the values, attitudes and predispositions of the staff group. Being a constituent increases the trust the staff have in Graham and the staff appear to accept that Graham will be able to represent their wishes. It is perhaps not just a matter of consultation, but also of representation.

3 Implicit in the process of staff selection is the fact that the appointing panel, if not school, has to determine what, for them, a 'good teacher looks like'.

Amongst the staff there was a measure of general agreement, which given the levels of consultation and sharing are not surprising. (Also, given the presence of a 'researcher' asking questions about what they are looking for it is even less surprising. The research may well have caused teachers to focus on something they otherwise took for granted. Carol on reading this chapter in order to 'clear it' for publication said that the school always worked this way.) However, these descriptions may not constitute what the literature advocates in terms of job and person specifics. This may indicate a difference in language (or jargon) between teachers and management pundits, a difference in level and intensity of description/prescription, or a difference in value.

However, Graham has said in subsequent conversation that he believes that the scope and frequency of discussion amongst the staff means that all the staff influence what the school is looking for in the appointment and this makes it precise and shared across the school.

4 These teachers emphasize personal qualities rather than instrumental ones. This may be a product of my questioning but long term acquaintance with the staff suggests, to me at least, that this is not the case. The comments point towards the teachers, particularly the headteacher perceiving teaching as more than preoccupation with children. There is, perhaps, a recognition of the importance of the primary staff being effective as a group (Yeomans, 1985). There might also be a value placed on 'affiliation'

(Nias, 1986). Or a sense of awareness that employment involves a psychological contract as well as a contract involving the exchange of labour for capital (Pascale and Athos, 1982). Possibly the clearest indication is that these primary teachers see the job of a teacher as a combination of professional and personal attributes, whereas much of the selection literature attempts to direct attention solely to professional concerns — functions, tasks, responsibilities etc. If primary teachers generally do not accept the professional/personal distinction which 'management' writers tend to offer, then there arises the issue of the appropriateness and match of some management theory in staff selection to primary schools.

5 The visit of candidates to the school is clearly a key event. It is the chief opportunity for staff to meet and gather impressions on the candidates (and *vice versa*). Morgan, Hall and Mackay, (1984) prescribe that the school visit should be an information event for candidates and not an assessment event for selectors (p. 36). The case study is obviously at odds with this and raises the question of whether the visit or the interview is the major face-to-face event.

6 The idea of teachers entering schools on a temporary or partial basis is quite common. Many schools have, when a suitable opportunity occurs, appointed supply staff as well as part-timers and temporary teachers to permanent posts. Prospective candidates are only too familiar with appointment procedures which simply 'go through the motions' because there already is an 'inside' candidate that the school is sponsoring. In this instance this was not the case. Yet the pattern of a trial period does exist in this school and it may well be a significant strategy for ensuring cohesion.

Evidence from PSSR, as well as from elsewhere (eg. Nias, (1986), Sikes (1985) Hargreaves and Woods, (1984)) points to the importance of relationships and value cohesion. Elsewhere, (Southworth, 1986(b)) I have posed the question 'how did schools with healthy, positive relationships come to be like that?' This case study begins to show that not only is the appointment of a staff member a building block towards positive relationships, but so too is the process.

Greenfields may have been less systematic than some writers would wish, but I would not say it was 'amateur'. It was simply different and perhaps more subtle than the instrumentalists and rationalists would be. The process was hardly precise in terms of job description but the absence of that kind of precision does not seem to have made the selection any less accurate. The literature advocates a process which could be called 'By Appointment'. That is, a teacher is appointed to a school by a panel who, except for the head, may not know with any sensitivity the staff group's values. Where these values are positive and productive the panel may run the risk of appointing someone who in the context of the particular school and staff is inappropriate. Staff Selection, in the sense of selection by the staff (within the limits of LEA rules of governance and employment law) may offer a less risky route. Hence this chapter's title, Staff Selection or By Appointment? and thus the question. This research does not resolve that question. More than anything else it points to the need for detailed research into how primary school staff are appointed and become members of the school.

References

BARRY, G.H., and TYE, F., (1975) *Running A School*, London, Temple Smith.
BUSH, T., (1986) *Theories of Educational Management*, London, Harper and Row.
CAMBELL, R.J., (1985) *Developing the Primary School Curriculum*, London, Holt, Rinehart and Winston.
COULSON, A.A., (1980) 'The role of the primary head' in BUSH, T., *et al.* (Eds.) *Approaches to School Management*, London, Harper and Row.
DAY, C., JOHNSON, D., and WHITTAKER, P., (1985) *Managing Primary Schools: A Professional Development Approach*, London, Harper and Row.
DEPARTMENT OF EDUCATION AND SCIENCE (1985) *The Curriculum from 5 to 16: Curriculum Matters 2; An HMI Series*, London, HMSO.
FERGUSON, S., (1979) 'The outmoded ritual we call teacher selection' *Education*, 25 May.
HARGREAVES, A., and WOODS, P., (Eds.) (1984) *Classrooms and Staffrooms*, Milton Keynes, Open University Press.
HILSUM, S., and START, K.B., (1974) *Promotion and Careers in Teaching*, Windsor, NFER.
ILEA (1985) *Improving Primary Schools*, London, ILEA.
MORGAN, C., (1981) 'The selection and promotion of staff' in Open University, E323, Block 6, Part III, *Management and the School; The Management of Staff*, Milton Keynes, Open University Press.
MORGAN, C., HALL, V., and MACKAY, H., (1983) *The Selection of Secondary School Headteachers*, Milton Keynes, Open University Press.
MORGAN, C., HALL, V., and MACKAY, H., (1984) *A Handbook on Selecting Senior Staff for Schools* Milton Keynes, Open University Press.
NIAS, D.J. (1986) 'Schools as well as children: Why mid-career teachers need their colleagues' Cambridge Institute of Education mimeo.
PASCALE, R.T., and ATHOS, A.G., (1982) *The Art of Japanese Management*, London, Penguin.
PHIPSON, G., (1986) 'Appointment of teachers' in MARLAND, M., (Ed.) *School Management Skills*, London, Heinemann.
POSTER, C., (1976) *School Decision-Making*, London, Heinemann.
RICHES, C., (1984) 'The Interview in education: Some research evidence and its implications for practitioners' in BOYD-BARRETT, O., *et al.* (Eds.) *Approaches to Post-School Management*, London, Harper and Row.
SAMUEL, G., (1986) 'How to appoint a deputy', *Education* 16 May.
SIKES, P.J., MEASOR, L., WOODS, P., (1985) *Teacher Careers: Crises and Continuities*, Lewes, Falmer Press

SOUTHWORTH, G.W., (1985) 'Changing management in primary schools' in *Education* 22 Nov.
SOUTHWORTH, G.W., (1986(b)) 'Managerialism revisited — 3; What makes for good relationships' *Education*, 14 March
SOUTHWORTH, G.W., (1987) 'Primary school headship and collegiality', chapter 4 in this volume.
YEOMANS, R., (1985) 'Are primary teachers primarily people?' *Education 3–13*, 13, 2, pp. 6–12.
YEOMANS, R., (1986) 'Hearing secret harmonies: How primary teachers learn to be staff members' BERA Conference Paper, Cambridge Institute of Education mineo.

Leading the Team, Belonging to the Group?

Robin Yeomans

We sit chatting in the staffroom. It's a quarter to four. The stragglers drift in from their classrooms, apologizing to the head, who sits there with apparent patience, a sheaf of papers on his lap. An unsignalled silence falls. After a pause the head hurries through the arrangements for next week's open evening, seemingly anxious that no one should interrupt. No one does. He then says he is handing over the rest of the staff meeting to the language co-ordinator. She sends him a hesitant smile, clears her throat, and explains that as they all know, it has been decided to completely overhaul the language policy document, and that it is important that all their views are considered. So everyone should feel free to say exactly what they think. An hour later the once-blank paper on the co-ordinator's lap overflows with her summary of the meeting's thoughts. Two colleagues working together in the second year junior team have been particularly vociferous in recommending the ideas on spelling that they have successfully developed during the term. The language co-ordinator herself has asked many questions. Four others staff have contributed intermittently. Three have sat in silence, one of them the head.

This may not be a typical staff meeting, but it reflects elements of many I have experienced and poses several intriguing questions about how primary staffs operate, as opposed to how they are told they should operate. Who is in charge? What is being said? What are the implications of who talks and what they say? Equally importantly, what are the implications of who remains silent and what could their silences mean? The members sitting together in a formally-constituted staff meeting are being constrained by informal, tacit, considerations which are no less powerful influences on actions for being unspoken.

Primary teachers could be forgiven for believing that the last thing they should do is talk to each other. Detailed curriculum documents, written statements of aims and objectives, precise job descriptions, appraisal schemes, increased bureaucratic burdens (disguised as greater financial control for schools) seem designed to separate heads from teachers by a paper wall and make personal contact between staff members redundant if not undesirable. It is as if thorough programming and efficient systems are perceived as superior replacements for messy negotiation and subversive individuality. 'Management' has become the key word, carrying with it all the overtones of shaping people as they ought to be rather than working with them as they are. Yet a spate of reports from DES and ILEA using such words as 'consultation', 'participation', 'discussion' and 'delegation', say primary schools should be efficient, tidy and 'organized'.

I want to look closely at the decision-making relationships within a primary staff. In particular, I am concerned with the interaction between heads and teachers and how this is reflected in issues of 'leadership' and 'membership'. Firstly, I suggest that primary school leaders have been given an inappropriate industrial model to copy. Secondly, I trace the implications for decision-making of the ILEA reports *Improving Primary Schools* and *The Junior Schools Project*. Thirdly, I suggest these reports have made the right noises but not for all the right reasons. Therefore, I examine the essential nature of primary school staffs as *small work teams* in which group processes have always been a powerful influence on outcomes, even though this has been given scant attention by management theorists.

Leaders and Followers?

The growth of large comprehensive schools brought the decline of the view that secondary schools could be run by gifted amateurs, who were simply ex-classroom teachers, and accelerated the rise of the professional headteacher-manager. Size and complexity left little choice. Concurrently, industry offered an academically respectable body of management theory, legitimized by the establishment of business schools.

National and local government economic policies from the late 1970s encouraged the belief in the equation efficiency = effectiveness and promoted the transfer of industrial management models from secondary to primary schools. The implicit logic seems to have been:

1. Secondary schools have become industrially-sized organizations.
2. Therefore, secondary schools need management structures appropriate for industrial organizations.
3. Management structures create efficient secondary schools.
4. All schools need to be efficient.
5. Primary schools as organizations are like secondary schools, only smaller and simpler.
6. Primary schools need management structures.

'The management team' is now part of the everyday jargon of many primary schools. The head is often regarded by the LEA as 'line manager', and even subject co-ordinators are sometimes conceptualized as 'middle managers.' The effect has been to reinforce hierarchical power assumptions and by implication, to legitimize a dominance/compliance relationship between leader and followers. The leader knows the right way and leads there. The followers' job is to do things the 'right way' by following where the leader directs. By inference, when things go wrong it is the followers' fault rather than a defect of leadership.

The flaw in applying such assumptions to primary schools is that they are not small secondary schools. They are not complex, multi-layered organizations in which each layer is insulated from others by distance, irregular contact, and diverse professional activity. Primary schools are usually groups of six to twelve people, often working in close physical proximity, interacting frequently, exhibiting a common set of professional skills, needing to be interdependent in developing an agreement about the continuity of the education children will receive as they move from year to year. Moreover, primary schools require active participation in which staff members share what they mean by talking, develop a common language through which they can negotiate with each other, and forge a commitment to values they feel able to reflect in their teaching. This is not the stuff that compliant followers are made of, nor all dominant leaders could allow.

Active *membership* as opposed to passive followership carries implications for how leaders lead and who the leaders are. Some heads consciously encourage members to lead in specific circumstances and there are schools where the level of mutual support is such that it is unnecessary to ask who follows and who leads. Equally many schools have leadership problems, especially when leadership is taken to mean more than headship. Deputy heads and curriculum postholders often feel themselves ambiguously placed, unsure whether they are leader or member. Sometimes heads put the blame on the inadequacies of teachers: 'Staff do not seem capable of becoming curriculum leaders. They have not shown the initiative in putting ideas forward'. (Gilbert, 1984, p. 16)

Ambivalent feelings of both head and postholder concerning authority and status can be at the root of difficulties in their relationship (Goodacre, 1984). Each may perceive themselves undermined professionally and personally by the actions or inaction of the other. The issue becomes transformed from who leads into who supports, who undermines, who threatens? The head can easily feel threatened by what s/he perceives as an invasion of head's sphere of authority, whilst a postholder feels s/he is undermined in relationships with colleagues by the lack of the head's support. This happens when leadership and membership are interpreted as delineations of personal territory.

Campbell's study of postholders in eight middle schools 'deemed primary' shows them exercising both curricular and interpersonal skills (Campbell, 1984). The latter involve such leadership and negotiation activities as leading discussions, liaising with heads, advising colleagues informally, teaching alongside them, maintaining their morale, and dealing with professional disagreement. He confirms the 'uncertainty, ambiguity and conflict in their role', derived chiefly from the wide range of demands on them, the tension between their school-wide curriculum responsibilities and 'perceived class-teacher autonomy', and their high degree of 'teacher-as-educationist' visibility to colleagues in curriculum development. Significantly he suggests that the mismatch between postholders' power and authority may explain participatory styles of decision-making:

> Staff could not logically or even legitimately complain that they were being dictated to, since they either participated in the production of the scheme, or consented to its final version. Thus it ensured that the postholder would not have to have recourse to power she did not possess in order to sustain or implement an innovation. (p. 355)

The constraints under which postholders operate affect primary heads too. Heads experience wide-ranging and often conflicting demands. Teachers, parents, governors, children and LEA seldom want the same thing. The head's responsibility for curriculum oversight is not matched by the power to control how teachers think, and thus how teachers will act in the minutiae of daily classroom interactions which constitute the active curriculum. On the other hand every action of a head teacher is a visible comment on the authenticity of the educational values s/he commends, whether it be remembering to say 'good morning' to teachers, talking to them or sending them pieces of paper, establishing a rapport with the children in assembly as the staff look on, being available in the staffroom at break, or smiling at a child as she walks along the corridor.

Developing as a Team

It has long been recognized that there are circumstances in which primary school leadership can be diversified and membership can be active.

> In the past head teachers were responsible for all schemes of work. Now that the primary school curriculum is being widened, it is increasingly difficult for them to be up to date with all the developments and sensible that they should invite *the help of assistant teachers* in preparing schemes, in giving advice to their colleagues and in the selection of books, materials and equipment. (Plowden 1967, para. 934)

> The authority of English headteachers is considerable, yet there are many schools in which a free interchange of ideas exists between the head and his staff *without his essential leadership being impaired.* (Plowden 1967, para. 1147)

However, these tentative suggestions go little further than saying membership might include offering some ideas to help the head lead. They cling firmly to the assumption that leadership is the head's task and that it is separate from membership. Campbell traces the move of the curriculum postholder to a position of curriculum 'centrality' in Bullock (1975) the Primary Survey (1978) and Cockcroft (1982). The emphasis had begun to move from members helping the head to lead towards members leading the staff. But there were still echoes of a dominant/compliant relationship model which hinted at a multiplication of benevolent masters rather than at a redefinition of primary school leadership. For example, postholders should learn:

> ... how to lead groups of teachers ... help others teach ... establish a programme of work in co-operation with other members of staff ... judge whether it is being operated successfully ... make the best use of the strengths of teachers ... help them to develop so that they may take on more responsibility. (HMI/DES, 1978)

By 1984 an important shift of emphasis had happened. Policy decision-making was being conceived as part of the function of each member:

> An HMI discussion document, to be published next month, will suggest that every school has teacher 'consultants' covering nine areas of learning. As well as having a class of their own, they would be responsible for drawing up subject guidelines, advising colleagues and in some cases, providing expert tuition to the top juniors. (*The Times Educational Supplement* 28 Sept 1984)

Close on its heels came ILEA's *Improving Primary Schools* recommendation that:

> Primary school teachers, except possibly in their probationary year, should take responsibility for advising the rest of the staff on major aspects of the curriculum or associated matters, for example assessment. (5.55, 1985)

The Report suggests that successful heads 'Have not been authoritarian, consultative, or participative as a matter of principle; they have been all three at different times as the conditions seem to warrant, though most often participative.' (3.25, 1985) It is also explicit that being an adviser means leading: 'The adviser does, from time to time, have to take the lead in revising the school policy document or scheme of work'. (3.40)

Finally, the transition to a more flexible view of leadership has been confirmed by the recent ILEA Junior School Project (1986). This has identified benefits of actively involving members in leadership. Its key factors for effective junior schooling include the following:

Purposeful Leadership of the Staff by the Headteacher

'Purposeful leadership' occurred where the headteacher understood the needs of the school and was actively involved in the schools work, without exerting total control over the rest of the staff.

In effective schools, headteachers were involved in curriculum discussions and influenced the content of guidelines drawn up within the school, without taking total control.

The Involvement of the Deputy Head

... Where the head generally involved the deputy in policy decisions, it was beneficial to the pupils.

... Thus it appeared that a certain amount of delegation by the headteacher, and a sharing of responsibilities, promoted effectiveness.

The Involvement of Teachers

In successful schools, the teachers were involved in curriculum planning and played a major role in developing their own curriculum guidelines. As with the deputy head, teacher involvement in decisions concerning which class they were to teach, was important. Similarly, consultation with teachers about decisions on spending was important. It appears that schools in which teachers were consulted on issues affecting school policy, as well as those affecting them directly, were more likely to be successful.

The emphasis on the role of every primary teacher as a curriculum postholder and adviser is confirmed in the Report of the Select Committee on Primary Education (1986). Thus, a unifying theme in the recent reports is the suggestion that virtually all primary teachers should exercise some curriculum leadership. The implications of this view are only hinted at, but affect how we define leadership and membership in a broader sense and, therefore, how leaders and members act. In particular, if membership is to mean more than 'followership' so leadership is redefined to mean more than directing. In suggesting that each non-probationer should have a leadership function as consultant, *Improving Primary Schools* leaves questions for its readers to answer. What is the head's function when s/he is one of the staff being led by a specialist colleague? Who leads and who follows when all are experts in some sense and all must accept the guidance of others in some context? The demarcation between leaders and members becomes blurred. Two examples illustrate this.

Firstly, Campbell shows that being a curriculum postholder and leader demands new membership skills which involve more than the exercise of authority — in *Improving Primary Schools* terms leading is 'a process of debate and negotiation not dictation' (3.40). Moreover, Goodacre's evidence suggests that some leadership skills elude many heads, particularly those of enabling others to be effective leaders. This is consistent with the views offered by Coulson and Southworth in this book. The head's close association with and responsibility for the school can make it difficult for them to 'let go' of the school. In that case those teachers who use heads as role models may be perpetuating an authority/dependence style of leadership rather than an enabling mode of leadership. Secondly, *Improving Primary Schools* describes successful heads demonstrating skills that might have once been thought more appropriate for effective members than for leaders:

> They like to talk ... but they also know when to keep quiet and let others have their say. Indeed they have a marked capacity to listen with care ... They obviously enjoy teaching ... Even though they may be very busy they seem to have all the time in the world for anyone in difficulty ... (3.26)

Leader and member behaviour are often indistinguishable because an effective leader legitimizes leadership from members. Membership-led initiatives may mean curriculum leadership from designated 'experts'. But more significantly they may be prompted by members perceiving staff needs and responding to them. Response may involve offering help with specific problems, sharing one's successes and acknowledging one's failures, praising the achievements of colleagues, generating curriculum insights in discussion, enabling consensus negotiation through perceptive staff meeting interventions, or providing sustained models of classroom excellence. When all are willing and able to talk and listen, all become leaders and members. Thus, a school has one responsible head, but may have any number of leaders for different organizational needs. When each member has a specific function performed for and valued by the staff we might legitimately describe it as a team.

The characteristic of a *team* is that it is an *interdependent task unit*. In particular:

1. Each member's function contributes to the team task.
2. Thus each member feels responsible to the team and valued by it.
3. Each member responds flexibly to emergent team needs as s/he perceives them.
4. Leading the team carries obligations as well as powers.

One of the headteacher's jobs is to ensure that individual professional actions are co-ordinated rather than that each member should accept the leader's prescription. Heads are not in the cloning business.

There is implicit evidence from *Improving Primary Schools* of awareness that creating a successful team makes particular demands on the interpersonal skills of heads who encourage teachers to be active staff members:

The Articles of Government make it plain that the last word within the school is the heads, though the final form may not be precisely what he or she would have chosen without the benefit of the staffs advice. (3.28) ... Heads who are secure in their role welcome agenda items from colleagues when staff meetings are being arranged. (3.31)

What holds true for heads holds true for members acting in any leadership capacity, namely the need to show sensitive leadership. Within the interpersonal complexities of the primary staff considerable damage can be caused by an overzealous peer consultant. This interpersonal dimension points to a further complexity in the primary school leadership/membership dichotomy, namely that teams have the capacity to become groups in a social and psychological sense.

Becoming a Group

Though the two ILEA reports highlight the developing pattern of curriculum partnership between heads and consultants, leadership/membership blurring is more than a product of curriculum complexity. It is also created by the interpersonal effects of group processes. A primary school staff may become a group. I define *group* as a collection of people who *behave* as a *socially interdependent unit* and mutually *perceive* themselves as a *psychologically interdependent unit* for known purposes or under known circumstances. In a primary school the headteacher and the person who exhibits leadership behaviour at a given moment may both be group members. They may or may not be the same person, but it is impossible to be leader of a group in any sense unless one is also a member.

A primary school staff may behave as a group *without* being a team. As a group it may concern itself with caring for and supporting members. Group leadership may be diversified so that members share leadership functions such as group counsellor, humourist easing daily pressures, carer who offers literal tea and sympathy, or source of grapevine information about children and their families. Group members might still go their independent unco-ordinated professional ways. Sometimes a staff which works as a team (an interdependent task unit) develops a group identity (as an interdependent social and psychological unit). When this happens powerful forces are generated.

I have argued elsewhere (1985) that primary school staff leaders and members are influenced by a group's capacity to meet personal needs. A primary school team may develop this sense of psychological interdependence which causes it to behave as a socially interdependent unit. This is because small size tends to intensify interaction between members, including the head, and interaction may lead to the development of rewarding personal relationships. Moreover, a primary school's structure gives the head responsibility for the staff, they depend on him/her to represent their interests with parents, LEA and other external agencies, whilst the head depends extensively on teachers' skill and support for a reputation as head of an effective school. Thus the leader and other staff members are encouraged to become interdependent, and the collective capacity of the staff to meet personal and task needs can further group development. As a team all members may become subject to the affiliative and affective rewards of successful co-operative activity, so that cohesion is intensified and the team/group becomes professionally and personally rewarding.

Collective activity is a strong cement. The team-as-a-group experience is sometimes enjoyed transiently after a particularly successful dramatic performance to which all have contributed. The staffroom fills with chatter and laughter, perhaps a bottle passes round in celebration of cohesion. Reluctant to leave, we remain glued to our chairs. However, if professional or interpersonal differences hamper team and group development, small size can create considerable tensions in primary schools, so that sub-groups can grow with their own internal cohesion which may fragment the staff and damage the school. Hartley's (1985) study of Rockfield Primary School shows staff sub-groups emerging in response to the head's stated purpose of creating in the school: '... an environment both physical and mental to compensate for the state of deprivation which exists in the child's own home'. (p. 55) An empty staffroom and huddles of two or three teachers in corridors and odd corners are often the visible evidence that fragmentation rules.

Belonging to a primary staff group makes it difficult to separate 'self' from 'teacher' or 'head'. This may be particularly difficult for the head who as 'person' is just another member who happens to have a particular organizational responsibility. If asked whether they were a member of the staff group most primary heads would want to say 'yes' and many staffs would agree with them. This peer relationship is encouraged by a *primus inter pares* view of the professional head/staff relationship in primary schools. The essence of the leader's membership is that s/he is as open to the dynamics of the group as is any other member. S/he becomes aware of how s/he makes other members feel. This can trigger uncomfortable feelings in response. Equally it can generate insights into colleagues' perspectives. Awareness of the disapproval of the colleague may be the kind of group pressure which affects a leader's actions, but it may also inform decision-making. It is surely helpful (though not necessarily comfortable) for a leader to know that a planned course of action may lack any support and commitment.

To suggest that notions of leader and member overlap is not to say that leadership and membership behaviour are the same. Broadly speaking, leadership is directed at achieving the task and includes encouraging members to lead appropriately. Membership is concerned with maintaining the group in that it is characterized by actions which help to preserve the group, such as supporting its goals and accepting appropriate leadership. However there are senses in which the distinction is tautologous. Any act consciously furthering group preservation, such as acceptance of a group view before individual preference, is an act of constructive *Membership* which *Leads* towards that fundamental group goal. Yet promoting group interests above individual preference might equally characterize a collaborative mode of *Leadership*, which simultaneously demands most of the designated leader and offers most to members.

In practice the distinction can be equally nebulous. Does a head lead when s/he listens, accepts, consults, delegates? Does the teacher support when s/he suggests, advises, disagrees, reports? Who has led when one teacher executes with skill and flair an idea the head has been suggesting for months? Is asking questions or providing answers the leadership or membership activity? It probably depends on the circumstances.

Though a leader is designated, all may expect to lead and support in some circumstance in a primary staff team. There are experts who are nominated leaders of particular activities, just as there are phases when each transiently leads. Membership involves responding sensitively to the actions of all other members if the team is to work effectively. The essence of skilful team performance is synchronized interaction. This involves co-operating with different individuals at different times and responding to the team as a whole. The likely consequence is the psychological interdependence which characterises the group.

Learning Together

Learning to accept leadership can be difficult. We don't all take the constructive view taken by one teacher I interviewed of her relationship with her head:

> If you feel not threatened, your ego is not threatened by whatever it is that's being suggested to you. You think 'Oh', as I did before

we started this way of working, 'Well that's not going to work but we'll give it a try anyway.' Then you can see — 'Ah, it is working. Ah well, there was something after all in what he said then'.

When heads delegate specific curriculum leadership they may find such membership too extreme for themselves and define it as abdication rather than participation. Perhaps the head's silence in the staff meeting I started with expresses distrust of a membership role to which he cannot even pay lip-service. Constructive membership at a staff meeting may require no more than an attentive nod signalling engagement in the discussion. It is preferable to the silence of the other two staff which probably doesn't even reflect followership, let alone membership. The unspoken message is often 'We don't agree, but as you just want us to rubber-stamp your decision, we see no point in expressing our view. We shall do our own thing anyway.' Perhaps they have noticed the language co-ordinator's selectivity in listing only those comments she thought the head was happy with.

Constructive participation is important for a decision-making group such as a school staff, where the effectiveness of a decision is closely tied to the willingness of the members to implement it. The leader who pursues his/her preferred solution may fail to identify the most effective solution for the group. Leading the group may require a form of membership behaviour which harmonizes individual goals with a compatible group goal by subordinating the leader's preferred goal. In the process s/he achieves the more desirable goals of leading the group in a direction it is able and willing to travel, increasing group task cohesion thereby, and strengthening the group's trust in its leader.

It is not the authority with which the designated leaders (including postholders) exercise leadership which distinguishes them from other members. It is their acceptance of responsibility for their part in the school organization and for the staff as a whole when they are leading. Heads are contractually responsible for their schools but responsibility can mean allowing others to take the lead at times whilst the head participates in the experience of membership. Paradoxically the ultimate test of heads' leadership may be the effectiveness of their membership — that they perform a valued function for and within the team and group.

Conclusion

The term 'collegiality' (Coulson, 1976) is increasingly used to describe primary schools adopting a collaborative form of leadership. I suggest that the distinguishing feature of such schools is the focus on the nature of the staff group rather than the style adopted by the head. The head is a member of that group, sensitive to its dynamics and conscious of its needs and goals, personal and professional, internal and external. There the head shares with all members of the group the characteristic that they behave as if their actions had consequences and implications for other members. The greatest demand on collegial leadership is that the leader as member is sufficiently secure to enable colleagues to lead effectively. Under that condition, the greatest demand of collegial membership is that the member as leader (eg. curriculum co-ordinator) helps colleagues to be led without damage to egos or the development of sibling rivalry.

The ILEA reports make an implicit call for collegiality. *Improving Primary Schools* (3.32) refers to the 'Janus-like quality' of primary deputy headship. I suggest that having two faces — leader and member — is an essential requirement for *all* primary staff members, whether they be head or teachers. This is because leadership and membership are activities performed by the same individuals at different moments within a designated framework of leaders and members. Though the recent reports are a move towards collegiality in policy terms, their greater significance is that they highlight a situation that has always existed in most primary schools, namely that since a primary staff is numerically a small group of adults, leaders and members cannot easily escape each other, and leadership and membership should not be treated as watertight compartments. Making this knowledge explicit is the first step in harnessing and using it for school effectiveness. The reality is that some primary schools are still run by dominant leaders and staffed by compliant followers and that some central and local authority management 'experts' are telling primary schools that dominance/compliance is the only way forward.

References

BULLOCK REPORT (1974) *A Language for Life*, London, HMSO.
CACE (1967) *Children and their Primary Schools*, London, HMSO.
CAMPBELL, R.J. (1984) 'In-school development: The role of the postholder', *School Organization*, 4, 4.
COCKCROFT REPORT (1982) *Mathematics Counts*, London, HMSO.
COULSON, A.A. (1976) 'The role of the primary head', in PETERS, R.S., *The Role of the Head*, London, Routledge and Kegan Paul.
GILBERT, D.J.D. (1984) 'A role for post-holders,' *Education 3–13*, 12, 1.
GOODACRE, E. (1984) 'Postholders and language assertiveness'. *Education 3–13*, 12, 1.
HARTLEY, D. (1985) *Understanding the Primary School*, London, Croom Helm.
DEPARTMENT OF EDUCATION AND SCIENCE (1978) *Primary Education in England*, London, HMSO.
ILEA (1985) *Improving Primary Schools*, London, ILEA.
ILEA (1986) *The Junior Schools Project*, London, ILEA.
Report of Parliamentary Select Committee on Primary Education (1986)
TIMES EDUCATIONAL SUPPLEMENT, (1984) 'Firmer HMI guidance drafted', Sept 28 4.
YEOMANS, R.M. (1987) 'Are primary teachers primarily people?' in this volume.

Section Three
Curriculum Management

Introduction

This section moves the focus away from roles, responsibilities and relationships and considers contemporary issues to do with managing the curriculum. Of course, in moving the focus this should in no way suggest a divorce between the curriculum and roles, responsibilities and relationships. In primary schools such a divorce is not possible nor profitable. However, the focus in this section is on the ideas and language now being employed to describe the primary school curriculum. The three chapters in this section make a compact set of perspectives.

In my first chapter, 'Perspective on the primary curriculum' I review the documents published in the early 1980s. I adopt a critical stance by continually asking how accurately and sensitively classroom issues and children's learning are reflected or overlooked in the documents. I use four questions to structure the chapter: What do children need to come to know?; What are the best means of helping children come to know these things?; How do we know the children have learned something?; and How do we let those outside school know what the children are doing? In conclusion I suggest that rather than hoping that prescriptions will 'end up' in the classroom I believe we should never leave the classroom in the first place. This stance is consistent with the chapters of Dadds and Holly in section four of this book.

The second chapter is by Colin Richards HMI and is the only commentary written by an HM Inspector and published outside a HMSO document. The chapter is a readable summary of HM Inspectors *The Curriculum from 5 to 16*, a document which is of immense significance to the way the curriculum may be conceived and described over the next few years. Richards' section on 'Implications' is extremely valuable and significant not least for the management issues raised or implied therein. For example, the demands on classteachers, collaboration and collegial approaches, planning and evaluation and staff development. Much that Richards' discusses relates back to sections one and two as well as to the companion chapters in this section.

Introduction

The third chapter is my sequel to the opening chapter in this section, hence the title 'Further perspectives on the primary curriculum'. Like Richards I too review HM Inspectors' *The Curriculum from 5 to 16*. However, I also review the DES White Paper 'Better Schools' which was published at approximately the same time and adds another flavour to the discussion. Readers will undoubtedly compare my review with Richards'. I conclude this chapter by outlining what I call a DIY course for primary school and curriculum management. This DIY course is similar to the ideas presented in other chapters (eg. Southworth in section one; Yeomans' second chapter in section two). As virtually all the chapters in sections one, two, three and four demonstrate such a DIY course is far from straightforward. The DIY course might also be compared to the ILEA Key Factors for Effective Schools in section four as well as Peter Holly's ideas for the developing school.

Perspectives on the Primary Curriculum

Geoff Southworth

Over the last six or seven years there has been a steady stream of documents concerned with the primary school curriculum. Since the Primary School Survey (1978) various perspectives have been published by the DES, HMI and the Schools Council. Perhaps these documents begin to develop something akin to Bourdieu's (1971) notion of 'master patterns' since the documents' prescriptions tend to organize school policies and processes not only because of the nature of the patterns suggested in them, but also by the frequency with which they are being offered. Partly with that idea in mind I shall refer collectively to these documents as the 'orthodox' perspectives.

This chapter seeks to consider certain issues contained in some of the published, 'orthodox' documents. There will also be an attempt to contrast them with other issues derived from personal experience as a primary school teacher. As a way of organizing this discussion four questions are framed:

1. What do children need to come to know?
2. What are the best means of helping them to come to know these things?
3. How do we know the children have learned something?
4. How do we let those outside school know what the children are doing?

By asking these questions it is the intention to develop a number of perspectives.

What Do Children Need to Come to Know?

(a) The 'Orthodox' Perspectives

As is usual much of this question is concerned with curricular aims. Since around 1980 schools have been literally bombarded with documents exhorting them to state their aims. Without doubt there is a major piece of investigation waiting to be done by analyzing the documents which have been published since 1980. For example, whilst each document brings with it some kind of suggested set of aims each also brings 'a set of predilections which predicate the structure' (Gray, 1973). Analysis of the documents may disclose certain preoccupations and priorities which in turn indicate assumptions which shape and constrain the curriculum (see Gibson, 1984).

The HM Inspectors' *A View of the Curriculum* (1980) considers in just five and a half pages the curriculum in primary schools under the headings: (i) Individual differences and common needs, (ii) Some necessary differences of programme, (iii) Conditions required for the inclusion of a modern language, (iv) Levels of difficulty in the work, (v) Skills, (vi) Content and Concepts, and ends with a summary. The bulk of space is devoted to skills, content and concepts. Out of five paragraphs on skills, three are devoted to aspects of language development, one to maths and one to a pot-pourri of observational and recording skills. This final paragraph also contains a sentence which suggests that music and art are useful ways of developing control over nervous and muscular systems ... which is an unusual way of describing and rationalizing the purposes of music and art education.

Within the content and concepts section attention is given to historical, geographical and scientific concepts. Religious education is mentioned and literature, drama, music and the graphic arts are thrown in for good measure five lines before the section ends.

The DES document *The School Curriculum* (1981) is even more detached. It offers a list of broad aims on page three and looks 'specifically' at the 'Primary Phase' in two and a half pages. High priority to English and mathematics is noted and applauded, although I find the subject title of 'English' rather restrictive compared to the title of language development which is now more commonly used. The same section also notes the Primary School Survey's finding that skills in the basic subjects may be improved where pupils are involved in a wider programme of work.

Later paragraphs acknowledge the multicultural aspects of Britain today and whilst this is a necessary extension of focus the wording may be rather insensitive to all those 'multicultural citizens' who have lived and worked in Britain before today. Mention is made of four curricular areas; topic work, science, art and craft, and French. I interpret their inclusion as signalling cause for concern since each is criticized in the Primary School Survey in one way or another.

By contrast *The Practical Curriculum* (1981) offers a rather fuller treatment. The scant attention which the above two documents give to primary education is possibly symptomatic of low esteem for the primary sector. In that sense one should be grateful to the Schools Council for seeking a broader and more carefully constructed review. For example,

The Practical Curriculum discusses the curriculum in terms of aims (providing a model set) and then goes on to consider learning through experience; forms of knowledge; modes of teaching and learning; values and attitudes; skills; and modes of expression, verbal and non-verbal. Out of this I can detect at least two issues of significance.

Firstly, the Schools Council document actually recognizes the connection between *teaching* and *learning*. A reader of the HMI and DES documents could be forgiven for thinking that they had very little to do with learning. The Schools Council booklet does acknowledge the inseparable linkage between teaching and learning in ways which do not necessarily see the latter as only a consequence of the former. Many of the reasons for this are to do with the greater appreciation the Schools Council documents demonstrate for the curriculum as an active set of processes rather than as an inert thing. Indeed, *Primary Practice* (1983) actually considers the curriculum in terms of subjects, process, as the study of problems, as areas of knowledge and experience, and *the curriculum through the child's eyes*. So that here at last is an understanding of the *received* curriculum as distinct from the prescribed curriculum.

Secondly, the notion of modes of expression, verbal and *non-verbal* is very valuable. The documents which have appeared on the curriculum are hide-bound by the verbal model even where expression is accommodated. *The Practical Curriculum* at least talks of the use of vehicles for thought, feeling and imagination and accepts the scale of the use of image and symbol in everyday life through the media and communication networks.

From this generalized 'review' a number of points can be proposed as possible issues for further consideration. Firstly, there is some need for a thorough examination of the philosophical confusions which are embedded in them. Secondly, although they offer summaries which are more or less useful, they also underestimate the richness of life in primary school classrooms. Thirdly, it is all too easy to detect a preoccupation with 'subjects' which is compounded by the fact that some subjects receive greater attention than others (Gulbenkian Report, 1982). Fourthly, the general tone is academic, sometimes aridly so. However, the publication of the two Schools Council working papers can be seen as a softening of the academic stance since they include more practical concerns. Perhaps this marks a closer relationship in terms of 'theory' and 'practice'? Fifthly, even though there is a movement towards an amalgamation of theory and practice there still exists a gap between 'planners' and 'performers' which is sufficiently large for important concerns to be neglected. The orthodox documents offer, at best, only a partial view of what children need to come to know. There are several other things which require inclusion or affect what is included.

Stating aims and promulgating ways of organizing schools are, of course, strategies of some utility but as presented in these documents they stress what is to be, rather than what we have now. They reside in the future, not the present. I would suggest that this tends to overlook the strengths of present practice and distances itself from classroom realities. Any attempt at introducing model sets of aims should be rather more in touch with what schools are like now. In separate ways the next two sub-sections will attempt to do this.

(b) The Materialistic Curriculum

Every school has a materialistic curriculum, it is the curriculum as purchased. It is, therefore, the curriculum of the major educational suppliers, book publishers and project producers. It is reading schemes, project kits, workbooks, worksheets, textbooks, workcards, hymn books, apparatus, posters and so on. For many schools it represents substantial curriculum subject structures. For some schools it is their only structure.

Twenty years ago the materialistic curriculum was 'designed' by such people as Marion Richardson, R.J. Unstead, Ronald Ridout, Hadyn Richards with Schonell and Burt's tests forming a large part of the assessment along with the 11+. Ten years ago it may have been Alpha and Beta or Fletcher maths, Ladybird reading books and Daniels and Diack monitoring reading. Today I suspect it is more likely to be structured by SMP maths, Ginn 360 Reading, Science 5:13, SRA language kits with Nelson-NFER evaluating.

Perhaps there is nothing inherently 'wrong' with this. Certainly teachers find these materials useful when coping with the demands of being general class teachers. However, there is a clear need to ensure a match between materials, aims and the children. To check that the processes which the materials embody are compatible with the processes the school's aims seek to promote and that both are consanguineous with the children. This is necessary because whilst not inherently inappropriate, the materialistic curriculum does present certain implicit dangers.

For one thing the materials often confuse curriculum development with acquisition and purchase (Southworth, 1983). For another, the materials can reduce curriculum awareness to products — one looks at the materials one is buying not the processes involved for either teacher or children. Next, because the materials are 'pre-packaged' they are often inflexible, sometimes 'frozen'. This exacerbates the fact that many materials require considerable amounts of time to be devoted to them so that they hamstring the shape of the child's timetable, if not the teacher's as well. Lastly, some of the materials underestimate the value of teachers. They require teachers to become 'operatives' — checking progress and servicing the material's sequencing — so that they often deflect teachers from actively teaching.

Of course, some materials are imaginative and useful. Many of the materials do relieve teachers of considerable amounts of preparation. Yet whatever their relative merits my main theme is to acknowledge that they exist and that they affect what children come to know. Because they exist they should be more obviously discussed than seems to me to be the case. *Primary Practice* does seem to acknowledge them; moreover, through its recommended reading list it seems to be selling some of them ... Perhaps following this level of recognition could come far greater awareness of the materials' benefits and costs; how do they structure classroom processes? How do they present the particular subject area? What skills and concepts do they engender? Looking at most of the orthodox curriculum documents one could be forgiven for thinking that this order of curriculum discussion was unimportant.

(c) The Teachers

An obvious set of perspectives which will influence the curriculum is that of the teachers. What children need to know will be directly affected by what the teacher thinks, feels and believes the children 'ought' to know. Yet, an examination of the orthodox curriculum 'testaments' shows that this hugely influential group are discussed in certain ways which imply an under valuing of the teacher's position, role and responsibilities.

The School Curriculum (1981) in its final paragraph (para. 64) talks about the achievements of the education service stemming from the contributions of all the partners in it. Yet much that goes before this paragraph suggests a notion of 'partnership' which exists within a hierarchical framework. Paragraph 10 of *The School Curriculum* says:

> It is the individual schools that shape the curriculum for each pupil. Neither the Government nor the local authorities should specify in detail what the schools should teach. This is for the schools themselves to determine. Existing articles of government commonly give to the governors the general direction and oversight of the conduct and curriculum of the school, although curricular matters are often in practice devolved upon the headteacher and staff ... There should always be the closest consultation and cooperation between the governors, headteacher and staff. The teachers provide their professional skills and experience and the fullest knowledge of opportunities and constraints and of individual pupils' capabilities and expectations. What schools teach is largely a measure of the dedication and competence of the headteacher and the whole staff and of the interest and support of the governing bodies.

Much of this appears to be sensible and straightforward (although it may not be compatible with the more recent Green Paper *Parental Influence at School* (1984)). The paragraph notes the autonomy of each school, and the contributions of teachers are cited. What intrigues me is the notion of consultation. Heads are recommended to *consult* staff. But note how the paragraph offers a model of consultation within a top-down framework. The drift is from central government to school to staff. Nowhere is there a counter current; perhaps the structure predicates the content. Plainly what is suggested is a consultative model of management within conventional frameworks for distributing authority and power. Clearly, what is not being suggested is a partnership of equals. The same structure is present in *Primary Practice* when it presents its five point plan for review, evaluation and development (p. 165). This behoves us to consider the notion of consultation since I suspect that consultation is often being employed as a piece of managerial rhetoric. It appears to be the negotiation of professional understandings, actions and ideas, but it could be just a well-lubricated version of 'sell and tell'. Given the structures implicit in paragraph 10 it is not too fantastic to speculate that the notion of consultation which is being pressed into service is actually a one-way channel of communication. It is more likely to ensure monologues from superiors to subordinates than dialogue between professionals.

Whilst this reservation needs further investigation before the case is proven, there are, I think, two concomitants of this style of consultation which make the argument more substantive. Firstly, what is implied in paragraph 10 and more clearly expressed in *Parental Influence at School* (DES, 1984) since it refers to the professional responsibilities of the head and staff requiring a 'firm legal foundation' (para. 32: 3) is the pursuit of *contractual* accountability as distinct from *moral* accountability. This concept of accountability raises the second issue. Contractual accountability begins to restrict teachers to the role of semi-professionals, allowed to work in 'our' schools provided they are guided by 'us' (Olsen, 1982) or as Bailey (1983) says it means that teachers should be seen to do what others would have them do'. This restriction also brings with it a reduction in the teachers' contributions to the curriculum because teachers will become curricular 'technicians' (Elliott, 1983), there only to implement policies rather than as designers and constructors of policies. Consequently, the whole process begins to look like a radical under-estimation of the teachers' involvement.

It is an under-estimation because one definition of the curriculum is to regard it as that which goes on between teacher and child as they work on certain tasks or activities. This is not a sinister view; rather, it describes an autonomous teacher. And it is the aspect of curriculum process which will always prevail so long as teachers are persons and not supplanted by microprocessors or robots. Whether schools develop collegial ways of working (Southworth, 1984) to overcome the 'cult of the individual' (Holly, 1984), whether the implications of DES (and others') policies continue to hobble the status of teachers, or even whether consultation is used as a softer version of autocracy, for the present we still have teachers whose values, beliefs, attitudes and feelings imbue the school, the classroom and the curriculum. This is too easily forgotten when official prescriptions regard teachers as '*resources*' to be worked on rather than as *persons* and co-professionals to be worked *with*.

(d) Balance

The materialistic elements and the contributions of teachers affect the scope and balance of the curriculum. Reciprocally, teachers and the producers of materials are affected by the views of the 'official' documents. The *Primary School Survey* (DES 1978) says:

> 8.29 The general educational progress of children and their competence in the basic skills appear to have benefited where they were involved in a programme of work that included art and craft, history and geography, music and physical education, and science, as well as language, mathematics and religious and moral education, although not necessarily as separate items on a timetable.

This is an often quoted section frequently used to roll back the advances of those who see primary education as purely concerned with basic skill acquisition. In that sense the section may be useful, but the section also carries with it a sense of priority *between* subjects. The heart of the matter is that this paragraph only makes the case for these subjects' inclusion. It seems to recommend their inclusion as being worthwhile but, and this is the denouement, it does not alter the status quo of subjects. It persists with the traditional arrangement of mathematical and language skills effectively forming the élite core of the curriculum. Now, I may not want to argue that they should be relegated from this position, but I do think that the focus on such a narrow core is prejudicial to many other aspects of the curriculum.

Generally speaking it is possible to draw up a list of 'second class subjects' comprising art and craft, drama, and history and geography when they are smuggled into the curriculum as language enriching 'topics'. They are second class in terms of the time devoted to them and the values placed upon them. All too often they are seen as 'practical' and not 'academic', as expressive but not cognitive, as coming 'after' the children have attained sufficient linguistic competences and so on (Southworth, 1982).

If the list is accurate then it suggests that all the declarations about the need for a balanced curriculum are based on prior judgments as to the elements between which you are to find a balance and to prior determination of the weighting of subjects (Dearden, 1981). Balance is presented as 'given' not as negotiable. Indeed, as Dearden demonstrates, the concept of balance is controversial.

What I would like to argue is that the present formulas for a balanced curriculum are imbalanced in respect of the weighting between subjects. It is my view that the 'balanced curriculum' in the 'orthodox' prescriptions afford too much emphasis on basic skills, and I believe this prescription brings with it certain harmful side-effects. For one thing the focus on basic skills translates into 'reading progress' (ie. decoding), 'number skills' (ie. arithmetic), and 'comprehension' (ie. finding answers to closed questions): and this is all done in order to confine the focus of attention to competences which are capable of being tested and quantified. The 'balanced curriculum' is only 'balanced' from the viewpoint of the testers. As Eisner (1980) says:

> the production of measurable competences in the three R's is creating an imbalanced curriculum that will, in the long run, weaken rather than strengthen the quality of children's education ... We need a curriculum for children that does justice to the scope of their minds and we need evaluation practices that do justice to the lives that students and teachers lead in classrooms.

At the moment we have neither because of the way we weight subjects and because of our preoccupation with assessing skills. The curriculum is imbalanced because we cling to the curriculum of the testers.

(e) The Learners

Like most of the curriculum documents already mentioned, it has taken me too long to arrive at the essential focus of the enterprise — children. Those who should come first are all too easily 'pushed down' the agenda.

Very little of the above sections has effectively addressed the question, what do children need to come to know? Perhaps there are two reasons. Firstly, for the purposes of this chapter I am less concerned with answering it myself than in demonstrating how others, more powerful and erudite than myself, have failed to provide adequate answers. Secondly, though, I am reasonably sure that I *cannot* answer the question. Before it can be answered I would need to know the children, their contexts, biographies, experiences and so forth. In short, I would need as Bruner (1977) says, to start with where the learners are. By starting with and from the children the task becomes both practical and urgent. It moves us away from indulgent discussions about aims and confronts us with the children who are trying to make sense of their worlds. At the same time it will put us into classrooms and amongst children. Efforts to answer this order of question are all too frequently conducted in staffrooms after school, or the head's study, or in LEA offices, or in Education Committee meetings, or

Elizabeth House or Institutes of Education. Of course discussion should go on there, but a reader of the orthodox documents could all too easily think that these are the only places where the discussion counts. The most obvious place is omitted, for to my mind the best place would be in classrooms whilst the learners are active. Possibly the verbiage of the documents has failed to convey that there are teachers and children who *are* working well. What this requires is a consideration of *processes* rather than *products*, but here too the documents are imbalanced in favour of the latter.

* * *

Not unexpectedly the bulk of this chapter is concerned with the first question. In devoting more space to the first I am simply reflecting the continued preoccupation with aims in the literature. In posing the other three I now want to touch upon issues which relate to this first one, and which may broaden the primary curriculum's frame of reference.

What Are the Best Means of Helping Young Children Come to Know These Things?

Here it would be easy to look at organizational issues such as class sizes, the nature of groups, resources and so on. My desiderata are rather simpler. *Primary Practice* (1983) includes consideration of assessment, self evaluation, staff development, management of small schools, refers to the use of parents and the community and provides some examples of selected schools' and teachers' approaches to subject areas (maths pp. 50–3; study of people past and present pp. 68–76; art, craft and design p.84; music pp. 87–9; personal and social development pp. 98–101; topic work pp. 106–115). Each is worthwhile and light years away from the bureaucratized comments in other documents such as *The School Curriculum*. These examples are illuminating and refreshing since they support the first item in my desiderata which is a willingness to focus on children, classrooms and processes.

Through an analysis of the documents published in the last four years it is possible to discern a movement away from the statement of abstract intentions and towards descriptions of actual practice. There is, of course, still further to go. We need to move on from straightforward descriptions to investigations of classroom processes. The documents are still a long way from portraying the complexities of life and learning in classrooms. By so doing there will be a shift in the focus of attention. Despite *Primary Practice* being an improvement on earlier documents it still continues to discuss the curriculum in terms of aims, objectives and assessment. In spite of its strengths, it is still rather weak on action and process issues.

This emphasis on process indicates my second point which is staff development and which I have outlined elsewhere (Southworth, 1984). Curriculum development can in substantial part only come through teacher development (Stenhouse, 1975). Therefore if this is seen as axiomatic schools should then become places of learning for all — children and teachers. By that I mean that teachers could be seeking to learn about themselves as teachers, wherever possible sharing this task and their knowledge with colleagues. In turn schools would begin to develop into learning collectives for all. Of course, this is easier to extol than to implement but there is some evidence of it taking place in some schools (see Southworth, 1984) and through the efforts of action researchers. Nevertheless, there are many questions to ask concerning the necessary pre-conditions which facilitate this approach, the kinds of LEA support and provision for INSET and, most fundamental of all, the staffing level of the school. However, before these can be discussed there is a need to ensure that the whole issue is put on the agendas of the DES and LEAs.

The third point which is pertinent both to this section and to the first is concerned with the ethos of the school. Looking at the balance of the curriculum subjects one can detect not only a hierarchy of subjects but also a corresponding attachment to the more 'academic' areas as the Gulbenkian Report (1982) demonstrates. In bold terms this means that there is a tendency for imagination, feeling and expression to be undervalued:

> In the recent rash of curriculum documents from the DES, HMI and Schools Council, there is a relative neglect of the emotions, establishing yet another curious tension between the practice of, and literature on, schooling. School life is utterly characterized by feeling ... I find only a stifled acknowledgment of the existence and importance of feelings and of the contribution that schooling can make to their education. (Gibson, 1983)

In the clamour to negotiate a primary school curriculum for the twenty-first century we are in danger of providing sets of aims whose 'instrumental rationality' (Gibson, 1983) is so strong that the heart of the matter is obscured. For me, the heart of the matter is summarized by Witkin (1974);

> There is a world that exists beyond the individual, a world that exists whether or not he exists. The child needs to know about this world, to move in it and manage himself in it ... There is another world, however, a world that exists only because the individual exists. It is the world of his own sensations and feelings ... If the price of finding oneself in the world is that of losing the world in oneself, then the price is more than anyone can afford.

How Do You Know They Have Learned Something?

> The inherent preferences of organizations are clarity, certainty and perfection. The inherent nature of human relationships involves ambiguity, uncertainty and imperfection. How one honours, balances and integrates the needs of both is the real trick of management. (Pascale and Athos, 1981)

I find that statement immensely helpful in terms of school management and if you inserted 'curriculum' before 'management' I think the statement is just as valid. So much of what is said about the curriculum implies that the learning that takes place is observable, quantifiable and certain. I tend to believe that quite a bit of curricular activity is difficult to observe and defies the current model of quantifying learning because it is 'uncertain'. Of course, because it is difficult it does not imply that we should give up. Rather, we should seek to refine our model and become more sensitive as Eisner claims above. The problem is that current moves towards developing ways of recording progress and devising continuous forms of education are rather clumsy.

The *Primary School Survey* (1978) contains a chapter entitled 'The Curriculum: planning and continuity' which draws attention to 'transition between classes' and 'continuity between schools' as well as teachers with special curricular responsibilities. The fact that just five pages are seen to constitute a chapter serves to highlight the importance which HMI attached to these issues. Through the First and Middle School surveys, and *Primary Practice* (pp. 128–130) and *The Practical Curriculum* (pp. 50–2) this attachment of importance persists.

In a general way continuity appears to be concerned with two sets of issues. One I will call *communicational*, the other *structural*.

Communicational issues involve such things as the plans teachers make for the groups they teach, the curricular policies the school adopts, the kinds of records teachers, schools, and LEAs design, the degree of liaison which occurs amongst teachers within a school and between schools when pupils transfer. In turn these raise such issues as the scope and methods of pupil assessment, interpersonal relations, the autonomy of individual teachers and the curricular areas which are (or are not) encompassed. To focus on just the last of these, since this also relates to curriculum balance, it appears that typically aspects of mathematics and language are centrally located in the network of curriculum communications. Other subjects tend to receive rather less attention. The materialistic curriculum plays a role here since reading and maths schemes offered by the publishers include take-away checklists and records. Consequently, because some curricular areas are less materialistically organized records are not kept. At the same time this is compounded by the values which create the list of second class subjects. Art, crafts, drama, PE, RE, and music are often the curricular areas which fall outside the purview of continuity (unless, perhaps, a particular child is deemed to be 'talented'). This exacerbates the diminution of their individual status and the balance of the curriculum is further affected.

Much of this concern for continuity may stem from HM Inspectors noting on their visits to schools that there is a lack of co-ordination which results in pupils experiencing rather too much repetition. Traditionally in schools September is the month of 'revision' and much of this, it is felt, could be reduced if schools and teachers involved in the transition of pupils were more carefully co-ordinated. Equally, co-ordination could avert the problems caused for pupils' continuity of learning if there was less reliance on the 'calendar curriculum' and on the 'broadcast curriculum'. The former can be caricatured as the succession of projects based on what-we-did-in-the-summer-holidays, harvest, autumn, halloween, bonfire night, winter and Christmas. The latter is the pursuit of the teacher who in the course of a week requires the children to watch half-a-dozen schools television programmes, listen to a radio broadcast and be interested in any extra media relishes such as The State Opening of Parliament! Both have considerable impact upon topic work (Benyon, 1981). Efforts to moderate the excesses of such practice seem sensible. The idea of co-ordinating is useful and the kinds of communication processes required are professional concerns. Yet, even if continuity is treated at this relatively obvious communicational level there are deep-seated issues to confront:

> Continuity is what is or is not experienced by the individual child.
> He is the one who experiences the discontinuity of demands by different teachers and different schools. (Dean, 1980)

This demonstrates the issue of the individual teacher's autonomy, and as Galton and Willcocks (1983) show this involves teaching styles and approaches to learning. Important as communication tactics are they are only the tip of the iceberg. At best they will not provide a continuous programme of learning, rather they will simply remove some of the discontinuities.

Galton and Willcocks suggest that there are deeper, underlying issues. These are the structural elements of teaching methods, learning processes, conceptions of developmental stages as well as epistemological structures. Continuity as a concept relies upon prior assumptions about how children learn, how they develop, how a form of knowledge (or alternative epistemological classification) is organized in terms of sequencing of key concepts. Without being in possession of such things how can someone logically prescribe continuity?

All of this is then compounded by the need for teachers to be able to recognize these things in their own and in the children's activities. Teachers will clearly need to have some evidence of the individual child's stage of development, the position at which the child now stands in any given subject or activity, the teaching approach now required. Two things begin to surface at this point. Firstly, the complexity of all this is not sufficiently appreciated in the prescriptions schools are offered. Secondly, a logico-linear view of learning is probably the prevailing model for continuity.

How far is it possible to be certain that a child has developed an appreciation of Ted Hughes' *The Iron Man*, or Tolkien's *The Hobbit*, or of Beethoven's *Pastoral Symphony*? And if it can be recorded, where do you go next to ensure continuity? Does Van Gogh come before or after Rembrandt? There may well be good reasons for ordering addition before multiplication, but my real point is that for some areas of knowledge the concepts are less easy to structure, let alone discern in children's actions.

Perhaps for the time being, at least, continuity whilst seeking clarity, certainty and perfection will have to put up with ambiguity, uncertainty and imperfection.

How Do We Let Those Outside School Know What the Children Are Doing?

The notion of continuity is interesting because as discussed in the documents the implication is that continuity of learning is something that only needs to be arranged inside schools, or if not inside schools it is solely to do with learning planned and processed by the school. Frequently the discussion fails to acknowledge the learning which takes place beyond the compass of schools. It might even imply that only school learning is legitimate, that somehow all other learning — at home, with family and friends — is 'unofficial'. Plainly such learning is outside the schools' control but surely some of it needs to be acknowledged and valued within the schools.

For example, those schools who have only lately received their first microcomputer may well be advised to enquire of their pupils the extent of their knowledge of computers since many of the children may be more familiar with computer-based learning than certain teachers. This is Bruner's point again of starting with where the learner is. It is also the daily routine of the reception class teacher who as the children are admitted searches to discover each child's levels of experience, awareness and knowledge. It is often this teacher who through induction schemes and parental help in the classroom works with the child's parents to be in a situation where she can capitalize on the child's prior experiences. By talking with the parents — and by listening to them — a dialogue and partnership is developed which supports the child and which communicates to those outside the school what the child is engaged upon inside the school.

Continuity of learning with its inherent inside school focus may infer that schools have a monopoly on learning. Whether that is an overstatement or not I feel that the discussion of continuity betrays a 'closed' view of learning and one which is not congruent with other attempts to open-up schools and involve parents and others.

Recent work in the area of reading development and parental involvement shows a picture of partnership between home and school whereby those 'outside' school are respected and involved with their child's learning. The research also suggests that significant gains are made. These are revealed by enhanced reading scores but, I might also speculate, that there are all kinds of gains for the parents, teachers and the school. It may not be possible to provide all aspects of curricular activity with parental involvement schemes but one of the things which needs to be considered in the light of these schemes is whether that style of communication can be harnessed so that other curricular areas might also benefit.

Certainly, along with giving out reading books and progress charts those parents who are so involved also witness, almost unintentionally, the teacher's skill and knowledge in dealing with the dynamics of attempting to teach large groups of children. In short, parents are provided with a view of the teacher's professional expertise. Also, the teacher witnesses the particular nature of the parents' relationship with their child. Hopefully, a level of communication is attained and sustained which transcends the more typical approaches to home-school communications. Without doubt it is qualitatively different to newsletters, parents' evening, reports, PTAs and such like — valuable as these may be in their ways. The main feature is that through parental involvement in reading schools are communicating an aspect of their curriculum to those outside. Maybe if more of the curriculum was communicated, more benefits would develop?

Conclusion

Out of this division some things need to be emphasized. One of my themes is that whilst teaching and learning issues are possibly gaining more attention, their centrality to the discussion is still not sufficiently recognized. If the intention of the documents is to try to help teachers become more proficient — in other words to learn about teaching — then the documents ought to begin with the teachers themselves inside classrooms. At the moment the discussion is outside classrooms trying to get in. Instead it should be inside-out!

Secondly, this 'review' of the documents is selective, prejudiced and partial. As such I make the same errors that many other writers do. Perhaps we need to be mindful of the story which is regularly told in primary school assemblies of the blind men and the elephant. Each blind man touched only one part of the animal yet each believed they knew the truth about elephants. Analogously, one might say that in this chapter the curriculum is the elephant and the documents and myself the blind men. No one knows all there is to know about the primary school curriculum. Rather, it should be regarded as a process of discovery not a point of arrival.

This raises a third thing. Ornstein (1972) wrote that assumptions can limit the contents of awareness. Before we attempt to implement the prescriptions currently on offer, we need to examine the assumptions which limit the prescriptions. Unfortunately the sheer quantity of documents which are bombarding schools at the present may force schools into submission and easy acceptance. This should be resisted. Critical analysis and vigilance is essential.

References

BAILEY, C. (1983) 'Education, accountability and the preparation of teachers' in *Cambridge Journal of Education*, 13, 2.
BENYON, L. (1981) 'Curriculum Continuity' in *Education 3–13*, 9, 2. pp. 36–41.
BOURDIEU, P. (1971) 'Systems of Education and Systems of Thought' in YOUNG, M.F.D. (1971) *Knowledge and Control*, London, Coller-Macmillan, pp. 189–207.
BRUNER, J. (1977) *The Process of Education*, Cambridge (MA,). 2nd ed. Harvard University Press.
DEAN, J. (1980) 'Continuity' in RICHARDS, C. (Ed.) *Primary Education: Issues for the Eighties*, London, A and C Black. pp. 42–52.
DEARDEN, R.F. (1981) 'Balance and coherence: Some curricular principles in recent reports', in *Cambridge Journal of Education*, 11, 2, Easter, pp. 107–118.
DEPARTMENT OF EDUCATION AND SCIENCE (1978) *Primary Education in England: A Survey by HM Inspectors of Schools*, London, HMSO.
DEPARTMENT OF EDUCATION AND SCIENCE (1980) *A View of the Curriculum*, HMI Series: Matters for Discussion No. 11, London, HMSO
DEPARTMENT OF EDUCATION AND SCIENCE (1980) *A Framework for the Curriculum*, London, HMSO.
DEPARTMENT OF EDUCATION AND SCIENCE (1981) *The School Curriculum*, London, HMSO.
DEPARTMENT OF EDUCATION AND SCIENCE (1982) *Education 5 to 9: an illustrative survey of 80 first schools in England*, London, HMSO.
DEPARTMENT OF EDUCATION AND SCIENCE (1983) *9–13 Middle Schools: an illustrative survey*, London, HMSO.
DEPARTMENT OF EDUCATION AND SCIENCE (1984) *Parental Influence at School, A new framework for school government in England and Wales*, Cmnd. 9242, London, HMSO.
EISNER, E.W. (1980) 'The impoverished mind', in *Curriculum*, 1, 2, Autumn, pp. 11–17.
ELLIOTT, J. (1983) 'School focused INSET and research into teacher education', *Cambridge Journal of Education*, 13, 2. pp. 19–31.
GALTON, M. and WILLOCKS, J. (1983) *Moving from the Primary Classroom*, London, Routledge and Kegan Paul.
GIBSON, R. (Ed.) (1983) *The Education of Feeling*, Cambridge Institute of Education.

GIBSON, R. (1984) *Structuralism and Education*, London, Hodder and Stoughton.
GRAY, D.W.S. (1973) 'Between Structure and Content and Beyond' in PIPER, D.W. (Ed.) *Readings in Art and Design Education, Vol. 2: After Coldstream*, London, Davis-Poynter, pp. 100–101.
GULBENKIAN, CALOUSTE (1982) *The Arts in Schools*, Calouste London, Gulbenkian Foundation.
HOLLY, P. (1984) 'Beyond the cult of the individual', unpublished Paper to Supporting School-Based Enquiry Conference September 21–23, Downing College, Cambridge. Mimeo. Cambridge Institute of Education.
OLSEN, T.P. (1982) 'School-based in-service education: Model or utopia?' in *British Journal of In-Service Education*, 8, 2, pp. 73–9.
ORNSTEIN, R.E. (1972) *The Psychology of Consciousness*, London, Penguin.
PASCALE, R.T. and ATHOS, A.G. *The Art of Japanese Management*, London, Penguin.
SCHOOLS COUNCIL (1981) *The Practical Curriculum*, Schools Council Working Paper 70, London, Methuen.
SCHOOLS COUNCIL (1983) *Primary Practice*, Schools Council Working Paper 75, London, Methuen.
SOUTHWORTH, G.W. (1982) 'Art in the primary school; Towards first principles', in *Journal of Art and Design Education*, 1, 2, pp. 217–29.
SOUTHWORTH, G.W. (1983) 'Curriculum implementation and the primary headteacher', in *Curriculum*, 4, 1, Spring, pp. 20–26.
SOUTHWORTH, G.W. (1984) 'Development of staff in primary schools: Some ideas and implications', in *British Journal of In-Service Education*, 10, 3, pp. 6–15.
STENHOUSE, L. (1975) *An Introduction to Curriculum Research and Development*, London, Heinemann.
WITKIN, F. (1974) *The Intelligence of Feeling*, London, Heinemann.

'The Curriculum from 5 to 16': Background, Content and Some Implications for Primary Education

Colin Richards

Introduction

The school curriculum matters. Through it, pupils develop their understanding of, and competence in, ways of knowing regarded as valuable in our society. Those professionally engaged in the education service and others with a personal interest in it attest to the importance of the curriculum. But such general assent is not sufficient to give direction to the formulation of policy or the improvement of practice. To do this, closer agreement is required as to the purposes informing the curriculum and as to the ways in which such intentions might be realized in schools and classrooms. This chapter examines the context, content and some implications of *The Curriculum from 5 to 16* (hereafter referred to as CM2)[1], a discussion document from HM Inspectorate. As part of the felicitously named 'Curriculum Matters' series, it suggests an approach to thinking about and designing the whole curriculum which might help to clarify and develop broad agreement concerning objectives and content. By focusing here on its implications for primary education, this chapter runs the risk of blunting one of the most important thrusts in the document — the provision of a common framework for considering the curriculum of primary, middle and secondary schools, a framework intended to promote communication and planning within and across the phases but without riding roughshod over legitimate differences in approach.

Context

During the last decade, primary education has had to contend with a formidable range of issues. Perhaps the most dramatic has been the large contraction in the numbers of primary-aged children, which has brought in its wake closures, amalgamations, staff redeployment, mixed aged classes and a host of professional and personal problems which demographic statistics have obscured, but which have loomed large in the day to day life of schools and education offices. The last ten years have witnessed continuing financial constraint with concerns for greater cost-effectiveness and with considerable repercussions on the funding of schools. Good 'house-keeping', always important in the primary sector, has become even more crucial and time-consuming. Growing public interest in schooling has led to schools being publicly accountable in ways and to a degree not previously encountered. Mechanisms and procedures for discharging accountability have had to be reconsidered and to some extent reconstituted. These developments have taken place at the same time as other major factors have affected British society and, directly or indirectly, primary schools: changing family patterns, the development of microtechnology, the growth in unemployment and the increasing recognition of discrimination on the grounds of gender and race. This changing social and economic context has made it important to review the primary curriculum and the way it is realized in schools to see what elements need to be reaffirmed, which redefined and which omitted.

This process of reappraisal to which CM2 is intended to contribute is already under way in a considerable number of schools. Professional development has been stimulated by a variety of factors including local education authority curricular reviews, school self-evaluation schemes, the programmes of work of the former Schools Council, the activities of the School Curriculum Development Committee and the provision of in-service education of both an award and non-award bearing kind. Publications such as *Primary Practice*[2] the Cockcroft Report[3] and HMI surveys of primary[4] first[5] and middle[6] schools have raised issues concerned with curriculum planning, breadth, differentiation, assessment, continuity, staff deployment and teacher education which have promoted discussion and action at local authority and school levels and in institutions of higher education.

The concern to reappraise the content and quality of education has also been shared by successive Secretaries of State for Education and Science and for Wales as part of the duty laid upon them by the 1944 Education Act to 'promote the education of the people of England and Wales.' Chapter 2 of the White Paper, *Better Schools*[7] reviews a number of initiatives in this respect and reiterates the Government's concern to reach a 'broad agreement about the objectives and content of the school curriculum' which can become the basis of the curricular policies of the Secretaries of State, the local education authorities and the schools. What is being sought is *not* unanimity within the education service, but a broad measure of agreement; *not* agreement about the *detailed* organization and content of programmes of work in schools but general assent to the purposes of education, the range of knowledge and skills to be included in

Colin Richards

the curriculum and the kinds of understandings and qualities children are to be helped to develop, or to acquire. *Better Schools* states:

> The definition of agreed objectives for the curriculum, in principle encompasses four strands: the purposes of learning at school; the contribution of each main subject area or element; the organization and content of the 5–16 curriculum as a whole; and what is to be attained at the end of the primary phase and of the compulsory years in the secondary phase. The objectives apply also where the age ranges of schools do not correspond with the typical pattern (page 13).

The publication of CM2 seeks to stimulate professional debate concerning the first three of these four strands and so inform the Secretary of State's national curricular policy. It is in part a response to the call made in his Sheffield speech of January 1984 for an open discussion aimed at clarifying and developing the objectives of the 5–16 curriculum.

Content

The document provides both a language in which to discuss the curriculum and a framework in which to plan it. Its use of non-emotive terms such as 'areas of learning and experience', 'concepts', 'skills' and 'attitudes' is intended to facilitate communication about the curriculum, which might otherwise be impeded by participants' preoccupation with 'subjects' and 'content' on the one hand and with 'children's needs and interests' and 'processes of learning' on the other. Use of such a common language, however ill-defined it may be around the edges, may help clarify areas of agreement as well as indicate more precisely areas of disagreement. Such a language may well be an essential pre-requisite for establishing curricular continuity both within and between primary and secondary phases.

To use a cartographic analogy, the document also provides a kind of curricular map or chart which aids analysis and planning. Projected on a small scale, it provides an overview of the large area of the school curriculum, outlines its shape, gives some indication of its contours, draws attention to its prominent features and traces some inter-relationships among them. It indicates the regions to be explored and illustrates some of the means which could be employed, but it does not provide directives as to the routes to be followed, the organization to be adopted or the precise equipment to be used. Its status needs to be made clear; it is provisional rather than definitive — subject to revision in the light of discussion and exploration and to evolution in the light of changes over time.

A six-fold framework for curricular review and development is offered comprising (i) general aims, (ii) areas of learning and experience, (iii)

'The Curriculum from 5 to 16'

elements of learning, (iv) cross-curricular issues, (v) general characteristics of the curriculum and (vi) assessment. It is important to stress that the framework is concerned with the factors that need to be borne in mind when appraising and designing a curriculum, not with the ways in which teaching and learning should be organized, whether in terms of subjects, broad areas, topics, activities or any combination of these:

> It is for individual schools to decide how the curriculum is to be organized for teaching purposes, but each of these ways of organizing the work in primary schools has to be assessed in terms of its fitness for purpose (page 9).

(i) General Aims

The document reaffirms the need to have educational aims which underlie and give guidance to the day to day work of schools. In particular, the goals of education outlined in the Warnock Report[8] and the aims proposed in *The School Curriculum*[9] are endorsed as providing the kind of broad guidance required to give a general orientation and thrust to a school's activities. CM2 argues for the importance of helping develop pupils' autonomy, rationality and self-confidence so that they 'grow up to become competent, confident, rational and self-reliant adults who can manage their own lives and play their part in society' (page 3). Such long-term purposes are best served in the present by approaches to teaching and learning which stress enquiry, questioning and challenge, which give enjoyment and satisfaction from the successful completion of tasks and which encourage children to use their imagination. In this way, the present is not to be sacrificed to the future, nor the imagination to the intellect, nor intrinsic satisfaction to instrumental considerations. In Aspin's terms[10] education is as much concerned with the 'possibilities of the present' as 'the cares of the morrow'. The purposes outlined in CM2 are avowedly pragmatic, derived from professional concerns with curricular policy and practice rather than finely argued educational theory with its base in epistemology, ethics, metaphysics or whatever. Underlying the arguments in the publication is a concern to achieve unity of purpose throughout the 5–16 age span so that all pupils of whatever race or gender have 'access to a curriculum of similar breadth and balance, irrespective of their level of ability, the school they attend or their social circumstances' (pages 3–4). Chapter Six of the Primary Survey (1978) indicates the scale of the problems facing primary education in providing that access.

Colin Richards

(ii) Areas of Learning and Experience

Though important, general aims need to be 'cashed out' in harder currency, if the task of transacting the curriculum with children is to proceed. CM2 argues that in pursuit of such aims, primary and secondary schools should involve all children in each of nine areas of experience and learning at all stages from 5–16. This approach to the curriculum through areas of learning and experience has been worked on through co-operation between HMI, local education authorities and secondary school teachers, but is here presented with a developmental perspective to stress the importance of each stage building on the foundation laid in earlier ones. Within the document, the areas are discussed in alphabetical order — deliberately so since *all* are regarded as essential to a child's education, though the relative emphasis given to each may properly vary somewhat at different stages in the educational process. The areas are (a) aesthetic and creative, (b) human and social, (c) linguistic and literary, (d) mathematical, (e) moral, (f) physical, (g) scientific, (h) spiritual and (i) technological. The characteristics of each area are offered 'not as definitive statements but as a basis for further discussion in schools' (page 17).

'They constitute a planning and analytical tool' (page 16) which school staffs or individual teachers might use to assess their current or proposed curricular provision before making modifications (either additions or, just as importantly, deletions). For example, if particular areas were missing or poorly represented in the work undertaken with particular classes or age groups of children, alternative provision could be made, perhaps in the form of new topics to be introduced in project work, or new processes to be introduced into creative activities, or new subjects to be put on the timetable. General acceptance of the view that children should have their understanding and capabilities developed in all nine areas during their primary education would have far-reaching implications; it would present a tremendous challenge for individual schools, let alone individual teachers, to meet.

(iii) Elements of Learning

To provide analytical 'bite' to planning based on areas of learning and experience CM2 introduces the notion of 'elements of learning'. These constitute the bases used to select what is it that children should be introduced to within each of the nine areas. Four major elements are distinguished: (a) knowledge (ie subject matter to be taught or learnt), (b) concepts (which, singly or in networks, enable children to organize knowledge and experience), (c) skills (many different kinds of capability related to the performance of tasks) and (d) attitudes (including dispositions and qualities of character). Further documents in the Curriculum Matters

'The Curriculum from 5 to 16'

series aim to relate these to particular subjects or aspects of the curriculum. CM2 does not discuss exactly how such elements might be incorporated into the curriculum planning process, but one possible way would be for schools (the whole staff or a working party) to (a) analyze an area of learning and experience in terms of significant concepts and skills, aided by local authority statements, Curriculum Matters publications and other published material, (b) consider the kinds of subject matter which could illuminate the concepts and involve the development of skills and (c) select and organize particular content which is comprehensible, interesting to the children and useful, either in terms of contributing significantly to their current understanding of the particular area or in terms of ready application in other contexts. Thinking about the primary curriculum in terms of skills, concepts, attitudes and subject matter is not new; what is significant is the advocacy by HMI of this self-conscious, analytical approach to curriculum planning for all primary schools.

(iv) Cross-Curricular Issues

An earlier section in this chapter briefly referred to developments within British society which have impinged on the work of primary schools. Such factors have given rise to a number of cross-curricular issues which complicate still further the tasks of curricular planning and review but which, if neglected, render the curriculum at the very least less vital and at the worst almost irrelevant. Environmental education, health education, political education and education for economic understanding are examples of such cross-curricular concerns which, though sometimes taught separately, 'are more frequently and often more appropriately mediated through topics, subjects, groups of subjects or the general life of the schools' (page 13). But most fundamental of all is the issue encapsulated in the Swann Report's[11] title *Education for All*. Equal opportunities for both boys and girls and for children from ethnic minority and majority communities presuppose a unity of purpose and a consistency of provision which apply irrespective of the size, type and location of the schools children attend. Curriculum planning and review have a part to play in achieving this more consistent provision.

(v) Characteristics of the Curriculum

The fifth component in the proposed framework comprises a set of broad criteria which can be applied when appraising the whole school curriculum or just one of its constitutent parts. The criteria reflect issues of perennial importance in curriculum design and to be applied and acted upon require professional discussion and decision-making involving not only the consideration of factual matters, but the making of value and other judgments. The criteria are more than rhetorical devices; they raise very significant questions relating to the curriculum as planned by teachers and as experienced by children. These criteria are:

(a) Breadth Are all primary children being appropriately taught in all nine areas of learning and experience and being introduced to the four elements of learning associated with them? Are children being given a broad range of activities within an area and within its component parts?

(b) Balance Is each area of learning and experience and each element given appropriate attention in relation to the others and to the whole curriculum as experienced by the child? What constitutes 'appropriate attention'? Over what period of time is this balance to be sought? Are the activities within an area of experience reasonably balanced? Are children experiencing a balanced range of teaching and learning approaches? The value judgments implicit in 'balance' cannot be avoided but need addressing directly.

(c) Relevance Is the curriculum relevant in terms of (a) improving children's understanding and competence in each area, (b) increasing their understanding of themselves and the world in which they live including the influences which bear on them, (c) developing their self-confidence and (d) equipping them with the knowledge and skills needed for adult living?

(d) Differentiation Does the work provided allow for differences in the abilities and other characteristics of children of the same age and yet at the same time does it have an overall unity of purpose which transcends individual differences?

(e) Progression and Continuity Within the primary school, is the work in each aspect of the curriculum reflecting and building on work done previously? Externally, do primary schools take adequate account of the influences to which their entrants have already been exposed and of the expectations entertained of their children by the schools to which they will transfer in due course?

Such general criteria and the challenging questions they entail need to be applied not only to the curricular policies and practices of individual schools but also to curricular policy statements emanating from whatever source.

(vi) Assessment

In addition to putting forward the broad criteria for curriculum evaluation outlined above, CM2 provides some guidance on assessment which, it argues, 'is inseparable from the teaching process' (page 51). Assessment is seen as serving two complementary purposes: (a) to improve children's learning through diagnosis of their strengths and weaknesses, discussion and self appraisal and the more effective matching of work to children's capabilities, and (b) to improve the curriculum through helping teachers to see how far their intentions are being realized and thus in what ways their teaching approaches may need modification. Although acknowledging that much assessment must be largely impressionistic in the crowded world of the classroom, it argues that assessment can be improved by getting expectations clearer (the Curriculum Matters series and the APU surveys should help here), by refining observation in the classroom and by judicious use of more objective forms of testing, which should be very closely related to the work in hand.

Some Implications

CM2 offers a fresh perspective on the curriculum, including a redefinition of what is 'basic' to primary education. Its argument that children should engage in a carefully devised, adequately justified and widely defined curriculum related to all nine areas of learning and experience offers a formidable professional challenge, already being taken up in a number of schools but with very significant implications for the self-sufficiency of the individual class teacher and the individual school.

The approach in CM2 demands conscious planning and evaluation from primary practitioners. It does not deny the importance of intuition or of 'tacit knowledge' when working with children, nor the significance of teachers' opportunism in capitalizing on children's interests aroused by those unexpected events which can prove so productive in primary classrooms. But it does assume that both intuition and opportunism are not sufficient to secure children's entitlement to a broad, balanced and relevant primary education.

The suggested approach places very great demands on class teachers, demands which, unaided, most cannot be expected to meet fully. A collaborative, rather than individualistic, approach to curriculum planning and review is implied — collaboration dependent upon teachers' deepened understanding of the areas of learning and experience and of how children might engage with them and upon the sharing of this expertise to teachers' mutual benefit and that of the children they teach. A key indicator of, and contributor to, this 'collegial'[12] approach to decision-making would be the formulation of curricular policies arrived at through staff discussion and setting out educational intentions and broad expectations relating to teaching and learning in various aspects of the curriculum or areas of learning and experience. Such policies would not deprive class teachers of all discretion in curricular matters, since the policies would not precisely prescribe content or methodology, but would be binding in a way that old-style schemes of work never were. Another manifestation of a collegial approach would be the preparation of what the 'Thomas Report'[13] terms 'school development plans', where primary schools 'set up arrangements to review where they are in relation to the many aspects of their internal and external environment, and to make plans for working on some of them ... [such] a plan should be operated by all teachers for it is a contract between the head and staff to which, in the end, all must subscribe' (pages 76–77). Work on particular areas of learning and experience believed to be less than adequately represented in the school's curriculum would be a suitable focus for such a development plan.

Far from devaluing the work of class teachers, collegial approaches, paradoxically perhaps, would increase their standing by fully recognizing the formidable range and levels of demand now being made upon them and by involving them, not just in the planning of the work of their own classes, but in the establishment of a school-wide curricular framework. The long-standing and valued primary tradition that one teacher should be responsible for ensuring that his/her class receives a curriculum adequate in range and depth is not in dispute, but the way this responsibility is to be properly exercised and supported is at least open to reinterpretation in the light of the changes and developments outlined earlier in this chapter. Support could take one or more of a variety of forms depending on the individual class teacher and the area of learning and experience in question: occasional advice from a post-hólder or other member of staff with specialist knowledge; a detailed scheme of work setting out elements of learning and giving advice on organization and methodology; school-based workshops or attendance at in-service courses organized by other agencies; a post-holder working alongside a colleague for a time, to introduce a new aspect of work or, perhaps more useful, to help her/him introduce it; or, in some cases, perhaps most often with upper juniors, a member of staff with specialist knowledge teaching someone else's class a particular aspect of the curriculum for a month, a term or a year, provided the class teacher retains overall responsibility for the work of the class, including the links that would need to be made between his/her own work and that of the specialist.

What is being discussed is not the dismantling of the class-teacher system, but its strengthening through sensitive deployment and development of the expertise which already exists on primary school staffs by means of a variety of ploys, varying from the one-off occasion, through short-term procedures, to more established long-term arrangements, all subject to renegotiation as circumstances change. Paragraphs 772 and 773 of the Plowden Report[14] could be cited in support of more flexible patterns of staff deployment to bring children into contact with teachers who have particular expertise.

A shortage of space precludes detailed consideration of the implications of CM2 for the self-sufficiency of the individual primary school, but such are the expectations of primary schools that most would need additional support to implement it effectively. Such assistance could take a variety of forms including: the formulation of local education authority curricular policies and guidelines and the management of the teaching force in the light of these; the establishment of 'clusters' of schools for the development and co-ordination of their work, as outlined in the Thomas Report, the deployment of advisory teachers to support work in particular areas of experience and learning; the provision of in-service education targetted on the needs of whole schools rather than simply individuals; the improvement of staffing levels to enable reductions to be made in the contact time of primary teachers; and the development of the skills of curriculum management at all levels. Such developments would still provide plenty of scope for individual schools' discretion on curricular matters but would help ensure greater consistency of curricular provision from one school to another across an authority. In this way, the concept of 'collegiality' might be extended beyond the individual school to encompass others in the locality.

Conclusion

In a speech in November 1985, Eric Bolton, Senior Chief Inspector, remarked on the lack of a sustained debate about, and scrutiny of, the curriculum in primary schools. He argued, 'It is difficult to identify sufficient common ground, or at least sufficient common language, to begin to discuss the primary curriculum nationally, let alone carry out the kind of scrutiny and development required to develop a primary curriculum framework and agreed objectives' (page 13).[15] The publication of CM2 is an attempt to provide such a common language and to provide some common markers to enable the search for a framework to proceed. The success or failure of the document and others in the Curriculum Matters series will rest on the response they receive from those striving to improve still further the education they provide. That 'sustained debate' is already beginning; do join it.

Notes

1 DEPARTMENT OF EDUCATION AND SCIENCE (1985) *The Curriculum from 5 to 16*, Curriculum Matters 2, An HMI Series HMSO.

2 SCHOOLS COUNCIL (1983) *Primary Practice*, Working Paper 75, Methuen Educational.
3 DEPARTMENT OF EDUCATION AND SCIENCE (1982) *Mathematics Counts*, HMSO.
4 DEPARTMENT OF EDUCATION AND SCIENCE (1978) *Primary Education in England*, HMSO.
5 DEPARTMENT OF EDUCATION AND SCIENCE (1982) *Education 5 to 9*, HMSO.
6 DEPARTMENT OF EDUCATION AND SCIENCE (1983), *9–13 Middle Schools*, HMSO. and DEPARTMENT OF EDUCATION AND SCIENCE (1985) *Education 8 to 12 in Combined and Middle Schools*, HMSO.
7 DEPARTMENT OF EDUCATION AND SCIENCE (1985) *Better Schools*, Cmnd 9469, HMSO.
8 DEPARTMENT OF EDUCATION AND SCIENCE (1978) *Special Educational Needs*, HMSO.
9 DEPARTMENT OF EDUCATION AND SCIENCE (1981) *The School Curriculum*, HMSO.
10 ASPIN, D. (1981) 'Utility is not enough: the arts in the school curriculum' in WHITE, J. *et al. No, Minister*, Bedford Way Papers 4, University of London, Institute of Education.
11 DEPARTMENT OF EDUCATION AND SCIENCE (1985) *Education For All*, HMSO.
12 See CAMPBELL, R.J. (1985) *Developing the Primary School Curriculum*, Holt, Rinehart and Winston, Chapter 10.
13 ILEA (1985) *Improving Primary Schools*, ILEA.
14 CENTRAL ADVISORY COUNCIL For EDUCATION (England) (1967) *Children and their Primary Schools*, HMSO.
15 BOLTON, E. (1985) 'Assessment: Putting the horse before the cart' *The Times Educational Supplement*, 22/11/85.

Further Perspectives on the Primary Curriculum

Geoff Southworth

Introduction

My article 'Perspectives on the primary curriculum' (Southworth, 1985a) attempted to critically review the documents published during 1978–84 which were concerned with the primary school curriculum. The article began by talking of a 'steady stream of documents' each of which offered a particular perspective on the curriculum. The article closed by saying that the 'barrage of documents' continued. Although the article covered a period up to Autumn 1984, even since then there has been another new set of documents from HMI and the DES which are sufficiently significant as to require looking at in some detail. The documents are:

(i) *English from 5–16*: Curriculum Matters 1 an HMI Series (DES, 1984a), October,
(ii) *Education Observed 2*: a review of HMI published reports (DES, 1984b), December,
(iii) *The Curriculum from 5–16*: Curriculum Matters 2 an HMI Series (DES, 1985a), March,
(iv) *Science 5–16*: A statement of policy (DES, 1985b), March,
(v) *Better Schools*, DES White Paper (DES, 1985c) March,
(vi) *Mathematics from 5–16*: Curriculum Matters 3 an HMI Series (DES, 1985d), April.

The month of publication is noted in order to show the timing of them. In just seven months there are six important documents to digest — the steady stream has indeed become a barrage, especially when the Swann Report (1985) and *Improving Primary Schools* (ILEA, 1985) are added to the list.

This chapter cannot do justice to all of these. Therefore, in order to make the task more manageable two of these named documents will be focused on: *The Curriculum from 5–16* and *Better Schools*. The reason for this selection is that these two present overviews of the primary curriculum as a whole, whereas the other documents tend to be more restricted in their scope. Another reason is that the first of these presents the current views of HMI whilst the second document is a DES one. The distinction is important, as HMI themselves are often anxious to explain, since a DES document although it may well have involved HMI in consultations is, in its final form, a Departmental publication on behalf of the Secretaries of State. It may well be interesting to contrast HMI views with the DES.

This article will attempt to cover a number of areas. First, some of the concerns and issues identified in the first article will be 'revisited' to see if there are any new developments or if any have been remedied. Second, each of the two documents will be considered. Out of this review the areas of agreement of both HMI and the DES will be presented as a common prescription. Finally, an indication of a way forward will be offered.

Concerns and Issues Revisited

Although not wishing to labour the issues outlined in the previous article there are a number of areas which need to be re-considered.

At a recent conference on HMI perspectives on the primary curriculum[*] the speaker presented HMI's views in a cogent and straightforward way. Many of the ideas were welcomed and accepted as useful. It emerges from that conference, and the HMI and DES documents, that what is now being constructed is a framework for the curriculum with the intention of reducing differences and inconsistencies between schools and LEAs. A feeling currently expressed by many HMI is that too often the sort of education a child receives is determined rather more by the lottery of geography (LEA or catchment area) than by curriculum design and practice. Such a sentiment is clearly more centralist than de-centralist so that a number of questions arise. Are we being offered a framework or a blueprint? Is difference always unacceptable? Will this framework allow schools the room to experiment? If the framework is accepted what role in the future will there be for LEAs? This is to view the 'framework' in its starkest terms but this is necessary. Quite markedly the documents since 1978 to 1985 mark a period of increased intervention in the curriculum and to perceive this clearly there is a need not just simply to list the numbers of documents but to headline the messages, particularly since all of the documents sound so very 'reasonable'.

[*]Cambridge Institute of Education Day Conference: H.M.I. Perspectives on the Primary Curriculum, March 1985.

Further Perspectives on the Primary Curriculum

Both *The Curriculum from 5–16* and *Better Schools* appear to be eminently *reasonable*; they almost exude *reasonableness*. The HMI document actually says in the Foreword that it represents 'what might reasonably be expected of schools'. Each talks of breadth, balance, coherence, consistency, progression, continuity, relevance and so on. Each of these terms is noticeably positive and laudable. Yet this sense of reasonableness needs to be handled with care for it is perhaps too seductive. By using labels which are pro-words it is difficult to challenge them. Who, for example, would want to argue for an irrelevant curriculum or an incoherent curriculum? A problem facing the reviewer of these documents is that a critique of them is all too easily understood in polarized terms. To criticize 'continuity' is to leave oneself open to the charge of wanting to maintain discontinuity. The very reasonableness of the language of the documents makes the critic appear unreasonable! Such binary logic needs to be dissolved so that a 'network of contrasts' (Gibson, 1984) might begin to be constructed which will help us to understand both the language and the concepts. In this sense the new documents are not much better than the earlier ones. There is some refinement in the definitions but my previous concern about balance and continuity remain. The documents use the words a great deal but fail to convey precise meanings.

Another issue which appears in these documents, and is a development of previous ones, is the strong sense of attachment to aims and objectives. Indeed both documents list the aims cited previously in *A Framework for the School Curriculum* (DES, 1980a), and *The School Curriculum* (DES, 1981). It is claimed that these aims generally command widespread support (DES, 1985a) and although 'there is room for legitimate disagreement about the priority to be attached to each element in this list' of aims, schools have reflected the content of this list in their own formulations of aims and in LEA lists too (DES, 1985c). I detect two things here. Firstly, if the compilation of aims which many schools have undertaken, or have been required to undertake, in the last five years or so has resulted in broad agreement, what does this imply for the notion of considerable differences and inconsistencies between schools and LEAs? HMI are anxious to stress that they report only on what is seen taking place in schools so if there are great differences in practice then it begins to look as if broad agreement on curriculum aims does not necessarily mean broad agreement on, or similarity in, curriculum processes. This has long been recognized in curriculum theory (Blenkin and Kelly, 1983) and perhaps demonstrates how long it takes for the ideas of theorists and researchers to filter through to those who write such documents. This points to questions about the appropriateness of aims and objectives. Perhaps aims only serve to mask the differences? Possibly all the discussion and promotion of aims has done is to create a spurious unity at central (DES) level. Certainly the aims listed are capable of numerous interpretations so that one has to ask of the documents whether, by their own criterion of seeking consistency, the lists of aims are any good? In part the documents acknowledge this since *Better Schools* talks of the need to attend to 'delivering the curriculum'. Clearly aims and objectives have failed to deliver the goods.

Secondly, there is the need to see aims and objectives planning with reference to primary schools. The view of education which underpins much of the primary curriculum is essentially developmental; the main focus is the developing child. This focus is largely concerned with where the child is now, rather than with where the child will end up. Consequently the approach is more process than product orientated:

> To view and to evaluate the curriculum of the Primary school, or of any other educational institution for that matter, by reference to goals or purposes external to it, no matter how those goals or purposes are defined, is to put at risk the essence of that curriculum which is its focus on the processes of education. If education is concerned with intrinsic value, then it cannot be defined by reference to any kind of extrinsic goal. That is the message of fifty years of curriculum development at Primary level. It is a message that cannot and should not be ignored. (Blenkin and Kelly, 1983, p. 21)

It seems to me that the process approach of primary education is at risk because of these documents. HMI are the more restrained and refer to areas of experience and flexibility in the primary years. *Better Schools* however is full of the heavy overtones of instrumentality: 'teachers are performing at a standard below that required to achieve the objectives now proposed for schools' (p. 50, para. 158); 'substantial and sustained improvement is realistic. It is also necessary in order to protect the nation's prosperity and well-being' (p. 3, para. 16); 'Education and training cannot always be distinguished' (p. 16, para. 48). These are just three illustrations which when added to the numerous references as to the needs of employers present a hard-nosed utilitarian conception of education which is probably at odds with much of primary education.

Clearly, there is a need to look at the appropriateness of stating objectives. *Better Schools* says there is a need 'to secure greater clarity about the objectives and content of the curriculum'. Two points arise from this. Firstly, there are questions to raise about the validity of curriculum design by objectives in general. The literature of curriculum study is full of the debate about objectives so it is something of a surprise to find the DES accelerating down this route. Secondly, there is the issue of the validity of objectives for the primary curriculum. Those teachers who prefer Bruner's (1971) approach of starting with where the child is are possibly being overlooked or maybe that approach is now undervalued.

As with the earlier documents there is a general lack of attention to children. Whilst it is true that both documents contain numerically more references to children than their predecessors, there is still insufficient attention paid. The absence of children is matched by an absence of concern for the contexts of teachers and children.

Only in *Education Observed 2* (DES 1984b) is mention made that 'about half the schools are in pre-1914 buildings and some are using rather old temporary classrooms' (para. 12). Behind such facts lie many challenges, frustrations and difficulties. An absence of its recognition suggests a lack of appreciation, firstly of the day-to-day contexts, and secondly of schooling in general. 'Overviews' dealing with national issues do tend to gloss over many things. When there is an added emphasis on consistency, then the tendency will be to homogenize. This may appear quite sensible to the DES and to HMI, but if so, then they are losing sight of a major section of their 'audience', namely teachers in primary schools.

Teachers in primary schools are very much concerned with 'their' class, 'their' children, 'their' school; their perspectives are specific. It is important though to understand this specific perspective more fully, and acknowledge it as a strength of the service. Teachers' viewpoints although specific are not just 'local', rather their perspectives are specific because of the *culture* of primary schools with its strong emphasis on individuality. There are two elements to this individuality. The first is that teachers have a strong belief in self-expression, and that primary school teaching appears to offer scope for initiative, the chance to use varied talents and above all to be yourself in the classroom. Teaching in primary schools is 'a career in which individualism is not only permitted but approved' (Nias, 1984). Secondly, individuality is a major value in terms of the children. Reading many of the aims primary schools have compiled, one is impressed by the constant references concerning the development of the individual child: 'The child should be an individual, developing in his own way' (Ashton *et al.*, 1975). Given this strong attachment to individuality it is quite possible that the documents under review may be philosophically incompatible with the target audience. The documents may be appealing for an homogeneous service when the teachers themselves value and maintain a heterogeneous service. The two, of course, are not necessarily in conflict since there are questions of 'level' and 'kind' to be taken into account. The existence of national guidelines on the school curriculum may still allow individual teachers to exercise professional judgment about exactly what to teach and when (Lawton, 1984). Dean (1984) similarly thinks that LEAs need to spend a great deal of time and thought on the curriculum at the primary stage, leaving teachers free to concentrate on how to help children to learn. However, the documents should now address these issues of 'level' and 'kind' of curriculum planning which they offer. Failure to resolve this will only add to the confusion and create suspicion.

What is clear is that the nature of the teacher's autonomy is being discussed and reconsidered. It is also clear that this is likely to have a particular impact upon primary education. There *are* differences in value concerning individuality, process, products, and most of the other things touched upon in this section. To alter in either scope or nature any of these is likely to alter primary education.

The Curriculum from 5–16 and Better Schools: HMI and DES

As a preface to reviewing aspects of these documents it is necessary to look at how HMI and the DES are seeking to effect change. It has been argued that in primary education the 1960s marked the 'progressive movement', the early 1970s the 'curriculum development movement' and the later 1970s and 1980s the 'accountability movement' (Blenkin and Kelly, 1981; Stenhouse, 1980). This argument is largely supported by Lawton (1980 and 1984) who suggests that the dominant metaphor in education has changed from 'partnership' to 'accountability' with the DES 'becoming more centralist and directive on curriculum issues in a bureaucratic, technicist and non-professional way' (Lawton, 1984). As Lawton demonstrates, this is not simply as a result of the plethora of documents but as a result of a variety of complex causes. Nevertheless, accountability is the current name of the game, as teachers are presently only too well aware.

It is helpful though to distinguish between HMI and DES documents. Although each is now caught up in the accountability movement the two are not the same. Central authority should be treated as a tension system not as a consensus (Lawton, 1984). Lawton goes on to classify the central authority into three groups: (1) the politicos (ministers, political advisers); (2) bureaucrats (DES officials); (3) the professionals (HMI); each of which has discernible 'beliefs', 'values' and 'tastes'. Although Lawton recognizes that this classification is overly neat, for me the problem is in separating the 'bureaucrats' from the 'politicos'. In *Better Schools* there are signs of the bureaucrats' belief in good administration and their valuing of 'efficiency' and of the politicians' belief in market forces and a high value being placed on 'choice'. Perhaps *Better Schools* not only marks a blurring of the edges between these two groups but is actually some sort of alliance between them. Lawton's work is useful in helping the reader examine the kinds of tensions and negotiations which are likely to have influenced these documents.

The Curriculum from 5–16

The first point to note here is the title, 'from 5–16'. In their quest for consistency and continuity HMI are producing a series of documents which look at the full range of compulsory educational provision rather than age sector interests. This is useful in one sense but it does tend to obscure phase issues such as middle years and middle schools. The most notable example though is to do with early years' education. One has to wait until the section on progression and continuity before HMI raise the challenge that most primary schools are already facing, that of catering for the fact that 'the majority of children enter school soon after their fourth birthday' (DES, 1985a para. 128). HMI are aware of the problem and difficulty but it is very muted in this document. *Better Schools* actually gives it rather more attention. Figures show (DES, 1985c) that some eighty per cent of children are estimated to be at school before they are five. Surely the title should read 'from 4–16', or at least 'from Rising Five to 16'? That though would only be the first mark of recognition. When I think back to the early 1970s I recall a tremendous period of activity and discussion caused by the raising of the school leaving age (ROSLA) from 15 to 16. When I compare all the activity that then took place in order to add on this extra year of schooling with what has subsequently happened with the lowering of the school entry age (LOSEA?) then one cannot help but note the massive contrasts. The former was heralded by national policies, discussions, funding, interest and concern. The latter has quietly happened almost unnoticed except to reception class teachers. Young children have been almost smuggled into schools to take up the spare capacity created by falling rolls. It looks as if to be young and in school means to be unimportant. Teachers of the very young have every right to feel neglected and *The Curriculum from 5–16* has missed an opportunity to really help them. Surely the first year in school is every bit as important as your last? Indeed, many primary teachers would argue that to 'make a good start' is absolutely vital. Yet the actions of so many outside school do not appear to agree. Primary schools have made significant strides in developing liaison and induction and parental involvement schemes which greatly aid progression and continuity when children start school. For HMI to cover all this in two bland paragraphs is barely even an acknowledgement. Such a paltry appreciation of the hard work schools have done is very discouraging. Teachers who have worked enthusiastically to establish links and contacts, and who have attended to the needs of four-year-olds, will read a document which fails to applaud this work, yet which is constantly pointing up many other required changes. Those teachers cannot help but feel that their endeavours are underestimated.

The majority of the document is concerned with 'designing the curriculum' (pp. 13–50). The overall curricular framework is viewed from two essential perspectives — 'areas of learning and experience' and 'elements of learning'. There is also a third section which considers 'characteristics of the curriculum'. The areas of learning and experience are listed (para. 33) in alphabetical order. This is done to avoid any sense of priority amongst them. Maybe that holds for this document, but when one looks at the HMI series, Matters for Discussion as a whole one finds that number one document is looking at English (DES, 1984a) and number three Mathematics (DES, 1985d). The Curriculum from 5–16 is number two and at the time of writing these are the only three published! It still looks as if the 3 Rs hold centre stage.

There are a number of points to be made about the conception of areas of learning and experience. One welcomes the idea of experience and learning; this, at least in name, indicates opportunities for a match between prescription and practice in primary education. There are some problems though. Since Hirst (1965) and Phenix (1964) curriculum discussion has been using similar labels to name different things. Curriculum theory is full of descriptions of mathematics or history as forms of knowledge (Hirst, 1965) or forms of understanding (Dearden, 1968), or areas of understanding and experience (DES, 1980), or now areas of learning and experience. It is also true that teachers and curriculum theorists speak of mathematics or history as *subjects.* Although many writers emphasize, as do HMI in the document, that the two are not the same, it does mean that a measure of confusion is actually built in simply because of the dual use of names. This is then exacerbated because teachers have been trained with a subject 'specialization' and this looks to be a continuing requirement (DES, 1985c para. 141). Parents and governors also tend to more readily understand the curriculum when it is presented in subject terms. Furthermore publishers produce materials which lend themselves to subject identities. Although HMI offer these areas of learning and experience in ways which are open to flexible adoption (ie. cross curricular links, integration), because schools are frequently engaged in discussions with parents, governors, teacher colleagues and LEA officers whose local patois is 'subjects' then it is difficult for schools to sometimes avoid being ambiguous or feeling ambivalent. I believe HMI are on the right track by not listing subjects since as Webb (1985) and Blenkin and Kelly (1981) show subjects are not always directly transferrable to primary schools. However, in another way HMI have been largely responsible for promoting the management of the primary curriculum through subject specialists (DES, 1978). It appears that the whole business of describing the content and management of the curriculum is fraught and confused. Primary schools badly need some help to make sense of it all. Perhaps most of all they need to be given the confidence to avoid attempting to carry the burgeoning load of content areas and continue the distinctive approach of primary education which is the development of processes that develop from the unity of the child's experience (Blenkin and Kelly, 1981).

Although there are criticisms to level at the present attempts to perceive the curriculum as separate bodies of knowledge and content, there is a need to recognize the achievements of HMI over the last ten years or so. During that time they have consistently championed a broad based curriculum and, it seems, resisted and thwarted the 'back to basics' lobby. This is a most welcome achievement. Consequently many teachers are delighted to see such areas of learning and experience as 'aesthetic and creative' on the list.

Further Perspectives on the Primary Curriculum

Breadth though is a double-edged concept. HMI have protected curriculum breadth but the schools now find themselves having to cope with a broadening curriculum. Aesthetics may be in but so too is technology. In 1981 HMI offered eight areas, now there are nine, and the 'new' one is technological learning and experience. This is illustrated in primary school terms as building a bridge or a crane, designing a model crane that will lift, or considering how to make things work better (para. 87). Although a great deal of this goes on in primary schools as a result of project work, visits, science, art, craft and CDT, the addition of a ninth area in just four years cannot but make teachers feel under pressure. Teachers who have read this document often agree with much that is in it but also say that they are left feeling they are being asked to do more and more. Since all teachers know you cannot 'fit a quart into a pint pot' a lot may not even try. HMI might be better advised to adopt a different approach. Rather than add on seemingly 'new' areas from 'outside' the school, they should work from the inside: with what teachers are confident at. This chapter (and its predecessor) promotes the view that primary teachers are more familiar and confident with the learning process. Rather than graft on things like technology or science we need to work from the teachers' understanding of process rather than content (see Playfoot, 1985; Skelton 1985). By so doing HMI might circumvent feelings of overload and make implementation rather less of a problem.

HMI illustrate many of the areas of learning and experience with samples of work going on in schools. This is a welcome development and answers a criticism in my first chapter. I would though ask that there is more of it. The snapshots offered are nothing more than vignettes and some are very superficial. Worthy though this development is, we need much, much more.

The 'elements of learning' are knowledge, concepts, skills, and attitudes. This is familiar stuff and is presented in a straightforward way. Knowledge and skills are given the greatest attention. Such a seemingly familiar discussion supports the sense of reasonableness. At first sight it appears to be perfectly acceptable. However, a closer look at observation skills, for example, makes me less satisfied. The sense of observation implied is simply that of looking and seeing 'what is there'. For some time art educators have been concerned that it might be of greater use to help children realize that there are many ways of looking and many ways of seeing (Field, 1970). The observation skills listed are fairly low level. There is no mention of critical appreciation or of the need to educate children for understanding the tremendous range of contemporary society's use of visual images (Southworth, 1985(b)). One must ask how relevant is HMI's list of skills?

The section looking at characteristics of the curriculum itemizes breadth, balance, relevance, differentiation and progression and continuity. Balance and continuity were considered in some detail in the first chapter and I find nothing here which counters my criticism there. All of their 'characteristics' are again presented as non-problematical. Such a stance drastically under-estimates the challenge of daily facing thirty six-year-old pupils who are very 'differentiated'. Indeed, differentiation in primary schools is readily acknowledged. It is part of the issue of four-year-olds, and it is the point of respecting the child's individuality which was mentioned earlier, as well as the integration of children with special educational needs.

The notion of relevance is interesting: 'relevance and practicality are closely related but not always synonymous' (para. 116). It looks like relevance is practical activity and in turn this is very much geared to a utilitarian view of the child's 'present and prospective needs'. Although the description of relevance seems to support many of the practical and experiential activities in primary schools, there are some things which undermine this characteristic. Earlier in the document, in the section looking at human and social learning and experience, HMI say that children are aware from an early age of the 'world of work' (para. 44). 'In infant schools, learning about the work of postmen, shopkeepers, nurses, policemen and other people who are seen at work by the children in their everyday lives lays a good foundation' (para. 45). How relevant is such an experience for the child whose parents are unemployed? What hidden curriculum message would that child be receiving about his/her own parents? It may well be that such a topic is neither relevant nor taking account of differentiation. Another concern is that the discussion of relevance ends with the statement that practical activities based on problem solving reveals to pupils the nature of problem solving in the 'real world' (para. 120). Surely this phrase 'real world' is offensive to all who contribute to life in schools. Are schools unreal worlds? Is solving problems the only reality? If this is the basis of relevance then we might be better off without it.

The Curriculum from 5 to 16 offers a great deal to think about and discuss. For primary schools it represents a mixed blessing. It preserves a broad curriculum but perhaps errs on a content overload whilst neglecting process. The characteristics of the curriculum still operate more as symbols than as substance. A significant weakness is in the language HMI adopt. A host of key words are used but their meaning is unclear. Furthermore, the adoption of such words as 'coherence' and 'balance' sounds reasonable but as the first chapter discussed such terms are problematical and this document does not provide any clearer definitions. However, it does still allow teachers quite a considerable latitude to determine curriculum guidelines and methods. Flawed though the document is, it still holds back from anything close to a curriculum blueprint. Indeed, what is offered is 'a planning and analytical tool' (para. 33), and it is offered in the spirit of stimulating professional discussion since the foreword invites feedback. When contrasted with *Better Schools* this document does appear to match the earlier points of Lawton's about HMI's preference for professionality and quality. It is also significant to note that HMI aim for 'effectiveness' (paras. 19 and 47) and not 'efficiency'. Efficiency is a key word in *Better Schools*.

Better Schools

Without doubt this is a significant document, in fact paragraph 59 suggests it is a 'statement of national policy' and warrants a detailed review on its own. Confining myself to the primary curriculum perspective it offers, means that the chapters on Teaching Quality, Parents and Schools, and the Legal Framework will be given less attention than they ought to have.

The document begins by outlining the present situation and mentions the progress made over the last thirty years. The progress of primary schools in curriculum development are simply listed as four sets of subject involvements plus active learning and computer awareness (para. 5)! This simple accounting is followed by the section 'The need for higher standards' which says: 'the standards now generally attained by our pupils are neither as good as they can be, nor as good as they need be if young people are to be equipped for the world of the twenty-first century' (para. 9). 'The government has a duty to take the lead in securing this improvement' (para. 11). Quite obviously the message is that whilst schools have improved this is not enough and the government intend that schools will have to do better. To support this the 'professional judgments' of HMI are outlined since their reports 'reveal an uneven picture' (para. 14). Again both sides of the picture are offered:

> By age 11 the best primary and middle schools have consolidated the pupils' positive personal qualities, have developed (to a degree which varies inevitably with pupils' abilities and home background) an almost universal competence in reading, writing and other language skills and in a wide range of mathematical skills and have established the foundations of understanding in science, in the humanities and in aesthetic and practical subjects ... two of the features found in the best schools — the commitment of the teachers to the education of their pupils and the orderly and civilised relationship between teachers and pupils — can be observed in the great majority of schools. (paras. 15 and 16)

But, the 'present spectrum of quality' is too wide for a national system. Primary and middle schools are charged with a weakness in curricular planning and implementation. Guidelines exist for English and mathematics but do not extend to other areas of the curriculum:

> Above all, there are rarely effective mechanisms for ensuring that declared curricular policies are reflected in the day-to-day work of most teachers and pupils. In only a minority of schools is the best practice of individual teachers in each area of the curriculum adopted as a standard to be emulated throughout the school. (para. 17)

Moreover there is a lack of designated subject consultants and where they have been appointed 'it is unusual for them to be given the time, status and the encouragement to enable them to prepare and support their colleagues'. There is also very little systematic approach to career development of staff (para. 22).

Having said that HMI have failed to acknowledge the strengths of primary schools, the DES appears to outline an even more depressing picture. Although concerned with efficiently managing the curriculum the document perhaps manages to only establish a sense of negativism. This hardly a climate conducive to change and its implementation.

Moving on to consider the primary and secondary curriculum there is an interesting comment about the HMI series, Matters for Discussion. These serve to inform and promote discussion but will also 'build up a general description of the objectives of the curriculum as a whole for all children of compulsory school age' (para. 32). In the eyes of the DES the HMI documents are not *discussion* documents but *descriptions* of what schools need to be focusing on. This surely means that HMI's invitations for feedback on their documents are largely irrelevant since the DES has already decided to act upon their descriptions and make them prescriptions. Later it is said that the Secretaries of State's policy for the range and pattern of the curriculum is not a determination of national syllabuses, although clearly the trend is towards a more centrally co-ordinated and advocated curriculum, and objectives are a major part of this. In all of this *process* is virtually absent. HMI talk of aims and objectives, but *Better Schools* speaks only of objectives.

Better Schools then adopts the characteristics of the curriculum, namely balance, breadth, relevance and differentiation, used by HMI. Here is evidence that what HMI presented as a matter for discussion is, in *Better Schools*, co-opted into policy. All of this not only supports much of the foregoing discussion in this chapter, it seems mark a change in tone. Schools are not up to the standards expected of them, although the standards are not very clear. The major criticism is that schools are inconsistent — that they are, in fact, too differentiated! Differentiation, rather like some of the other slogans, is ambiguous and allows the central authority (DES bureaucrats and politicians) to look both ways at once. As Lawton says (1984) 'this new centralism will only be acceptable if it is based on sound educational principles; bureaucratic or political dogma will not do'.

Specific consideration of the primary phase is limited to two pages. The content of the curriculum is confined to nine items which do not immediately correspond with the nine HMI list. It is legitimated by an instrumental rationale in terms of technology and 'how people earn their living'. Although it is believed that what is offered is capable of application 'the main constraints lie in the number of teachers and their collective qualifications and skills and in the size of the school' (para. 64). It is a relief to find an acknowledgement of constraint, until one turns to the relevant chapter (Ch. 5 'Teaching Quality'). Here teaching success is simply equated with pupil progress (para. 131) which may sound right but fails to convey the sheer dynamics of pupil 'progression', and I wonder why progression is preferred to development? This same chapter also raises the issue of 'curriculum delivery' (para. 133) which I take to mean implementation of agreed policies and guidelines. It is interesting that only now in 1985 is implementation being posed as a challenge in the 'official' documents. Curriculum study has long recognized that implementation is a central issue (Southworth, 1983; Hoyle, 1970). The responsibility now looks like being placed on the teachers for failing to implement change. If so, this is unfair. Firstly, there have been many changes implemented in primary education, particularly since the 1978 *Primary School Survey*. Microcomputers have been introduced, science education is now much more widely to be found, as are post holders for that area, children start school earlier (see Ch.4 *Better Schools*), observational drawing is common-place and many schools have introduced CDT and parental links. Secondly, all this has gone on against a background of falling rolls, reduced promotional opportunities, amalgamations, closures, uncertainty and financial cut-back. Thirdly, during this period schools have spent considerable amounts of time revising their aims in order to comply with the DES (ie. Circular 6/81) and to respond to the 'accountability movement' and the 1980 and 1981 Education Acts. All of this depicts a period of considerable turbulence and to suggest that schools are not 'delivering' something only recently 'ordered' is insensitive to the challenge which schools have faced and managed extremely well.

What emerges from *Better Schools* and *The Curriculum from 5 to 16* is a prescription as to how schools should become 'better', it looks something like this:

1 Accept the 'broadly agreed aims' and employ the objectives advocated in Better Schools and those currently being published in the HMI series.
2 Secure commitment to these objectives through consultation:
   2.1 internally with teaching staff,
   2.2 externally with parents, governors, employers, the community.
3 Itemize the elements of the curriculum (knowledge, concepts,

skills, attitudes) for each area of learning and experience:
- 3.1 this planning should be recorded in curricular guidelines and made available to 2.1 and 2.2,
- 3.2 cross-curricular issues should not be left to chance but assured through consultation.
4. Curricular characteristics of breadth, balance, relevance, differentiation, progression and continuity should be constantly used to foster consistency and uniformity.
5. This should be supported by ensuring that teachers with posts of responsibility act as consultants in respect of specific subject areas of the curriculum across the school:
   - 5.1 ensuring that the benefits of class teaching in primary schools is made more effective (and efficient) since it is not expected that a class teacher can or should cover the whole curriculum unaided,
   - 5.2 ensure that consultant teachers have the time, status and encouragement to work alongside colleagues,
   - 5.3 emulate the best practice of individual teachers in each area of the curriculum across the school,
   - 5.4 ensure a match between objectives and practice.
6. Organize pupil groupings and teaching approaches with reference to the characteristics of the curriculum and with a sense of flexibility.
7. Involve teachers so that they contribute to the corporate development of the school, particularly in such areas as objectives, marking, records and assessment.
8. Systematically plan teacher development and INSET needs.
9. Foster 'outreach' schemes such as home visiting, parental involvement, links with play groups and nurseries, and organize times of pupil admission and transition.
10. Assess and record pupil progress; appraise the performance of teachers.

As a DIY list for primary school and curriculum management it looks straightforward. In one sense it has things to commend it, setting aside the preoccupation with objectives. Many writers are currently seeking to promote collaborative ways of working which correspond to, say, items five and seven (see McMahon *et al.*, 1984; Campbell, 1985). The problem of this prescription is what it overlooks or assumes.

One assumption in all of this is that collaborative work is not just desirable but also achievable, if not actually 'easy'. Collaborative ways of working though will encounter tensions created by the size of the school. Collaboration in a Group One school is a different issue from collaboration in a Group Five school. Then there are issues of individually and autonomy mentioned previously. Allied to all of this will be the formal and informal groupings of the staff group, the effect of the school's building and layout, and the role of the head. Then there is the particular composition of the staff group (sex, age, values, interests, philosophies, career status, 'subject' strengths, professional experience, personal qualities, teaching competences). Even this short list of additional factors begins to complicate the straight-forwardness of the prescription. Far from being neat and tidy, it begins to look rather messy and misshapen.

What also needs to be distinguished is collaboration which enables the schools to work more effectively and collaboration which might foster and perhaps even defend comfort and complacency. At the moment we only have HMI's word that collaboration does improve primary school practice. A number of others may agree but this agreement is largely based on hunch and intuition. In terms of research evidence we do not know what actually does make an 'effective primary school'! Before this prescription can be accepted we need rather better evidence that the diagnosis is accurate. That is why ESRC's funding of a research project at this Institute, to investigate Inter-Adult Relationships in English Primary Schools is so apposite. Also as this chapter is being written HMI are preparing to publish a booklet describing excellent practice in primary education (DES, 1987). Both are steps in the right direction and offer ways forward. However, by way of concluding this review I would like to offer some personal views as to other ways forward.

A Way Forward

Firstly, teachers, and others concerned with primary education, indeed with education as whole, must respond with energy to the present spate of documents. Certainly those at the 'centre' (politicians, bureaucrats, HMI) must not be allowed to believe that it is only they who want to improve schools. All those who work in or with schools strive towards that same goal.

Secondly, those at the centre need to be shown that they do not have a monopoly on educational wisdom. In fact, this whole notion of centralism needs to be considered. Who is *really* at the centre of education? Is it the Secretary of State or the teacher in the classroom? Perhaps it could even be both? This is not to try to shift the metaphor back from 'accountability' to 'partnership', it is to recentre the whole enterprise. Curriculum delivery and implementation will always be problems so long as teachers, those who actually implement and deliver, are left outside in the cold. School improvement surely relies on the consent, if not the consensus of teachers. At present any thought of curriculum 'consensus' is rather false because it is increasingly managed only by those at the centre (Whitbread, 1985).

Thirdly, primary education needs to be awarded not only greater status, but equal status. At the moment primary education is in danger of being marginalized by the 'imperialism' of such curriculum innovations as GCSE, TVEI and CPVE. It can be shown that much of our present curriculum theory has been generated from the practical problems of the secondary schools (Blenkin and Kelly, 1981). This is in part why curriculum objectives and subjects hold sway over processes and the idea of the child as unifier of the curriculum he/she experiences. It may also begin to explain why the contemporary solutions of curriculum-led staffing and subject-orientated roles for staff have currency.

A move towards satisfying these three needs would be to positively involve teachers because they can offer perspectives on the curriculum that are broad, balanced, relevant and differentiated. And maybe this positivism would begin from the teachers being allowed to communicate the achievements of primary education. Although all concerned with schools seek developments the inexorable publication of successive documents asking for change and improvement puts teachers on the defensive and corrodes their confidence. Of course we all need to look forward, but we must not lose sight of the present. Both documents focused on here underestimate the achievements of schools. One has to look to another HMI document to find something like a positive perspective:

> The great majority of these (primary) schools show themselves to be stable and well-ordered, with friendly relationships between teachers, non-teaching staff and children. The children are keen to learn; they enjoy their work and are helped to be sensitive to the needs of others and to care for their environment. Visitors are encouraged and parents are made welcome. Many schools have developed close links with parents, some of whom share in the work of the school ... (DES 1984b. para. 13).

Is not that a significant achievement? In terms of a climate for learning, personal and social development, interpersonal skills, feelings and attitudes that is surely a tremendous attribute. Just imagine what primary schools would be like without that. It is interesting to note in *Better Schools* the references about the needs of employers. This is taken further in the current rash of school management courses which include visits to industry and commerce since there is an assumption that schools can learn from commercial managers. Perhaps they can, but the ethos which HMI describe as prevalent in primary schools is an ethos identified in 'excellent companies' (Peters and Waterman, 1982); maybe the less than excellent companies should visit primary schools since they already possess the foundations of success?

We need now to build on this. Teachers need to be encouraged to share their strengths: in schools, on courses and through the literature. The endeavours, challenges and successes of primary schools should be recognized and promoted. The present unfavourable climate of change based on criticism and criteria unacceptable to primary schools needs to be altered. The status of primary schools, children and teachers also needs to be revived. Positive reinforcement offers a more appropriate route than exhortations to do better. We need to celebrate primary education: now is the time to praise primary education.

References

ASHTON, P., KNEEN, P. and DAVIES, F. (1975) *Aims into Practice in the Primary School*. London, Hodder and Stoughton.
BLENKIN, G.M. and KELLY, A.V. (1981) *The Primary Curriculum*, London, Harper and Row.
BLENKIN, G.M. and KELLY, A.V. (Eds.) (1983) *The Primary Curriculum in Action: A process-approach to educational practice*, London, Harper and Row.
BRUNER, J. (1977) *The Process of Education*, Cambridge, Mass, Harvard University Press.
CAMPBELL, R.J. (1985) *Developing the Primary School Curriculum*, London, Holt, Rinehart and Winston. See Part 3: Towards the Collegial Primary School, pp. 149–169.
DEAN, J. (1984) 'Ours is not to reason what', *Times Educational Supplement*, 11 May, p. 21.
DEARDEN, R.F. (1986) *The Philosophy of Primary Education: an introduction*, London, Routledge and Kegan Paul.
DEPARTMENT OF EDUCATION AND SCIENCE (1978) *Primary Education in England: A survey by HM Inspectors*, London, HMSO.
DEPARTMENT OF EDUCATION AND SCIENCE (1980) *A Framework for the School Curriculum*, London, HMSO.
DEPARTMENT OF EDUCATION AND SCIENCE (1980) *A View of the Curriculum: HMI Series — Matters for Discussion No. 11*, London, HMSO.
DEPARTMENT OF EDUCATION AND SCIENCE (1981) *The School Curriculum*, London, HMSO.
DEPARTMENT OF EDUCATION AND SCIENCE (1984a) *English from 5–16*, London, HMSO.
DEPARTMENT OF EDUCATION AND SCIENCE (1984b) *Education Observed 2*, London, HMSO.
DEPARTMENT OF EDUCATION AND SCIENCE (1985a) *The Curriculum from 5–16*, London, HMSO.
DEPARTMENT OF EDUCATION AND SCIENCE (1985b) *Mathematics from 5–16*, London, HMSO.
DEPARTMENT OF EDUCATION AND SCIENCE (1985c) *Better Schools*. Cmd. 9469, London, HMSO.
DEPARTMENT OF EDUCATION AND SCIENCE (1985d) *Science 5–16: A Statement of Policy*, London, HMSO.
DEPARTMENT OF EDUCATION AND SCIENCE (1987) *Primary Schools: Some Aspects of Good Practice. An HMI Publication*, London, HMSO.
FIELD, D. (1970) *Change in Art Education*, London, Routledge and Kegan Paul.
GIBSON, D.R. (1984) *Structuralism and Education*, London, Hodder and Stoughton.
HIRST, P. (1965) 'Liberal education and the nature of knowledge', In ARCHAMBAULT, R.D. (Ed.) (1965) *Philosophical Analysis and Education*, London, Routledge and Kegan Paul.

HOYLE, E. (1970) 'Planned organizational change in education', *Research in Education*. No. 3, May 1970, pp. 1–22.
ILEA (1985) *Improving Primary Schools*, London, ILEA.
LAWTON, D. (1980) *The Politics of the School Curriculum*, London, Routledge and Kegan Paul.
LAWTON, D. (1984) *The Tightening Grip: the growth of central control of the school curriculum*. Bedford Way Papers 21, London, University of London Insitute of Education.
MCMAHON, A., BOLAM, R., ABBOTT, R. and HOLLY, P. (1984) *Guidelines for the Review and Internal Development in Schools*, (Primary School Handbook). York, Longman/Schools Council.
NIAS, J. (1984) 'The definition and maintenance of self in primary teaching', *British Journal of Sociology of Education*, Vol. 5 No. 3, pp. 267–280.
PETERS, T.J. and WATERMAN, R.H. (1982) *In Search of Excellence: Lessons from America's Best-Run Companies*, New York, Harper and Row.
PHENIX, P.H. (1984) *Realms of Meaning*, New York, McGraw Hill.
PLAYFOOT, D. (1985) 'Do magnets mean much?' *Times Educational Supplement*, 22 March.
SKELTON, M. (1985) 'It's the context that counts', *Times Educational Supplement*, 10 May.
SOUTHWORTH, G.W. (1983) 'Curriculum implementation and the primary headteacher', *Curriculum*, Vol. 4 No. 1 pp. 20–26.
SOUTHWORTH, G.W. (1985a) 'Perspectives on the primary curriculum', *Cambridge Journal of Education*, Vol. 15 No. 1, pp. 41–49.
SOUTHWORTH, G.W. (1985b) 'Drawing is discovery', *Times Educational Supplement*, 3 May.
STENHOUSE, L. (Ed.) (1980) *Curriculum Research and Development in Action*, London, Heinemann.
WEBB, D. (1985) 'Primary curriculum under threat', *Forum*, Vol. 27 No. 3, pp. 70–72.
WHITBREAD, N. (1985) 'Managing consensus on the curriculum', *Forum*, Vol. 27 No. 3, pp. 68–70.

Section Four
Evaluation and Effectiveness

Introduction

Evaluation and notions of effectiveness are important, indeed central to school management. 'Managers' are frequently making judgments about change, innovation, development and performance. A problem with these judgments is that they are often made too quickly and upon partial evidence and that judgment is confused with evaluation. The chapter in this section accept the central place of evaluation and effectiveness but regard evaluation and effectiveness as not simply the sole responsibility of management (if that means only headteachers) but of *all* teachers.

Marion Dadds' offers a critical view of teacher appraisal. She asks a series of probing questions which can be summarized as wanting to know what contribution teacher appraisal will make to the children's learning and the teacher's development? Dadds' sees appraisal as an opportunity for helping teachers learn about their teaching and the children's learning. However, such a view requires appraisal to be regarded as a learning process and this will only be achieved if the process of appraisal creates the appropriate conditions in which teachers will feel secure to reflect and share their insights and feelings about their teaching. Therefore, appraisal relies on the quality of relationships inside the school. In this sense much of what Marion Dadds says relates to the chapters in section two.

The second chapter in this section is an extract from 'The Junior School Project'. The ILEA Research and Statistics Branch has carried out a research project to identify factors common to effective schools. This extract is the summary of the main report and presents the twelve key factors of effectiveness which the research team have identified. Prior to offering these twelve factors there is a review of those features which appear to make it easier to create an effective school. Although only a summary it makes fascinating reading. I believe a number of the factors are dealt with in this volume of readings. Readers might also compare the ILEA's findings with both my 'DIY course of school and curriculum management' in section three and Peter Holly's chapter in this section.

The third chapter in this section is Peter Holy's survey of self evalua-

Introduction

tion in primary schools. This is an ambitious chapter which provides an overview of classroom action-research, LEA schemes for school self evaluation and school-based reviews such as the GRIDS scheme. The chapter draws extensively on the literature and provides a useful summary of many of the recent findings in the literature, particularly with reference to American studies into school evaluation, effectiveness and improvement. Throughout the chapter Holly explores the tension between developing the individual teacher and developing the individual institution. Whilst he accepts the two are connected he is concerned to avoid the promotion of an approach which overemphasizes one to the detriment of the other. To this end Holly suggests an alternative model of self evaluation which he calls 'the developing school' and which contains an implicit view of school management which is appropriate to school development. The chapter also revisits a number of issues touched upon in earlier chapters: collaboration, collegiality, teacher development, and effectiveness.

Although Holly does not say it as such, his idea of the developing school, based upon 'collegial ownership of development' and 'self-confrontation', requires management to orchestrate a considerable array of factors and forces. This I try to illuminate in the Endpaper.

Learning and Teacher Appraisal: The Heart of the Matter

Marion Dadds

As long as we are not losing sight of the qualities of a good learning experience these days and are prepared to defend our perspective, we should be able to field the avalanche of documents and directives coming at us. Incidentally, on talking to four dozen or so primary and middle school teachers recently, most admitted to having heard of *The Curriculum from 5 to 16*[1], none had had time nor motivation to read it, and most admitted that it wouldn't be very likely to change their lives radically unless reinforced with legislation (which is not beyond fantasy). This may be less a reflection of the nature of the documents than of the style and shape of class teachers' full and demanding lives. It seems all too easy to push a battery of policy and advisory documents people's way and then wait for Nirvana to materialize. But we all know that learning and change for schools, for teachers and for children, just do not happen in this simple way. In contrast it was of no surprise that most of these teachers could talk incisively about the red hot topic of teacher appraisal. All felt it would be beneficial if handled with sensitivity and respect, though by whom and in what way was more difficult to say. All would welcome a constructive dialogue with other professionals about their teaching with a view to improving in both strong and weaker areas of performance. In essence, they were open to a constructively critical appraisal that could add to their own learning and development as crafts people in the art of teaching. It is difficult to predict, at the time of writing, how local authorities will interpret the demand for appraisal, in terms of the styles of appraisal adopted, and the negotiating procedures that will precede 'schemes'. But let's suppose that there is still time for dialogue and constructive debate to influence how teacher appraisal will shape up, and that the participants in the system have a contribution to make. How might we conduct that debate given that all of us teaching at whatever level in the system will be affected at some point in the future?

Perhaps we could start with a basic common sense question such as

'Why are we getting involved?' This should stop us all rushing headlong into hours of extra work, worry and other people's blueprints of how it should be done, with no guarantee of acceptable nor justifiable outcomes. It seems almost too obvious to say, but these forty teachers assumed, unquestioningly, that the whole point of any such exercise, however it were to be conducted, and by whom, would be the improvement of learning opportunities and experiences for their pupils. If it is not about that for us even under the compulsion of legislation, why spend such scarce resources of time and energy on the exercise? If the investment does not enable us to teach more effectively, so that our pupils have a richer educational experience, then we ought to be looking to other ways in which that can be achieved. These teachers were clearly signalling that their own professional learning, by definition, subsumes a deepening understanding of pupil learning and will lead to improved teaching. Caution should be a rule, therefore, in specifying criteria for appraisal if we are uncertain of their contribution and relationship to children's learning. Where is the evidence, for example, that a Jaeger skirt is worth more points than cheesecloth and worry beads? Or that brightly triple mounted displays are any more beneficial than *ad hoc* here-today-lets-move-on-displays? Or that brightly triple mounted displays don't produce tired teachers who are short in their interactions with children? Of course there are several other dimensions to the teacher's role, outside the classroom. S(he) needs to function in the school at large, contribute to school life and developments, relate to other teachers and parents, keep abreast of issues and thinking in education, be aware of the social and political context in which s(he) is working. But central to all of that, at the heart of the matter, is the relationship between teaching and pupil learning and development. Forgive me for quoting that well worn opening sentence from the Plowden Report[2], but 'At the heart of the educational process lies the child' still seems to hold good for many primary school class teachers as a yardstick with which to measure the worthiness of their multiple, complex efforts. One of our major difficulties at present is that teacher appraisal has not been adequately tried and tested in the light of these aspirations. Who knows but that other ways of trying to improve practice might be more effective? Even evidence in two of the most recent publications on teacher appraisal[3,4] is confusing or conflicting. Some teachers have reported finding the exercise valuable, in that they have been required to think more about certain issues, and it has given them time to talk about their teaching with the Head. But they also admit to it neither changing nor helping their practice. Other local research, conducted by Cambridge Institute students, offers similar findings[5]. Reports from the AMMA conference[6] suggest that certain approaches can be intensely problematic and in some cases ineffective, even in well tried schemes in industry and the police force. The extent of the success of appraisal schemes in improving teaching is far from clear.

Given the doubts, perhaps there are further questions to which we need good answers before we proceed, such as 'Who is it for?' and 'What are they going to do with it when it's done?' If responses to either of these do not include the words 'children', 'teachers', 'learning', 'classrooms', 'support' and 'development', then perhaps something is amiss. Some distinguish between appraisal for teacher learning and development, and appraisal for accountability purposes, as though they were discrete requirements[7]. There is, of course, an obligation to convince the consumer (as parents, taxpayers and industrialists have become known) that we are working hard, doing our best, trying to improve things for pupils, achieving acceptable standards. But equally, the consumers should be in a reciprocal accountability relationship, ensuring that the demands placed on our time, the kinds of activities with which they require us to engage and the kinds of questions to which they require professional answers, are appropriate and reasonable, aiding our attempts not hindering them. Appraisal schemes that involve us in addressing a string of questions which lead nowhere in practical teaching are patently a waste of scarce professional time. Asking a primary teacher, for example, what she is doing to cater for children with severe learning difficulties might do no more than reveal a glaring gap to the consumer of which the teacher already was well aware, but was unable to remedy — few in-service courses on the issue, no release from school to attend what little there might be around, no extra resources for coping with the difficulties, an overstretched advisory team, and so on. Similarly, an appraisal document that requires a teacher to respond to ninety-eight aspects of class and school performance (and there are some around) is more likely to overwhelm the mind and spirit of most than to lead to constructive and focussed analysis of teaching. Given, also, that there might be little more than an hour or two in the year to talk over these responses with the appraiser, such a complicated document, leading to an impossibly onerous catalogue of uncertainties about one's performance might do more harm than good, the areas of concern thus revealed only adding to the frustrations of having little or no support to remedy them. A ninety-eight point analysis of ourselves seems a fool-proof recipe for exacerbating existing feelings of inadequacy, which most of us have from time to time. Likewise, a scheme that is deemed finished when the form, questionnaire or tick list is completed and filed away in some bureaucratic drawer, does not do justice to a genuine professional desire to benefit from appraisal. Schemes that are not closely related to resources for their initiation and follow through or that cannot be translated into practical action are no schemes at all and those who require teachers to be thus engaged are not fulfilling their reciprocal obligation and accountability to the profession. No one should have the power to waste others' professional time under the disguise of accountability. We cannot improve things for pupils in schools by harassing their teachers with complicated and redundant paper exercises.

Yet it should be possible to reconcile the teacher's need for professional development with the consumer's need for reassurance. This may demand a well thought through scheme founded on some basic principles of learning. At the same time it should convince the consumer that the professionals are developing their work as well as they are able.

Whilst an attempt to systematize teacher appraisal is fairly new, insights gained from well developed learning theory are not. We have much that can guide us in planning and evolving approaches that could lead to sound professional development for the teacher and contribute to the life of the school. What might some ingredients in such a learning based approach be? Let me offer a few hypotheses, none of them entirely original, since learning has been around for a long time, none of them exceptionally profound, since most people interested in the subject will have drawn similar lessons from their own observation.

Perhaps learning is most effective when we feel thoroughly and actively involved in the process ourselves. This kind of involvement might be generated by an enthusiast whom we respect — witness how well primary school topics go when teachers share enthusiasms with children. But the motivation and involvement generated from self-initiated learning is, perhaps, even more powerful. We need to see the relevance of the work to questions, ideas and problems that have come from within us. If we don't see the point of it, we have difficulty making sense of the activity. 'Children work best at problems they have set themselves'[8]. It may also be true of adults. The implications for teacher appraisal are fairly obvious. An approach that allows us to recognize and identify problems in our own teaching, for ourselves, might also maximize the degree of motivation required to do something about them: a voluntary response by us to our own learning needs. Appraisal can be something we do to ourselves, in our own way, on our own terms. Teacher classroom action research[9] epitomizes such a philosophy of self-government and has a respectable history of success in classroom improvement. At the other extreme there are approaches that deny the individual's competence in this. Here, self-appraisal means that some authority figure, who may be the appraiser, hands over their questionnaire, or tick list for the appraised to complete. There may have been little, or no, opportunity for the appraised to determine its format, nor to negotiate ways forward as a result of the appraisal. It is something that is done to you by someone else even though you are allowed to complete their format. The authority figure chooses the gun, loads it, points it at you and you pull the trigger. Therein lies involvement and self-appraisal.

At the optimum level of involvement, a sense of personal control over the process may be the best recipe for successful learning. Does this then mean that the agenda for the appraisal is best left for the appraised to compose? Clearly there must be an opportunity for just that, if the teacher's own learning is to be an outcome. Now an external observer, the

Headteacher, local inspector, HMI or Secretary of State might very well argue that some are blind to the most worrying aspects of their performance, or, in a more positive light, are unable to evaluate their own strengths. They might not be able to identify the problem or prowess that the external eye can see. This brings us to the notion of learning being interactive, a process that is set in motion, and sustained, through constructive interaction between the learner and an outside source, the constant to-ing and fro-ing between what is inside our head and what is outside it. Piaget called it assimilation and accommodation, as we all remember from those dreary psychology lectures[10]. We don't always need a teacher for this kind of learning to take place, but in many cases, the right kind of teacher can be crucial in holding up the other end of this process. Also the value of the external seeing eye to our own perspective can be immeasurable. Yet, as we have said, there needs to be a degree of mutual respect and concern between the two parties. Do we learn well from those whose judgment we mistrust? Can we identify with the problems and strengths they see in our teaching if we do not value their perspective? The choice of the appraiser, therefore, can be neither arbitrary nor standardized. They may have to be the one who can offer the best kind of feedback possible and can support the most effective and constructive dialogue. This may be the Headteacher, fellow teaching colleagues or other professional peers. In looking at and appraising ourselves we will need to be mindful of the purposes and direction of the school or institution in its wider sense. Taking control of our own development does not mean doing our thing independently of corporate aims. The perspective of others looking from different places in the institution might help us to clarify where our professional endeavours fit into the jigsaw. Likewise, our perspective can contribute to an evolving view of the whole. Appraisal may be about learning where we may help as well as learning to know what we can contribute towards others' growth. The support issue is strong here, too. Do we learn best when we know there is the kind of support necessary for the process of change we wish to undergo? This might take the form of personal interest being shown in our learning, regular reinforcement of strengths as well as sympathetic help with weaknesses, time and space to stand back and reflect, systematic analysis of classroom provision and teaching, visiting other schools or financial backing to attend appropriate courses. At the minimum, it might mean regular follow up discussions after the termly or yearly appraisal interview with a sense of genuine interest shown in our work and our learning. The appraiser obviously has a vital part to play. Their role is continuous not static. How can they know us and help us in our continuous learning process on a one-off or two-off basis? Close involvement is crucial if they are to act as support and to sustain the other end of the dialectic. Since we are in an interactive context, there is a reciprocal obligation on us to enter that with an open mind, open to others' perspectives and judgment, willing to explore alternative ways of describing and addressing an issue. Many schools are already moving forward with joint negotiated agendas, drawn up by the appraiser and the appraised and many of these leave plenty of room for everyone to manoeuvre and grow. If we can respect our appraiser for the respect s(he) is prepared to show us as a learner then we should both come out of this reciprocal context having gained something. It will also, probably, make it much easier to accept the learning potential of appraisal if we know everyone is taking advantage of it, from the Secretary of State, right throughout the system. We might even be able to help and support our own personal appraiser in her/his processes. Without this communal commitment we could perhaps be forgiven for thinking of appraisal as rather akin to 'work' in the saying: 'If work were really so good for us as the rich would have us believe, they would have kept it all to themselves.'[11]

Most people do not learn well under stress and duress. Behaviourist learning theory has at least demonstrated that rewards are more powerful as an aid to learning than punishment. True, it may be possible to get most learners to adopt new behaviours by holding out the threat of punishment or pain, by withholding an annual increment or instilling a fear of losing promotion prospects or a useful reference, or by serving other various helpings of negative reinforcement. But behaviourist learning theory also teaches that there is a price to be paid for negative reinforcement; along with it may go negative attitudes, resentment, hostility, low self-esteem, feelings of inadequacy, apathy, withdrawal. What good are those kinds of attitudes and emotions to the nation's children or to a healthy teaching profession? The mature learner eventually becomes her/his own guru, outgrowing the need for extrinsic rewards and punishment as a motivating force. Many teachers who have voluntarily entered into self-evaluation through classroom action research report the growing intrinsic reward that the activity brings. Learning about, and developing one's professionalism take on their own stimulus and momentum. Such teachers continue it for no less reason than knowing they are improving life in schools and classrooms for their pupils[12]. Furthermore, they control their own evaluation and learning processes, neither ducking from analyzing the large concerns in their teaching, nor flinching from honest confrontation of weaknesses. None of them need the prodding of an external authority figure and appraiser to drive them down their self-initiated, self-appraisal path. What they do seem to need is an open, caring and supportive group of colleagues with whom they share a common knowledge of the task and with whom they can conduct a constructively critical debate about their achievements and aspirations within it. This approach, involving group support for self-initiated self-evaluation, has much to commend it as a context for teacher development. And for many of the participants, it has already been tried and tested. The relative smallness of the staff group in primary schools had distinct advantages here. Talking is essential for good communication. Good communication is essential for healthy relationships, and healthy relationships are essential for constructive appraisal. The chances of face-to-face contact and getting to know our colleagues as people are enhanced if we all work in one building, share one staff room and have only a few relationships to build. These in themselves, though, will obviously not bring about a healthy ethos. Life is never as simple as that, for the smallness of the group could be as equally deathly as it could be life-giving. If things are not too good in a small group, there are fewer relationships to escape into. When an only child falls out with the parents s/he cannot take refuge with brothers and sisters. The onus is on building a community where positive and negative feelings can be aired, shared and worked through. Whatever trust is, a good deal of it is needed. Whatever psychological safety is, that needs to be felt too. Constructive and supportive appraisal, at its best, could add to the growing quality of relationships and begin to create the ethos in which it can best continue to flourish. Neither comes easily nor cheaply.

A badly conceived and administered appraisal scheme can add unproductive stress to a teacher's life. If it takes up more time than we can comfortably give it, other aspects of our work may suffer — preparation, marking, teaching, in-service, time for parents, reading etc. No Secretary of State has yet found it within his/her wisdom to bless primary school teachers with a few free periods for those myriad tasks surrounding the classroom act, and which are essential to it. If primary teachers feel short of time already, what sense is there in trying to squeeze appraisal into the already overflowing pot. To respect appraisal and its professional potential it would be helpful to respect the professional and their potential for appraisal. Individual differences in need and emotional tolerance for self-evaluation may require individual approaches to appraisal. Ninety-eight questions may very well suit the more boisterous and analytical personality but may undermine the less secure person, or one who needs to develop at a more measured pace. Do we learn best when we are allowed to bite off just as much as we can chew? If an outcome of our appraisal is to be faced with far more change than we can possibly handle, the stresses and strains of the job will be increased rather than alleviated. That won't lead to better teaching. Too much anxiety gets us nowhere but the local surgery. Most people learn well in a productively relaxed and accepting context, freed from the excesses of anxiety and tension that lead to confusion[13]. Nor does more work necessarily lead to better teaching performance for those already working at full stretch. An hour tending our roses or taking a bath might produce better outcomes in the classroom than many other intense professional activities. It is often in the relaxed luxury of those spaces that the inside of our head gells in a most unpredicted way. Continuity in our own learning does not always mean continuity in the task or the workplace[14,15]. We may need to think carefully about the timing, pacing and loading of an appraisal scheme for if we get it wrong it might work counter to its purposes.

Finally, we should be looking for some reflection of the problematic nature of learning in the structure and conduct of the appraisal scheme. As our pupils' learning is very often a puzzle to us, because the whole business of learning is puzzling, so too will be our own. It will not go in straightforward, painless and predictable directions. There will be highs and lows, fears and excitements, clarity and confusions, certainties and doubts, advances and regressions. A blueprint scheme that sets up a framework of teaching for the appraised to emulate is built on an erroneous model of learning. We cannot look at a model and assimilate it whole and quickly. Nor are we empty vessels to be filled with ingredients that will suddenly be baked into a perfect and complete cake, any more than our pupils are pots to be filled with our own particular brand of knowledge. To say that we must strive to be just like Teacher A down the corridor, or to be told that we need to mend our professional ways so that we will perform like Teacher B, is to overlook that what we bring to the context is ourselves, at our particular stage of growth and development. And that is all the raw material we have to work on. We can only move forward in our own way, at our own pace, down paths that we believe are leading somewhere valuable; sometimes by ourselves, sometimes in the company of a range of fellow travellers alongside whom we sharpen our thinking and our doing. There are many and varied notions in the profession of what those paths are, and to where they will lead, so we also need to reserve a healthy modicum of tentativeness along the way when we meet people with the 'right' answers who claim to know beyond doubt what a 'good' teacher is or what 'effective' teaching looks like.

There seems to be much fear around at present about teacher appraisal, principally amongst those to whom others wish to do it. Perhaps we need not fear it in itself if we have the confidence to mould approaches that serve us, in our schools, with our colleagues, and our pupils and are allowed to do so. What we must question (and perhaps fear) are approaches that are handed us from 'outside', unnegotiated, unproven, devoid of flexibility, theoretically unsound and that overlook our own needs and learning processes at the heart of the matter.

Notes

1 DEPARTMENT OF EDUCATION AND SCIENCE (1985) 'The Curriculum from 5 to 16 HMSO.
2 DEPARTMENT OF EDUCATION AND SCIENCE (1967) Children and their Primary Schools, HMSO.
3 SUFFOLK EDUCATION DEPARTMENT (1985) Those Having Torches.

4 TURNER, G. CLIFT, P. (1985) *A First Review and Register of School and College-based Teacher Appraisal Schemes*, Open University.
5 Anonymized for ethical purpose — Unpublished research study CIE.
6 *Appraisal in Education*, (1985) 166, 18, November.
7 RODGER, I.A. and RICHARDSON, J.A.S. (1985) *Self-evaluation for Primary Schools*, Hodder and Stoughton.
8 ELLIOT, J. (1980) *Science 5 to 13 in Curriculum Research and Development in Action*, Heinemann.
9 NIXON, J. (Ed.) (1981) *A Teachers Guide to Action Research*, Grant McIntyre.
10 PIAGET, J. (1952) *The Origins of Intelligence in Children*, International Universities Press.
11 Overheard in a downtown Nottingham pub.
12 DADDS, M. (1986) 'Group support for self-directed teacher research' *Forum*, 28,2, January.
13 BANDLER, R. and GRINDER, J. (1979) *Frogs into Princes* Neuro Linguistic Programming, Real People Press.
14 BRUNER, J.S. (1983) 'Intuitive and analytical thinking' in DONALDSON, M. *et al. Early Childhood Developing and Education*, Blackwell.
15 POINCARE, H. (1970) 'Mathematical creation' in VERNON, P.E., *Creativity*, Penguin.

Key Factors for Effective Junior Schooling

ILEA Research and Statistics Branch

This section has described the positive or negative effects that a variety of factors and processes had upon pupils' educational outcomes. Many of these factors had an impact on several different outcomes. Similarly, school and classroom processes were frequently related to each other. Thus, through a detailed investigation of these links, a picture evolves of what constitutes effective junior schooling.

This picture is not intended to be a 'blueprint' for success. Inevitably, many aspects of junior schooling could not be examined in the Junior School Project. Furthermore, schools are not static institutions. This survey was carried out between 1980 and 1984, and it has, therefore, not been possible to take full account of all the changes (particularly in approaches to the curriculum) that have taken place since that time. Nonetheless, this section identifies the key factors that were consistently related to effective junior schooling.

Initially, before examining factors over which schools and teachers can exercise direct control, consideration is given to less flexible characteristics of schools. It was found that certain of these 'given' features made it easier to create an effective school.

Schools that cover the entire primary age range (JMIs), where pupils do not have to transfer at age seven, appear to be at an advantage, as do voluntary-aided schools.[1] Smaller schools, with a junior roll of under 160 children, also appear to benefit their pupils. Class size is particularly relevant: smaller classes, with less than 24 pupils, had a positive impact upon pupil progress and development, especially in the early years.

Not surprisingly, a good physical environment, as reflected in the school's amenities, its decorative order, and its immediate surrounding, creates a positive situation in which progress and development can be fostered. Extended periods of disruption, due to building work and redecoration, can have a negative impact on pupils' progress. The stability of the school's teaching force is also an important factor. Changes of head and deputy headteacher, though inevitable, have an unsettling effect upon the pupils. It seems, therefore, that every effort should be made to reduce the potentially negative impact of such changes. Similarly, where there is an unavoidable change of class teacher, during the shool year, careful planning will be needed to ensure an easy transition, and minimize disruption to the pupils. Where pupils experience continuity through the whole year, with one class teacher, progress is more likely to occur.

It is, however, not only continuity of staff that is important. Although major, or frequent changes tend to have negative effects, change can be used positively. Thus, where there had been no change of head for a long period of time, schools tended to be less effective. In the more effective schools, heads had usually been in post for between three and seven years.

It is clear, therefore, that some schools are more advantaged in terms of their size, status, environment and stability of teaching staff. Nonetheless, although these favourable 'given' characteristics contribute to effectiveness, they do not, by themselves, ensure it. They provide a supporting framework within which the head and teachers can work to promote pupil progress and development. The size of a school, for example, may facilitate certain modes of organization which benefit pupils. However, it is the factors *within* the control of the head and teachers that are crucial. These are the factors that can be changed and improved.

Twelve key factors of effectiveness have been identified.

The Twelve Factors

1. *Purposeful Leadership of the Staff by the Headteacher*

'Purposeful leadership' occurred where the headteacher understood the needs of the school and was actively involved in the school's work, without exerting total control over the rest of the staff.

In effective schools, headteachers were involved in curriculum discussions and influenced the content of guidelines drawn up within the school, without taking total control. They also influenced the teaching style of teachers, but only selectively, where they judged it necessary. This leadership was demonstrated by an emphasis on monitoring pupils' progress through the keeping of individual records. Approaches varied — some schools kept written records; others passed on folders of pupils' work to their next teacher; some did both — but a systematic policy of record keeping was important.

With regard to in-service training, those heads exhibiting purposeful leadership did not allow teachers total freedom to attend *any* course: attendance was allowed for a good reason. Nonetheless, most teachers in these schools had attended in-service courses.

2. The Involvement of the Deputy Head

The Junior School Project findings indicate that the deputy head can have a major role in the effectiveness of junior schools.

Where the deputy was frequently absent, or absent for a prolonged period (due to illness, attendance on long courses, or other commitments), this was detrimental to pupils' progress and development. Moreover, a change of deputy head tended to have negative effects.

The responsibilities undertaken by deputy heads also seemed to be important. Where the head generally involved the deputy in policy decisions, it was beneficial to the pupils. This was particularly true in terms of allocating teachers to classes. Thus, it appeared that a certain amount of delegation by the headteacher, and a sharing of responsibilities, promoted effectiveness.

3. The Involvement of Teachers

In successful schools, the teachers were involved in curriculum planning and played a major role in developing their own curriculum guidelines. As with the deputy head, teacher involvement in decisions concerning which classes they were to teach, was important. Similarly, consultation with teachers about decisions on spending, was important. It appeared that schools in which teachers were consulted on issues affecting school policy, as well as those affecting them directly, were more likely to be successful.

4. Consistency amongst Teachers

It has already been shown that continuity of staffing had positive effects. Not only, however, do pupils benefit from teacher continuity, but it also appears that some kind of stability, or consistency, in teacher approach is important.

For example, in schools where all teachers followed guidelines in the same way (whether closely or selectively), the impact on progress was positive. Where there was variation between teachers in their usage of guidelines, this had a negative effect.

5. Structured Sessions

The Project findings indicate that pupils benefitted when their school day was structured in some way. In effective schools, pupils' work was organized by the teacher, who ensured that there was always plenty for them to do. Positive effects were also noted when pupils were *not* given unlimited responsibility for planning their own programme of work, or for choosing work activities.

In general, teachers who organized a framework within which pupils could work, and yet allowed them some freedom within this structure, were more successful.

6. Intellectually Challenging Teaching

Unsurprisingly, the quality of teaching was very important in promoting pupil progress and development. The findings clearly show that, in classes where pupils were stimulated and challenged, progress was greater.

The content of teachers' communications was vitally important. Positive effects occurred where teachers used more 'higher-order' questions and statements, that is, where their communications encouraged pupils to use their creative imagination and powers of problem-solving. In classes where the teaching situation was challenging and stimulating, and where teachers communicated interest and enthusiasm to the children, greater pupil progress occurred. It appeared, in fact, that teachers who more frequently directed pupils' work, without discussing it or explaining its purpose, had a negative impact. Frequent monitoring and maintenance of work, in terms of asking pupils about their progress, was no more successful. What was crucial was the *level* of the communications between teacher and pupils.

Creating a challenge for pupils suggests that the teacher believes they are capable of responding to it. It was evident that such teachers had *high* expectations of their pupils. This is further seen in the effectiveness of teachers who encouraged their pupils to take independent control over the work they were currently doing. Some teachers only infrequently gave instructions to pupils concerning their work, yet everyone in the class knew exactly what they were supposed to be doing, and continued working without close supervision. This strategy improved pupil progress and development.

7. Work-centred Environment

In schools, where teachers spent more of their time discussing the *content* of work with pupils, and less time on routine matters and the maintenance of work activity, the impact was positive. There was some indication that time devoted to giving pupils feedback about their work was also beneficial.

The work-centred environment was characterized by a high level of pupil industry in the classroom. Pupils appeared to enjoy their work and were eager to commence new tasks. The noise level was also low, although this is not to say that there was silence in the classroom. Furthermore, pupil movement around the classroom, was not excessive, and was generally work-related.

8. Limited Focus Within Sessions

It appears that learning was facilitated when teachers devoted their energies to one particular curriculum area within a session. At times, work could be undertaken in two areas and also produce positive effects. However, where many sessions were organized such that three or more curriculum areas were concurrent, pupils' progress was marred. It is likely that this finding is related to other factors. For example, pupil industry was lower in classrooms where mixed activities occurred. Moreover, noise and pupil movement were greater, and teachers spent less time discussing work and more time on routine issues. More importantly, in mixed-activity sessions the opportunities for communication between teachers and pupils were reduced (as will be described later).

A focus upon one curriculum area did not imply that all the pupils were doing exactly the same work. There was some variation, both in terms of choice of topic and level of difficulty. Positive effects tended to occur where the teacher geared the level of work to pupils' needs.

9. Maximum Communication between Teachers and Pupils

It was evident that pupils gained from having more communication with the teacher. Thus, those teachers who spent higher proportions of their time *not* interacting with the children were less successful in promoting progress and development.

The time teachers spent on communications with the whole class was also important. Most teachers devoted the majority of their attention to speaking with individuals. Each child, therefore, could only expect to receive a fairly small number of individual contacts with their teacher. When teachers spoke to the whole class, they increased the overall number of contacts with children. In particular, this enabled a greater number of 'higher-order' communications to be received by *all* pupils. Therefore, a balance of teacher contacts between individuals and the whole class was more beneficial than a total emphasis on communicating with individuals (or groups) alone.

Furthermore, where children worked in a single curriculum area within sessions, (even if they were engaged on individual or group tasks) it was easier for teachers to raise an intellectually challenging point with *all* pupils.

10. Record Keeping

The value of record keeping has already been noted, in relation to the purposeful leadership of the headteacher. However, it was also an important aspect of teachers' planning and assessment. Where teachers reported that they kept written records of pupils' work progress, in addition to the Authority's Primary Yearly Record, the effect on the pupils was positive. The keeping of records concerning pupils' personal and social development was also found to be generally beneficial.

11. Parental Involvement

The research found parental involvement to be a positive influence upon pupils' progress and development. This included help in classrooms and on educational visits, and attendance at meetings to discuss children's progress. The headteacher's accessibility to parents was also important, showing that schools with an informal, open-door policy were more effective. Parental involvement in pupils' educational development within the home was also beneficial. Parents who read to their children, heard them read, and provided them with access to books at home, had a positive effect upon their children's learning. One aspect of parental involvement was, however, not successful. Somewhat curiously, formal Parent-Teacher Associations (PTAs) were not found to be related to effective schooling. It could be that some parents found the formal structure of such a body to be intimidating.

Nonetheless, overall, parental involvement was beneficial to schools and their pupils.

12. Positive Climate

The Junior School Project provides confirmation that an effective school has a positive ethos. Overall, the atmosphere was more pleasant in the effective schools, for a variety of reasons.

Both around the school and within the classroom, less emphasis on punishment and critical control, and a greater emphasis on praise and rewarding pupils, had a positive impact. Where teachers actively encouraged self-control on the part of pupils, rather than emphasizing the negative aspects of their behaviour, progress and development increased. What appeared to be important was firm but fair classroom management.

The teachers' attitude to their pupils was also important. Good effects resulted where teachers obviously enjoyed teaching their classes and communicated this to their pupils. Their interest in the children as individuals, and not just as pupils was also valuable. Those who devoted more time to non-school chat or 'small talk' increased pupils' progress and development. Outside the classroom, evidence of a positive climate included: the organization of lunchtime and after-school clubs for pupils; teachers eating their lunch at the same tables as the children; organization of trips and visits; and the use of the local environment as a learning resource.

The working conditions of teachers contributed to the creation of a positive school climate. Where teachers had non-teaching periods, the impact on pupil progress and development was positive. Thus, the climate created by the teachers for the pupils, and by the head for the teachers, was an important aspect of the school's effectiveness. This further appeared to be reflected in effective schools by happy, well-behaved pupils who were friendly towards each other and outsiders, and by the absence of graffiti around the school.

These are the twelve key factors that have been identified in the study. Some had a stronger effect than others on the cognitive and non-cognitive areas investigated, but all were positive. Unlike the 'given' characteristics discussed earlier, these factors depend on specific behaviours and strategies employed by the headteacher and staff. It is essential to realize that the school and the classroom are in many ways interlocked. What the teacher can or cannot do depends, to a certain extent, on what is happening in the school as a whole.

Whilst these twelve factors do not constitute a 'recipe' for effective junior schooling, they can provide a framework within which the various partners in the life of the school — headteacher and staff, parents and pupils, and governors — can operate. Each of these partners has the capacity to foster the success of the school. When each participant plays a positive role, the result is an effective school.

Note

1 On the whole, the latter tend to have more socio-economically advantaged intakes than county schools.

Making it Count: Evaluation for the Developing Primary School

Peter Holly

Introduction

This chapter is concerned with one of the educational growth industries of the last fifteen years — self-evaluation. Self-evaluation in the primary school has taken many forms, all of which share the one intention of being alternative forms of evaluation to that commonly practised by Her Majesty's Inspectorate and many LEA Inspectors. It is internal as opposed to external evaluation; it is done *by* the members of staff — with appropriate support — *for* the members of staff. The prepositions here are important. They are symbolically — even psychologically — important. Self-evaluation aims to be accomplished *for* and *with* the participant practitioners; it is not a case of the work being done *to* or *at* these same participants. The goal is self-confrontation (see P.A. and R.A. Schmuck, 1974) for self-improvement.

Having said this, the different forms of self-evaluation tend to span a spectrum of accountability concerns (see Elliott, 1979). The major factor is the question of who retains *ownership* of the exercise. And, consequently, what is the conducive management style to foster and not undermine staff commitment to the various schemes? It will be argued in this chapter that a school with a particular management ethos gets the brand of self-evaluation it deserves; perhaps it ought to be the other way round. Indeed, it will be argued that, in the developing primary school, the achievement of a reciprocity of styles — of both evaluation and management — is crucial.

In 1985, in the DES publication entitled *Quality in Schools: Evaluation and Appraisal*, HMI reported on their 'first hand' studies of 'a small number of school-based schemes for institutional evaluation and staff appraisal'. They visited eight primary schools and one middle school drawn from eight local education authorities. Predictably, they found a variety of approaches to evaluation in operation; eg:

Evaluation for the Developing Primary School

- self-initiated schemes devised by the schools themselves
- the GRIDS scheme (Guidelines for Review and Internal Development in Schools), developed under the auspices of the Schools Council/University of Bristol and now being co-ordinated by a team based at the Schools Curriculum Development Committee (SCDC)
- a joint Schools Council/LEA scheme
- a quadrennial LEA-inspired scheme
- an approach based on the guidelines contained in the NUT document 'A fair way forward'

Despite this impression of a patchworth of provision, three forms of self-evaluation have tended to receive most attention:

(i) classroom self-evaluation (often referred to as action-research) and
(ii) school self-evaluation, which has commonly taken two forms:
- institutional review according to LEA 'booklet' schemes
- school-based review (SBR) which aims to involve the whole staff in reviewing and developing the whole school according to a suggested framework of 'process guidelines'. The GRIDS Project mentioned above is an example of this approach (see Holly, 1983).

While these three approaches have received most attention in primary schools (and, consequently, are surveyed in the first half of this chapter), it is noted that the young pretender, ie. teacher/staff appraisal, is a significant force to be reckoned with — and thus receives separate attention from Marion Dadds in this volume.

Classroom Self-Evaluation

The period 1980–83 was some sort of heyday for self-evaluation in this country. The Schools Council, through its programme structure, espoused the cause of self-evaluation and actively supported a great deal of school- and locally-based activity. The Programme One team (armed with the goal of encouraging 'purpose and planning' in primary schools) organized a major conference at Stoke Rochford in 1981 to review the effectiveness of self-evaluatory approaches (see Nuttall, 1981). Arising from the discussions at this conference was the determination to find a route through the self-evaluation minefield — which would prove a viable, effective alternative to the (perceived ineffectiveness of) prevalent LEA 'checklist' schemes — thus the instigation of the GRIDS Project. Meanwhile, the Programme Two team were commissioned to 'help the individual teacher become more effective' — through classroom self-evaluation. A myriad of small

Peter Holly

activities was launched to encourage classroom practitioners to adopt the approach known as action-research.

The action-research 'movement' in the UK was a child of the late 1960s, early 1970s, although its parentage can be traced back to the USA in the 1940/50s. Holly (1984) has shown that the work of Kurt Lewin (in the social field) and Stephen Corey (in the educational field) took some time to percolate across the Atlantic. Three points are relevant here: first, action-research was taken up in the late 1940s by the Tavistock Institute and there was an enthusiastic but relatively short-lived encounter with 'action learning' (see Revans, 1980) in the post-nationalization period in the coal industry; second, when action-research entered the educational arena it was under the aegis of the EPA movement (Halsey, 1972); third, in 1970, a conference was organized at York University to explore the educational potential of action-research. Rapoport's seminal paper (entitled 'Three dilemmas in action-research') was delivered at this conference and aimed to provide an overview of the 'Tavistock Experience'. One of the conference participants was Lawrence Stenhouse who, at that time, was not only directing the Schools Council's Humanities Curriculum Project, but was also beginning to put together the rationale which would eventually provide the philosophical underpinning for the teacher-as-researcher movement (see Stenhouse, 1975). Stenhouse's HCP colleagues was John Elliott and it was Elliott's work with Clem Adelman that produced both the Ford Teaching Project and the Classroom Action-Research Network (CARN), both of which fueled the rise of the action-research movement, which experienced wider recognition in the period 1980–83 under the enthusiastic support of the Schools Council's Programme Two, directed by Don Cooper.

Of some importance to the central themes of this chapter is the fact that, during its Atlantic crossing and its entry into the educational 'culture' in the UK, 'action-research was hijacked by cultural mobsters' (see Holly, 1986). Whereas Lewin (for example, 1946 and 1948) had always stressed the group orientation of action-research (that is group solidarity in order to collaboratively research and take collective action within social situations) and Corey (1953) had emphasized the importance of approaching 'school problems', action-research in the UK in the hands of Stenhouse and Elliott, etc. became synonymous with individual teacher-based enquiry and clasroom self-evaluation. And this has remained its identity.

As I have argued elsewhere (Holly, 1986), this allegiance as a 'teacher-based' change strategy is both its greatest strength and its greatest weakness. Classroom action-research is most successful — and this is its greatest strength — in energizing the improvement of the teaching and learning process in an individual's classroom. It realizes the conception of the 'reflective practitioner' (see Schon, 1983) and, consequently, the 'practice' in that individual's classroom can benefit enormously. This success, I would contend, is caused by three main reasons:

First, action research is teacher-centred, ie. self-centred; the individual teacher lies at the heart of the process. It is teacher-based in that it is conducted by the teacher (with appropriate external support) for that same teacher. As I have also argued (Holly, 1986), this approach is not only 'highly personal and highly personalized', but also 'sits comfortably with the cellular isolationism recorded by Joyce et al, (1983)'. Action-research, as we know it, feeds into the culture of teacher classroom autonomy which is so embedded in the 'philosophy' of the English educational system. Perhaps, to be accepted within the 'culture', action-research has had to sell itself in terms of the same cultural currency.

Furthermore, while much of this activity is orchestrated within collaborative teacher groups (whether in-school or within external networks), membership of the group tends to be viewed instrumentally; that is, that the other group members are used instrumentally to enhance the interests of the individual practitioner. The emphasis tends to be on taking from the group rather than sharing and giving to the group. Creative individuals are not culturally bound to creative synergism; solidarity within the collective is an ideological goal not shared by many educational action-researchers. Thus, when Elliott (1976–77) drew up 43 'practical hypotheses' connected with the issue of developing teachers' abilities to monitor their own work, he was able to state that: 'the more access teachers have to other teachers' classroom problems, the more they are able to bring about fundamental changes in their practice, (pp. 20–21).

In the period 1981–83, Elliott directed a Schools Council action-research project entitled 'Teacher-Pupil Interaction and the Quality of Learning' (TIQL) (see Elliott and Ebbutt, 1986). While several primary schools were connected to this work, in practice, this involvement meant that one or two individual members of staff were actively engaged in the project. Whether this constituted 'school involvement' is another question. On the one hand, action-research is pitted against the 'bureaucratic understanding' of those employed to promote institutional constraints (on individual 'freedom') ie. school managers. Action-research, according to this argument, becomes a political, destablizing force; the managed versus the managers.

It feels subversive. The rhetoric centres on personal emancipation. And some teachers revel in this 'heady' invitation to join the educational barricades, while others probably shudder at the thought. Action-research tends to invite the taking up of stances which are anti-bureaucratic and anti-managerial. Consequently, it is rare to find the energy and commitment (to the improvement of the teaching and learning process in the classroom) invoked by action-research having *meaning* across the staff of a primary school. It has proved difficult to 'make it count'. If the 'underlying purpose' of self-evaluation is 'to improve the teaching and learning process in the school' (see McMahon *et al*, 1984), it has to be said that action-research, in terms of its teacher-based approach grounded in the professional development of an individual teacher's 'curriculum', fails to achieve success in the all-important arena of staff-based inquiry, staff development, and the collegial development of the whole curriculum. It is relegated, by its own allegiances, to being influential in individual classrooms, not in (that is, grounded in) the school. It remains at the level of 'teacher problems' as opposed to 'school problems'.

School Self-Evaluation

Approaches within this category of evaluative activity tend to differ on two counts: first, there is an emphasis on either *accountability* — ie. contractual accountability — or *internal development* (indeed, many observers have questioned whether the two are incompatible); second, there is the promotion of either *normative frameworks* or *procedural frameworks*. The normative approach stresses what a school self-evaluation should be reviewing; typically, as with the LEA 'checklist' approach (see Clift, 1982), the approach is constituted by the posing of prompting questions concerning *what* to look at within the evaluation. The ILEA document entitled 'Keeping the School Under Review' (1977) is a good example of this approach. Born out of the post-Tyndale hiatus, this document could be viewed as 'inspection by proxy' — a desperate attempt to fill the inspection vacuum. In less emotive times, however, the checklist approach has been popular — especially amongst LEA officials (who, according to G. Elliott, 1980, compiled most of the earlier schemes) — because of its ability to encapsulate an implicit view of good practice within the prompting questions. This approach is not just a 'ready reckoner'; if the question asks whether pupils' work is on display in classrooms and around the school, the very question suggests that this is in fact a 'good thing' to do. The procedural approach, on the other hand, rests on the promotion of process guidelines — the 'how' of evaluation as opposed to the 'what' — with much talk of cycles, steps, stages and phases. Incrementalism is the key concept here.

The LEA 'checklist' approach has been criticized in terms of the nature of its practice for the following reasons:

- it elevates external accountability concerns at the expense of internal development
- the approach rests on mandation and wrests *ownership* away from the teachers; the questions belong to the LEA, not to the teachers. As experienced, the approach is redolent of line management
- there is no emphasis on the importance of the *process* of improvement and development. The review is the thing. The action stage is not seen as having an integral role to play. The emphasis, then,

is on giving an account rather than moving forward on the strength of such a review of current practice in terms of action for development
— the prompting questions mask the subsidiary, follow up questions which, for the sake of brevity, have to be left unasked
— the curriculum in action (or the received curriculum) is ignored
— according to the Open University research (see Clift and Turner, 1985) the approach was resisted and negated by schools and, therefore, had little effect. While it may have temporarily filled a gap in political terms, its very anchorage in accountability was often enough to condemn the resulting booklet to the headteacher's desk-drawer.

The 'hard-line', 'top-down' flavour of the LEA 'checklist' schemes did have one major consequence. When a chief education officer wrote in the foreword to such a document that 'this self-appraisal document is intended as a tool to help a headteacher to gather, analyze and interpret information relating to the various aspects of the work of a primary school' and when G. Elliott (1980) showed that, up to that point, all the LEA schemes — thirty-one of them — had been produced either by LEA administrators/advisers or as joint ventures between these same officials and headteachers (and none by teachers themselves), a reaction was bound to set in. And this reaction came in both theory and practice. From the theoretical standpoint, Simons (1980, 1981 and 1984), Elliott (1979), Adelman and Alexander (1982), Clift (1982), Holly (1984a) and Shipman (1979) all weighed in with images of, and strategies for, an alternative in-school evaluation scenario. In practice, many schools began to explore the efficacy of schemes which emphasized internal development at the expense of accountability considerations.

Yet some LEAs persevered with the booklet approach, attempting to learn some of the lessons mentioned above along the way. For the past three years I have been meeting on a yearly basis with those *teachers* responsible for drawing up what is known in this particular LEA as the 'School Profile' (for primary schools only). The following points are of some pertinence:

— in being put together by teachers (mainly headteachers), it aims to be a professional document
— the intention is to provide both a focus for staff discussion and the promotion of internal school development by offering a review — within the profile, albeit briefly — of all the facets of the whole curriculum. Consequently, there are two or three pages on 'good practice' in Art, Craft and Design Education; Drama; Health Education; Language; Mathematics; Micro-computers; Music; Personal, Social and Moral Education; Physical Education; Religious Education; Science; and Social and Environmental Education.

There are also sections on the School Environment; Relationships; Teaching Skills; In-Service Training and Leadership. The latter contains sub-sections entitled Children; Home, School and Community; The Curriculum; Class Organization; Staffing; Staff Meetings; Head Teacher; and Safety Procedures. Some examples of the questions contained in this section are as follows:

Staffing
What are the duties of those teachers who have posts of responsibility?

Do all staff know of these duties and are they subject to revision?

Do they contribute to the needs of the school in terms of curriculum or are the posts allocated for other reasons?

A staff may offer a wide variety of abilities. In assessing whether these are used to the best advantage it may also be apparent that there are potential sources of help among ancillary staff, parents, or people in the local community.

In what ways are probationary teachers helped?

Are there guidelines for occasional teachers to ensure continuity in classwork?

Are the duties of ancillary staff clearly defined and are other staff aware of them?

What steps are taken to train them and to review their relationships within the school?

Staff Meetings
When meetings are held are they part of a regular routine or are they only called for specific purposes?

During the past year what meetings were held, who initiated them and why were they held?

If there was an agenda, how was it originated and were decisions minuted?

Are staff agreed about the timing and mode of meetings and the arrangements for implementation of decisions?

When decisions on future policy are made are there clear statements of the objectives and the priorities for the next term or year?

Headteacher
To what extent is delegation a feature of your leadership?

Are decisions effectively communicated?

Is there an accepted method of disseminating information and instructions among staff?

Is the work load in organizing, teaching and voluntary activities evenly shared?

Do you consider that the time available to you is used to the best advantage in achieving a balance in curriculum development and monitoring teaching, and administration work?'

The members of the working party who drew up the profile included the following procedural considerations; first, the self-evaluation process should be on a five-yearly basis; second, the principle of self-selection from the list of sections should be central; third, that the accumulating 'file' of review material, responses, decisions, monitored actions, etc. should be the basis for staff reflection and further action; and fourth, the schools should be given 'guidelines for responding to the profile'. A member of this working party has reported at length on this involvement.

At the time of completion, we felt some satisfaction that the document had emerged as practical and rational, and could be seen as worthwhile in schools, because it had been produced by groups of practitioners, for use by other practitioners. We were also apprehensive since we wished to avoid any feeling that the views of a few were going to be seen as an imposition on many. Nevertheless, we still felt that the profile presented the best opportunity to date for schools to control internal development, with self selected lists of priorities, at an individual pace.

The profile is intended to form the basis for self development in primary schools for the next ten or fifteen years. Having invested in the profile in terms of time, thought and self analysis, we were all anxious to assess its reception in schools, not least because we felt that it would be of great assistance in our own schools.

The response guidelines were felt to be the essential catalyst which would make the whole scheme work. It fell to me to attempt to crystallize the thinking of the panel.

The profile was never seen as a definitive document, or an end in itself. It will be subject to regular revision, as will the response guidelines. Neither should really remain in the present form at the beginning of the next five year cycle, and already changes are needed to the section on in-service training, in the light of the forthcoming GRIST developments.

I approached the problem by asking myself the question: 'How would I have felt about the profile had I not been involved in its preparation? Where would I begin?' The agenda for priority for my school might not be that of my neighbour's, and so self-selection of starting points related to identified needs is suggested in the guidelines.

There is, in fact, no set pattern of working through from page one until all sections have been completed. It is for the staff of a school to decide where they need to begin.

The next question which arose was: 'How long should the whole exercise take?' We could have produced a neat package, with a prescribed time scale for each section, but this would have missed the point. Certain areas will take up far more time in one school than another, and the length of time spent on a specific review will depend upon individual circumstances.

Nevertheless, there are general guidelines, because to have ignored a time scale completely would have been to have left the whole process drifting. Thus a five year cycle is suggested as a suitable span for a full in-depth review, with one area being examined each term.

A shorter time scale of perhaps one or two years would mean that the exercise would be rushed and would leave deeper issues untouched. Certainly, during any five year period, staff changes will occur. Here, the profile may offer additional support.

By recording minutes of discussions on specific issues such as organization or the school environment, the new head or class teacher may have a useful insight into the reasons why things happen in a certain way. Criteria which might have applied to class organization a few years ago will probably have changed when falling rolls have been experienced. Understanding the reasons for decisions, as well as being aware of school policies will certainly be enlightening, and may be a useful supplement to the curriculum guidelines which are handed to the newcomer as a means of introducing him to the school.

Minutes of meetings held to discuss specific issues might also form the basis for future action, which could range from ordering more Science equipment to deciding to spend more time teaching handwriting during the Autumn term.

At this point I began to wonder if I would be entirely happy to carry out such an extensive review of my school in isolation. What would happen if I experienced problems which seemed to be insoluble? Might there be a danger that changes in my school would throw it out of step with my neighbour's? In any case, how do I know at present if my school's standards, routine and organization are generally compatible with other similar schools?

Here there seemed to be an opportunity to use the profile to bring schools closer together, so that experiences might be shared to improve learning for the pupils. There might also be an opportunity to improve continuity and consistency between area groups of Primary schools feeding into the local Comprehensive.

The response guidelines suggest that area groups of schools should meet at least once a year to produce group summaries of school reports, which would be set out in the form of common problems and postive solutions to difficultjes. This collaborative approach might have certain advantages.

Financial implications will inevitably arise from self evaluation. Increased co-operation between schools might allow some pooling of resources, which could help individual schools to overcome particular shortfalls, even if only on a short term basis.

Collective reports might also identify solutions as well as common problems, and these would be brought to the attention of the LEA. Sending annual reports to County Hall would also mean that there would eventually be a collection of views which would provide an insight into patterns of experience over a wide spectrum. At the end of a five year span, the views of all Primary Schools in the County on major issues would be available through these area summaries.

The acid test would still be: 'Who will read the reports at County Hall, and what will happen when they have been received?' Taking a pessimistic view, and assuming that very little will happen in the way of follow-up, what direction should the profile next take?

It is clearly essential that the initial impetus is maintained, and also that the profile remains the property of those who have invested in it, ie. the teachers.

To ensure control of the document, it is suggested that a working party, with a membership representing area groups of schools should be set up to monitor developments, and to ensure that recommendations for action are taken up and supported. All schools would have the opportunity of being represented on this panel, since its membership should change annually. Finally, the profile is in an embryonic form. It does not yet seem to have been given a fair chance to flourish. It is important because it is more than a curriculum review, but covers far more, including relationships and management. These guidelines are intentionally brief, yet precise enough to provide a reasonable structure. The profile ought to be of assistance because it asks many telling questions. It also encourages mutual self help, which is needed. The new governing bodies mean that there are fewer opportunities for headteachers to meet on a regular basis. The profile offers a new opportunity for dialogue between schools.

If the profile implies any accountability, it is of an ethical nature, which we demand of ourselves as professionals. We all appreciate the need to refine existing good practice.

For me, the pay-off for successful self evaluation, will, I hope, be threefold. First of all, my school should become a better place to be, for all of us. Secondly, staff development ought to bring out the best in my teachers, and myself. If I have the first two, then it ought to follow that my overall aim will be realized, and that is to improve the quality of experience for all the children in my care. This is ultimately the driving force behind the profile, to which all other considerations will be subordinate.

Unfortunately, the enthusiasm on the part of the members of the working party has not been matched within the LEA itself. The same teacher concludes:

When the editorial panel met to consider the final form the profile should take, we were more concerned with the problems of introducing it to schools, than dotting the 'i's and crossing the 't's.

There were in fact several issues about which we felt very strongly. We were concerned that every teacher, not only heads, should receive a personal copy of the profile, since we were convinced that any meaningful self appraisal would depend upon all members of a school's staff becoming involved at certain stages.

We were also concerned that adequate explanations of the motives for producing the profile should be given to those who would be asked to make use of it. We fully appreciated, having listened to a consultant's accounts of previous self evaluation programmes, that our introductory moves would have a critical effect on the profile's reception in schools.

A 'user's guide', the response guidelines, should have formed an integral part of the profile. Unfortunately, these guidelines failed to be included in the final document. A year ago I noted that the worst thing that could happen in the future would be for the profile to arrive without warning on the headteacher's desk. We were very dismayed to find that the expert advice we had been given concerning the crucial nature of the introduction of such a document into schools had been ignored.

As already mentioned in this chapter, the GRIDS project epitomizes the approach which rests on the articulation of process guidelines.

GRIDS (Guidelines for Review and Internal Development in Schools) has been a pilot project, a publication and has been described as a 'simple tool for planning, development and (self-)evaluation'. I would argue that, despite its somewhat straightforward published format, GRIDS is underscored by a sophisticated 'theory' of the potential of whole school review and development for putting into practice the theory of change in organizations. Like Organization Development (O.D.), GRIDS is an attempt to change schools at the cultural (ie. institutional and, therefore, deep-seated) level. When the project was launched in 1981 the following rationale was offered in the Schools Council's publicity leaflet:

> There is now widespread professional agreement that a systematic process of self-review is an important first step in the process of institutional/internal development in schools. However, there are at least four major barriers to the successful adoption of this approach. First is the inter-relationship between the two purposes of such self-review — school development and social accountability: only too often these two purposes are perceived as being in direct conflict. Second is the lack of time and resources for teachers, heads and external support agencies to carry out the process. Third is the lack of validated self-review schedules and development procedures. Fourth is the general lack of experience of successful ways of carrying out the diagnosis phase and extending it into the planning and development phases. There is clearly a need for development and research work to tackle and overcome some of these barriers and this project is seen as an initial step in this direction.

In the same bulletin the 'guiding principles' underpinning the project were enumerated:

(i) The aim is to achieve internal school development and not to produce a report for formal accountability purposes.
(ii) The main purpose is to move beyond the review stage into development for school improvement.
(iii) The staff of the school should be consulted and involved in the review and development process as much as possible.
(iv) Decisions about what happens to any information or reports produced should rest with the teachers and others concerned.
(v) The head and teachers should decide whether and how to involve the other groups in the school, eg. pupils, parents, advisers, governors.

(vi) Outsiders (eg. external consultants) should be invited to provide help and advice when this seems appropriate.
(vii) The demands made on key resources like time, money and skilled personnel, should be realistic and feasible for schools and LEAs.

The principle aims of this action project are:

(a) to collaborate with schools in the planning and implementation of a systematic self-review and development process over a one year period
(b) to produce two sets of guideline materials (one primary, one secondary) for use by schools undertaking self-review
(c) to pilot these materials (GRIDS) in five LEAs and approximately thirty schools

The execution of these intentions constituted the first phase of this, a pilot project. The materials were produced in concert with the participating schools and the 'structure' (the five stages — see the accompanying diagram) finalized.

Reflecting on my involvement in the GRIDS Project (as both a member of the development team and then its national co-ordinator), I was able to make the following observations (Holly, 1984a) concerning six possible 'criteria for success' in going about the complex task of school self-evaluation using something like the GRIDS method.

Staff Development The development of the teachers as a staff can be a crucial by-product of their involvement in a self-evaluation scheme. The members of staff involved need to feel that there is a 'pay-off', a tangible, demonstrable gain for them for all the hard work, long hours, anxiety induced by scrutiny, etc. This pay-off might be better working conditions, improved career prospects, higher morale, more intellectual stimulation, more resource support, more team 'spirit', enhanced collegiality, etc.

Whole Staff, Whole School The aspiration should be for the whole staff to look at the whole school. The deliberation should (at least at some stage) include all members of staff so that they all feel involved in, and committed to, the enterprise and all feel to some extent under review. I have called this the 'democracy of discomfiture', an equilibrium of the threat involved.

Self-evaluation is not something that 'other' people (classroom teachers?) ought to be doing; it is good enough for everyone. In addition, *collaboration* in school self-evaluation can lessen the personal anxiety (see Holly, 1984b)

Evaluation for the Developing Primary School

The five stages of the internal review and development process

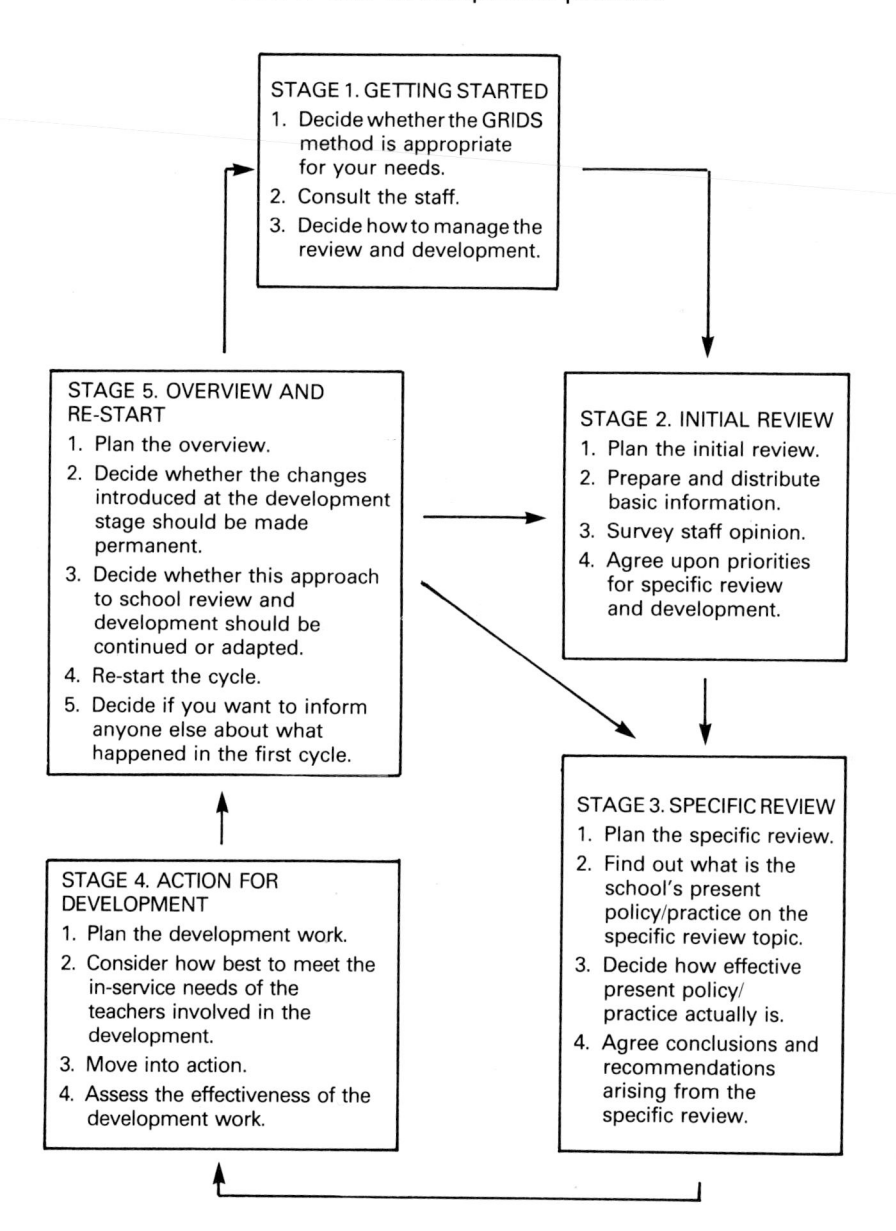

STAGE 1. GETTING STARTED
1. Decide whether the GRIDS method is appropriate for your needs.
2. Consult the staff.
3. Decide how to manage the review and development.

STAGE 2. INITIAL REVIEW
1. Plan the initial review.
2. Prepare and distribute basic information.
3. Survey staff opinion.
4. Agree upon priorities for specific review and development.

STAGE 3. SPECIFIC REVIEW
1. Plan the specific review.
2. Find out what is the school's present policy/practice on the specific review topic.
3. Decide how effective present policy/practice actually is.
4. Agree conclusions and recommendations arising from the specific review.

STAGE 4. ACTION FOR DEVELOPMENT
1. Plan the development work.
2. Consider how best to meet the in-service needs of the teachers involved in the development.
3. Move into action.
4. Assess the effectiveness of the development work.

STAGE 5. OVERVIEW AND RE-START
1. Plan the overview.
2. Decide whether the changes introduced at the development stage should be made permanent.
3. Decide whether this approach to school review and development should be continued or adapted.
4. Re-start the cycle.
5. Decide if you want to inform anyone else about what happened in the first cycle.

221

Confidentiality The staff should have rights of ownership of the data collected; the access to this data needs to be negotiated with the staff and going public must be a staff decision. On the other hand, the evaluation process should not be allowed to become cosy and anodyne. The aim is to marry protection with rigour, not cosmeticism and blandness.

Institutionalization The process of self-evaluation needs to become cyclical and organic to the school (see Simons, 1980). The 'top down' LEA approach did not win staff commitment; hopefully, the more 'bottom-up', organic approach will encourage the staff to accept the need for change and to identify with the process of innovation and its institutionalization (see Holly, 1984b). It is a question of embeddedness, ie. an acceptance across the staff that 'this is the way we do it around here'.

The Nature of Innovation School self-evaluation is in itself an innovation; like all innovations it is a *process* (with by-products and side-effects) leading to *products* or outcomes. The process is important, not all-important. Outcomes deserve equal billing; it is not worth just 'going through the motions'. Teachers deserve the best deal possible in return for their self-evaluatory efforts (see Hargreaves, 1983).

External Support To ensure a valid product, it is important to involve external consultancy and support. The concepts of 'peer group appraisal' and the 'critical friend' are central here. In recent experience external support can enhance, not undermine, internal development. The emphasis is on a school-focused, school-centred approach; there is a need for a collaborative INSET partnership to support school-based inquiry in all its facets.

In this same paper I also reflected on the complexity of attempting a whole school evaluation.

School self-evaluation is not easy to define as it exists in various forms. It is my contention that this problem concerning definition is exacerbated by the fact that, in practice, the three components — 'school', 'self' and 'evaluation' — can all be taken to mean different things. There is, therefore, a problem of the permutation of meanings.

If the three terms are all problematical, what is the range of definition within each?

(i) I see in the use of the term 'school' a question of *focus* or *scope*. What aspect or property of the school is being focused upon? It could be a single classroom, a few classrooms, a 'subject' area, a section of the school, eg. a year group, the whole school (for instance, the whole curriculum; the pastoral structure; post-holder responsibilities, etc.), relationships, management processes, etc. It is a question of where to pitch the evaluation in terms of *what* and *how much* is under scrutiny.

(ii) It has been asked, 'what is the 'self' in self-evaluation?' *Who* constitutes the self? Is it just the teaching-staff or does the self include other involved and/or interested parties? Some schools, when tackling an evaluation, have included a selection of people from the following categories: ancillary helpers, support staff (eg. nursery nurses), visitors (eg. welfare workers), pupils, parents, governors, members of the local community, employers and LEA officials. Again, it is a question of where to pitch the evaluation — this time in terms of the *scale* of involvement. Research has tended to show, however, that the more external involvement there is, the less those internal to the evaluation (the teachers) are committed to it (see Clift, 1982). There is a tension between the moves towards increased accountability on the part of schools and the successful development of an in-school evaluation: the more the emphasis on the accountability component, the more is the tendency to produce a 'white-wash' as opposed to a true evaluation.

(iii) And this leads on to the third perspective which is a question of *degree*. Is the evaluatory aspect taken seriously or not? What is a 'true evaluation'? Most commentators would agree that there are four basic stages in any evaluation:

— identifying the area to be studied
— gathering evidence, information and facts pertaining to the case (the stage sometimes referred to as 'reconnaissance')
— the analysis of the data; making judgments concerning the quality of the situation under review; these judgments can then become recommendations to the internal decision-makers, an agenda for action
— making decisions and moving into change and development; taking the action; monitoring the changes

As part of an in-school evaluation, the teaching staff are responsible for all four stages.

Arising from the points made above were two major lessons from the GRIDS involvement:

- it is impossible to evaluate simultaneously all those aspects that constitute the 'whole school'. Priorities have to be established.
- it is also impossible to involve the whole staff throughout the exercise. Working groups operating for their colleagues would seem a productive way forward. Interestingly, however, differences between the operation of GRIDS in primary and secondary schools did emerge over time and were touched upon in a project interim report:

> In practice many of the primary schools involved all the teachers in each stage of the process but understandably secondary schools made greater use of small working teams. It can be difficult to move from review into action but the majority of the schools appear to have achieved this. For example, in one primary school where there was no specialist music teacher the staff identified music as a topic for specific review and development. The development work that has resulted from this review has included a school-based in-service course for all the teachers, recorder lessons introduced for each class, an increase in the general musical activity in the school and a determination on the part of the staff that each child should be musically literate by the time he/she leaves the school. A considerable change from the position a year ago when music for the majority of the pupils meant a sing-along session for half an hour each week. Most of the primary schools worked only on one priority area but secondary schools often selected three or four.

Further evidence of GRIDS in practice is contained in a report written for the final issue of the 'Schools Council News' (no. 44). The report concerns a GRIDS project team meeting in one particular primary school and is entitled 'Who will look after the fish tanks?'

> The meeting was held in the head's office after school, beginning at 3.45pm and lasting until just after five o'clock. It was attended by five members of staff, including the headteacher, the deputy head (the GRIDS school co-ordinator and the specific review co-ordinator, and a teacher with a scale two post of responsibility. Four members of staff did not attend. As soon as lost coats had been found, the new senior area education officer had departed and tea and coffee served, the meeting began with a recapping of progress thus far (mainly for the benefit of the visiting consultant).
>
> All the primary schools participating in the project had been prepared for their involvement during the summer term, 1983. At the beginning of the autumn term all the schools embarked on the *initial review* to identify priority areas of concern which seemed in need of specific review and development. This staff had focused

on the question of 'post-holders' and had decided to explore the possibility of changing the staffing policy of the school along the lines of establishing members of staff with 'curriculum responsibility'. A member of staff was asked to lead this exploration at the *specific review stage* and the external consultant was able to introduce into their initial discussions several Schools Council publications and reports on the subject of post-holders and specialisms in the primary school.

By means of collaborative discussion the staff had begun to explore the role of post-holder — what it entails and what it can entail for them — and had identified four components: the marshalling of resources, the preparation (with staff involvement) of curriculum guidelines, the dissemination of current ideas among the rest of the staff and acting as a consultant-cum-evaluator. It was this last component which was considered 'iffy' and most contentious. They had come up against the possible tension between the creation of curriculum leaders and teacher autonomy in the classroom. It was pointed out, however, that if the members of staff had pooled their experience and expertise in the creation both of the post-holder's area of responsibility and in the production of the guidelines themselves, they had created the yardstick by means of which their future progress could be monitored; they had set their own parameters for success, their own level of expectation. Hopefully, you are not threatened by your own creation.

The staff had also mapped out their (desired) curriculum and how the number of posts of responsibility available (six) should be allocated to each area of this curriculum. Their scheme was as follows:

> Language and Literacy (two post-holders)
> Mathematics, Science and Technology (two)
> Creative and Physical Skills (one)*
> The World Around Us (one)*
> *   with back-up being provided by either the head, the deputy head or scale one teachers

It was also realized that, rather than have one member of staff to be responsible for each cross-curricular concern, eg. multiculturalism, racism, sexism, liaison with the feeder infants' school, etc., each post-holder would have to be concerned about such important issues in their own area. As was pointed out at the meeting, this would also encourage staff discussion across the areas of responsibility; the primary school should not jettison its undoubted strength — the potentiality for on-going, informal discussion across the staff. Indeed, the staff of this particular school, in designing their curriculum, had already identified several areas of overlap where it would be important to maintain cross-curricular links.

In this meeting the question was asked, 'Where do we go from here?' The short answer was 'back to the guidelines of the GRIDS process itself'. The longer answer involves dissemination of their current thinking — both amongst the rest of the staff and at LEA level (as their plans have staffing implications). The consultant's advice? Keep on exploring and probing the issues; keep on growing as a staff within your discussion and, once certain of your ground, begin the task of convincing your doubtful colleagues. But, one of the team finally exclaimed, *'Who will look after the fish tanks?'*

(a longer version of this report is available in Bollen and Hopkins, 1987)

Various lessons have been learnt from the GRIDS experience:

— certain roles are crucial, e.g. both internal and external co-ordination
— in the increasingly participative primary school the role of the head (as head and team-member) is still equally important. While heads demonstrated all kinds of leadership styles in the project schools, 'enthusiastic neutrality' seemed to capture the spirit of the enterprise. Certainly, GRIDS was enhanced by the negotiation of (as opposed to the imposition of particular) personal/group agendas

Various participants in the pilot project have reflected on their involvement by focusing on these central issues:

Initially it can seem threatening to the head, but it need not be. My initial concern was that the staff would identify for specific review an area of the school which threatened me, eg. consultation and decision-making procedures or an area like health and safety procedures that I would not be interested in spending time on. Now, seeing the whole GRIDS process in focus, I realize that whatever the staff identify in the first instance is important because it is a matter of concern to them. Giving it attention and acting on the recommendations made will mean that ... the staff will realize that what they say and feel matters and they will respond to the next review. Staff discussion becomes much more meaningful if the staff feel that they are influencing policy ...

(Headteacher of a project school, quoted in McMahon *et al*, 1984)

Unlike the stance of this particular headteacher — who attempted to 'take a back seat' — most primary school heads were centrally involved in the process. In the original pilot schools heads frequently assumed the role of school co-ordinator. As confidence in using the scheme grew, however, it was increasingly the case that other members of staff were called upon to play the pivotal role.

In one particular LEA, in which twelve primary schools entered the project as a collaborative network, the LEA co-ordinator was able to reflect on the nature of the develping involvement:

> In this LEA GRIDS has now run for one year. It began after a group of primary headteachers had identified the need to find an evaluation model for schools to use. Seven headteachers in that working party liked what they had heard of GRIDS and agreed to present it to their staff and, if the teachers agreed, to pilot the GRIDS model in the LEA. A further five schools joined the ranks.
>
> In the early days many staff were cautious and suspicious of the motives and intentions of their headteachers and the Authority in general. What did the Authority expect to gain from introducing GRIDS? What interference/monitoring could be expected? Were schools to be accountable through GRIDS? All these questions were raised before a consensus of opinion took the school into the project. I think it is fair to say that after the initial introduction of the Guidelines, headteachers took no further part in the decision-making. To stand a chance of success it had to have a full staff commitment to it, and a show of confidence that it was a worthwhile venture.
>
> For some headteachers this was a management style which would be quite innovatory in their school and which could undermine the 'authority' they had previously enjoyed. For others it was the opportunity to enjoy corporate decision making; it was a chance to *share* the responsibility.
>
> Some anxiety was expressed that post-holders might feel under pressure and experience harassment if their particular area of responsibility was found to be operating inadequately in the school. Of course this was possible, but in the atmosphere of sharing, growth and responsibility this was not found to be the case.
>
> Twelve schools decided to adopt GRIDS as a way of looking at their school. Each appointed a co-ordinator, never the headteacher, usually the deputy head, occasionally a lower scale teacher. In each case, it was a person who could command re-

spect, and who could organize GRIDS and cope with the additional workload. Yes, it did require a willing person to take on extra work. It meant external meetings, record keeping, and the overall co-ordination of the review in their school. In each participating school this person has been the pivot around which the project work has revolved, far more being required in that role, than I have described, but failing all else someone who could motivate colleagues to make a commitment to a team approach. It is interesting that in each of the pilot authorities the co-ordinator was the headteacher and yet it was unanimously agreed in this LEA that this should not be the case. There are numerous arguments to support such a decision. Will the workload be unreasonably heavy and exert too much pressure upon a full-time class teacher? Can a 'teacher' have an adequate over-view of the school? Can the status of headteacher marry with the corporate approach required? Is there a temptation to use the innate authority of the headteacher to guide the review in the direction 'they' would like? I leave the answers to these questions open — there are many and persuasive points to be made and in the end GRIDS is a flexible model and must be used to suit each individual school ...

As LEA co-ordinator — what do I do?

I see my role as having several facets. As *organizer* I convene meetings for school co-ordinators and heads and organize workshops for co-ordinators, in which we focus upon small, but important areas of the Guidelines, or use the small group situation to discuss problems which co-ordinators might face in their schools.

The GRIDS material needs to be carefully understood and followed, if a rigorous approach to evaluation is to be attempted. I am an *adviser* on the process and seek to 'train' the co-ordinators, so that in managing the project in their schools, they will feel confident. The Guidelines, themselves, are general material and, as adviser, I try to make them relevant to all the chosen areas for review. I have found the tendency in some schools to rush through the evaluation stage and make for the remedies, the results. As an outsider it is possible to slow down the review, suggest changes in course and encourage deeper examination of the particular area.

During the specific review stage, schools are expected to collect information internally on their chosen area and I have been able to produce appropriate reading materials, and audio visual aids. At another time in the project contacts are made with outside consultants and having collected resource information, I would be able to make that contact myself on behalf of the school. On these grounds I consider myself having the role of *facilitator* whilst as an outsider with an objective viewpoint I can act as an *observer* and 'critical friend' which seems an appropriate term, for one who can question the working method, but who poses no threat to the individual schools and teachers.

The school co-ordinator's job is a very crucial, yet difficult one. I think I have been a *'sounding board'* and tried to be a sympathetic ear, when at times the difficulties seemed insurmountable. Having time to listen and an overview of the project has enabled me to give full attention to problems and the opportunity to encourage and discuss objectivity.

Finally, whilst intrinsic in all the other aspects of my work, is the task of *communicator*. We have used a monthly bulletin to ensure that all people, in every school, know what members of the project group are doing and what plans are being drawn up for the future. Contact with officers in the LEA has been encouraged and, whilst respecting confidentiality, progress reports have been compiled and, with the consent of the group of schools, circulated to all interested people.

In short, I help the process along and in the future I would hope to be a saleswoman and take the Guidelines to those schools who might do well to consider them, as well as support to those schools already involved (Osborne, 1984).

Other important lessons emerging from the GRIDS experience have included the following:

— the existence of preconditions for staff collaboration, if established prior to the project involvement, certainly enhanced the process. These same conditions could, however, emerge from the involvement

— unlike the school described above in the case study, most primary schools identified aspects of the curriculum as key/priority areas of focus

— it has been argued (see Holly, 1984) that, as with action research, the GRIDS approach does not 'count' over time. That is, initially, it is most successful at galvanizing whole school/staff involvement (often for the first time), but, in the longer term, it is questionable whether individual practice in the classroom changes as a result of the initiative. The energy for change fails to percolate down through the 'culture' of the school (ie. the staff's attitudes, norms, values and expectations) in any meaningful way.

PROJECT	FOCUS (short-term)	TARGET (long-term)
TIQL (Teacher-Pupil Interaction and the Quality of Learning)	The classroom; Individual Practice	Institutional Development (?)
GRIDS	The Institution; Whole school staff	The Classroom; Individual Practice (?)

Alternatively, however, a primary school teacher was able to reflect more optimistically about her GRIDS experience:

> I honestly don't mind (giving up) the time because I feel that as a staff we are moving forward and an important area of the curriculum is being tackled and hopefully in the future the children will benefit ... (the project) is compelling teachers to reflect and to come up with answers to such questions as 'why am I teaching that?', 'should I be?', 'is it effective?', and, hopefully, 'what is best for the children?' (quoted in Holly, 1984b).

What seems to be needed is a change strategy which combines the effective aspects of both action-research and the process guidelines approach — thus generating a systematic commitment to the development of classroom practice across the staff. Holly (1985) has attempted such an accommodation within his conception of the Developing School — see also Reid, Hopkins and Holly (1987).

The Developing School

The Developing School constitutes a school with a *development culture* — in which evaluation (for development) is an organic feature (see Fullan, 1981). It is partly, therefore, the Evaluative School (see Simons, 1980).

The staff of the Developing School concentrate on developing and managing the learning process in the classroom. In doing so these teachers learn about learning. It is partly, therefore, the Learning School (see Holly, 1986a).

In the Developing School the staff effect and implement worthwhile changes effectively. It is partly, therefore, the Effective School (see Reid, Hopkins and Holly, 1987).

The Developing School has a capacity for being innovative. But innovations are introduced in a certain (developmental) style. The dictionary definition of 'development' (the bringing out of potential; bringing to a more advanced, highly organized state; evolutionary growth; the exploitation of natural resources; a gradual unfolding) provides the terms of reference. Strengths are identified (and retained); other areas in need of priority attention are investigated. The aim is to synthesize the best of the old with the best of the new. And the responsibility for this work should be grounded in the body of the staff. The Developing School rests on staff development and is energized by the supportiveness of staff collaboration within school-based INSET.

All these themes are interrelated, as has been recently evidenced in the Carnegie Report (1986) published in the USA:

> The focus of schooling must shift from teaching to learning, from the passive acquisition of facts and routines to the active application of ideas to problems. This transition makes the role of the teacher more important, not less.
>
> Teachers must think for themselves if they are to help others think for themselves, be able to act independently and *collaborate with others*, and render critical judgment.
>
> (What is required is) a transformation of the environment for teaching. School systems based on bureaucratic authority must be replaced by schools in which authority is grounded in the professional competence of the teacher, and where teachers work together as colleagues, constantly striving to improve their performance ...

Furthermore, the Developing School eschews instrumental and factional collaboration in favour of a more collegial approach (see Holly in Reid, Hopkins and Holly, 1987). Collaboration is necessary but not sufficient for collegiality. Like self-evaluation itself, collaboration is a mechanism for staff involvement within which the transfer of ownership can be accomplished. Moreover, Purkey and Smith (1985) have claimed that collaboration is 'most likely to occur in an atmosphere that supports innovation and risk-taking' Lieberman (1986), in turn, maintains that, within collaboration, 'problems emerge from the team's mutual concerns and inquiries'; and Fullan (1985) has drawn our attention to the work of Little. The latter (1981) has contended that:

> There is some evidence that organizations ... which have participatory leadership, administrator support for an innovation (both psychological and resource support), intra-staff co-operation, and support and exchange of ideas among organization members are more likely to effectively implement innovations which they attempt.

Holly (1986) expanded on this theme:

In addition, 'Collegiality' seems to have both a quantitative and qualitative importance. It rests on both *breadth* and *depth* (Southworth, 1986); breadth of involvement and depth of commitment/insight. Yet collaboration itself serves three central purposes: it provides the framework of process involvement (and thus the shared benefits of the team approach, involving staff development based on supportiveness and the excitement, indeed 'high' of building together), membership of a learning group (producing 'better' research — more varied data, more insightful analysis, joint action, etc.) and participation within a medium — the group — for (personal) change.

'Collegiality' then, is being explored in all its (potential) facets. As Walker (1985) has maintained, collegiality can arise out of a collaborative process and school-based research/evaluation can be the vehicle for this process. His argument is that conditions can be fostered within, and by, the research process itself. Self-evaluation constitutes a process of involvement; it is the medium (with accompanying messages) of interactive dialogue. According to Walker, a teaching *staff* can become a 'community of knowledgeable users' — thus breaking down the barriers between those who do research, those who are subject to it, and those who make use of it. As Little (1981) has pointed out, there are schools where 'classroom observation is so frequent, so intellectually lively and intense, and so thoroughly integrated into the daily work and so associated with accomplishments for all who participate, that it is difficult to see how the practices could fail to improve teaching'.

Those primary schools which are trying to fuse staff ownership of the development programme (collegiality) with a meaningful commitment to the improvement of classroom processes across the school have found the following five approaches of some importance:

- staff conferences/workshops which concentrate on the practicalities of the management of learning
- 'open house' classrooms — for staff discussion
- paired or mutual observation leading to the extraction of pertinent issues which are then fed into the staff dialogue
- the formation of research and development 'interest groups'. This approach has been used most successfully in elementary schools within the Danforth Project in St. Louis in the USA
- the provision of process guidelines as enabling, flexible frameworks

Holly (1986b) has compiled the Teachers' Guide which rests on a simple matrix, the two axes of which are the *key areas of focus* (to be prioritized) and the *procedural (action) steps*.

What is crucial, however, is that the Developing School demands to be 'managed' in a certain style — a style which, ideally, should reflect the nuances of the management of learning at classroom level. School management should facilitate teachers to learn how to facilitate learning. The conducive style of management should be as follows:

- participative and consultative. All staff should be *involved* — both dialogically and in terms of their consequent practice in the classroom
- invoking and facilitating of staff commitment and ownership
- supportive, collaborative and collegial; it should provide an enabling framework
- preoccupied with the orchestration of talent and expertise that is the staff. This involves the identification of personal strengths within a team approach. It also involves the fostering of responsibility across the staff. It is not inappropriate for the developing primary school to have an Institutional Development Plan.
- keenly aware of the importance and affectiveness of staff relationships and the climate of the school. Cultural values and norms lie at the heart of this climate. Thus, openness, trust, a preparedness to face risk and ambiguity, a positive attitude to criticism, etc., may well be vital 'principles of procedure' for the Developing School (see Reid, Hopkins and Holly, 1987).

Like evaluation, management should belong to the teachers. The goal for both is internalization as opposed to externalization; they are internal functions of the effectively collegial school. When this symbiotic relationship between evaluation, management and development is harnessed for the primary school then we can really talk in terms of making 'it' (ie. the reciprocal relationship) count.

In conversation with a headteacher recently, he made the following observations concerning 'his' school's involvement in whole school evaluation along the lines suggested in the Teachers' Guide: the whole staff involvement provides the vehicle to break down cultural (ie. traditional) barriers, between, for example, 'improvers' and 'improvees' and the managers and the managed. As Fullan (1985) has reminded us, the 'instrumental rationality' of someone else's enthusiasm feels like 'brute sanity' to the person(s) being imposed upon. It has been argued in this chapter that, for this very reason, both action-research or classroom self-evaluation and the LEA 'checklist' approach to self-evaluation tend to reinforce and, therefore, perpetuate the divide — to the detriment of the improvement of the teaching and learning process across a school.

Indeed, it would appear that the utilization of the bottom-up, top-down distinction, is not an appropriate means of sign-posting the way forward. Fullan (1985) echoes the themes of this chapter when he argues that 'innovations that focus on classroom changes' (like action-research) 'can result in major change in the classroom and this is no small feat. However, for school-wide change, more top-down/bottom-up combinations are required, and it is, of course, much more difficult because more fundamental changes are being attempted'. Fullan continues:

> Most of all, it is imperative to understand and appreciate the actual dynamics of the change processes as they unfold. However change is initiated, once it begins, it involves anxiety and uncertainty for those involved and (if successful) the development of new skills, cognitive understandings, beliefs and meanings. Whether the process is successful depends on certain organizational conditions that support and propel the process ... leaders must alternately and simultaneously balance and contend with several dilemmas, paradoxes, and subtleties: simplicity — complexity, top-down/bottom-up, tightness — looseness, evaluation — nonevaluation, and commonness — uniqueness of situations.

What is required to begin to resolve some of these central dilemmas is an exploration of the 'middle ground' of collegial ownership of the development process. Collective 'purposing' involves general staff participation in both agenda-setting and implemention of this same agenda. Some critics (see Tangerud, 1986) have rather disparagingly labelled this approach as the 'harmony — consensus model', but this need not be the case. If self-confrontation (see the Schmucks, 1974) is written into the scenario, the collegial *process* will involve the central task of exploring value differences. What this collaborative process can also do, however, is create shared understandings of what it is like for those who exist on either side of the divide. Members of staff come to appreciate the problems and dilemmas of management and managers come to appreciate (or relearn) the nature of the daily vicissitudes of classroom life. Awareness and sensitivity are heightened across the staff and the myth of certainty (perpetrated by many managers in their own self-interest) is laid to rest. This new, shared domain of practical knowledge and understanding encompasses all the facets of the enterprise that is primary schooling. It is more democratic, inevitably less patriarchial (or even matriarchal) and is synergistic in intent. The 'building-blocks' for school development (see Holly, 1985) are seen for what they can be — not separate 'treatments' but elements which are mutually inclusive and interdependent. 'Evaluation', 'collaboration', 'staff development', 'management', etc., constitute the internal linkage for organic school development. And in this fusion process they cease to have any independent meaning.

It could be argued that it is inappropriate to use terms like 'democratic' to refer to the participative primary school. As Naisbitt (1984) has observed:

Participatory democracy sounds like a political concept and it basically is. Yet the role we play as citizens is but a small part of our lives. We also belong to a variety of institutions where we are governed as well: schools, churches, clubs.

Furthermore, he argues, the way institutions are governed influences the quality of life for the participants. As a consequence, we should be 're-evaluating the contradiction between our democratic political values — which are growing ever more participatory — and the archaic traditions that govern us in our jobs'. Naisbitt's solution — from an industrial standpoint — is worker participation, because 'only one group can make the most pervasive changes, the employees of a corporation — the life-blood of its success ...'

In his analysis of general social and economic trends, Naisbitt (1984) raises two further issues of some relevance to this chapter. Firstly, he maintains that certain social divisions (reinforced by hierarchicalism) create 'breeds apart' and prevent the attainment of a balance of interests. Again from an industrial standpoint, but echoing Fullan above, Naisbitt identifies the continuing tension between the pursuit of technological achievement and the achievement of human and spiritual satisfaction. As Naisbitt points out, if one 'side' is over-played, the other will demand compensation ('each feeds the other', he says). Naisbitt's argument is that the industrialization of the 1950s produced the reaction of the 1960s, the 'self-help or personal growth movement, which eventually became the human potential movement'. This trend has culminated in the prevalence of quality control circles — which are essentially collaborative, self-evaluative groups of colleagues discussing work-related problems and solutions. Action-research in schools can be viewed in the same light — it constitutes the human alternative which feeds on a 'highly personal value system'. Secondly, Naisbitt, in describing the 'new health paradigm', refers to three basic ways to improve health care — and in so doing charts the course of this chapter:

> You can introduce outside agents such as drugs and surgery ... or you can try to improve either the human being or the environment. What began happening in the 1960s is that we shifted over to working on the human side, the idea being that a stronger population can better resist disease.

His prediction is that 'the next big shift will be to focus more on the environmental influence on health'. The educational parallels are unmistakable.

References

ADELMAN, C and ALEXANDER, R.J. (1982) *The Self-Evaluating Institution*, Methuen.
BOLLEN, R. and HOPKINS, D. (1987) *School Based Review: Towards a Praxis*, (OECD/CERI), ACCO.
CARNEGIE FORUM (1986) 'A nation prepared: Teachers for the 21st century', *Report by the Carnegie Forum's Task Force*
CLIFT, P.S. (1982) 'LEA Schemes for school self-evaluation: A critique' *Eudcational Research* Vol. 24, No. 4; with TURNER, G. (1985) 'Teachers' perceptions of a voluntary LEA scheme for school self-evaluation', *Educational Research* 27, 2.
COREY, S. (1953) *Action-research to Improve School Policies*, Teachers College Press.
DES (1985) *Quality in Schools: Evaluation and Appraisal*, HMSO.
ELLIOTT, G. (1980) *Self-Evaluation and the Teacher*. An annotated bibliography and report on current practice (parts 1–4) School Council
ELLIOTT, J. (1976) 'Developing hypotheses about classrooms from teachers' practical constructs; An account of the work of the Ford Teaching Project', *Interchange* 7(2)
ELLIOTT, J. (1977) 'Evaluating in-service activities: From above or below?' *Insight* November
ELLIOTT, J. (1979) 'The case for school self-evaluation' *Forum*, 22 (1)
ELLIOTT, J. and EBBUTT, D. (Eds.) (1986) *Case Studies in Teaching for Understanding*, Cambridge Institute of Education.
FULLAN, M. (1981) 'The relationship between evaluation and implementation', in LEWY. A and NEVO, D. (Eds.) *Evaluation Roles in Education* Gordon Breach
FULLAN, M. (1985) 'Change processes and strategies at the local level? *The Elementary School Journal*, 85, 3, University of Chicago.
HALSEY, A.H. (1972) *Educational Priority* volume one (see chapter 13 EPA Action-Research) HMSO.
HARGREAVES, D.H. (1983) 'School self-evaluation', *Inspection and Advice*, 19, Autumn.
HOLLY, P.J. (1983) 'The GRIDS project, '*NUT Primary Education Review* (The Schools Council's Primary Contribution) Autumn, 18.
HOLLY, P.J. (1984) 'The development of action-research: Charting a paradigm shift', CIE Seminar Paper. October.
HOLLY, P.J. (1984a) 'Clarifying the concepts involved in institutional self-evaluation', CIE Conference Paper
HOLLY, P.J. (1984b) 'The institutionalization of action-research in schools', *Cambridge Journal of Education*, 14, 2, Easter Term.
HOLLY, P.J. (1984c) 'Beyond the cult of the individual: Putting the partnership into in-service collaboration', Conference Paper, Downing College, Cambridge.
HOLLY, P.J. (1985) 'The developing school', CIE/TRIST Working Paper
HOLLY, P.J. (1985a) 'Teachers as course members and their practical concerns' CIE unpublished paper.
HOLLY, P.J. (1986) 'Action-research: Teacher-based, teachers-based or staff-based?', Symposium paper, University of Murcia, Spain.
HOLLY, P.J. (1986a) *Teachers Learning, about Learning* INSET Materials for Staff Discussion, CIE/TRIST Working Paper.
HOLLY, P.J. (1986b) *The Teachers' GUIDE*, CIE/TRIST Working Paper
ILEA (1977) *Keeping the School Under Review*, ILEA Inspectorate.
JOYCE, B., HERSH, R. and MCKIBBIN, M. (1983) *The Structure of School Improvement*, Longman.
LEWIN, K. (1946) 'Action-research and minority problems', *Journal of Social Issues*, 2.
LEWIN, K. (1948) *Resolving Social Conflicts*, Harper and Brothers.

LEIBERMAN, A. (1986) 'Collaborative research: Working with, not working on ...'. *Educational Leadership*. February.
LITTLE, J. (1981) 'The power of organizational setting: school norms and staff development', AERA Conference Paper, Los Angeles.
MACPHERSON, C.B. (1962) The *Political Theory of Possessive Individualism*, Oxford.
MCMAHON, A., BOLAM, R., ABBOTT, and HOLLY, P.J. (1984) *Guidelines for Review and Internal Development in Schools. Primary School Handbook*, Longman/Schools Council.
NAISBITT, J. (1984) *Megatrends*, Futura/Macdonald.
NUTTALL, D. (1981) *School Self-Evaluation-Accountability with a Human Face?* Longman/Schools Council.
OSBORNE, F. (1984) 'Reflections of a GRIDS local co-ordinator', Unpublished Paper.
POPKEWITZ, T.S., PITMAN, A. and BARRY, A. (1986) 'Educational reform and its millenial quality', *Journal of Curriculum Studies*, 18, 3, July — September.
PURKEY, S.C. and SMITH, M.S. (1985) 'School reform: The district policy implications of the effective schools literature', *The Elementary School Journal*, 85, 3.
RAPOPORT, R.N. (1970) 'Three dilemmas in action-research', *Human Relations*, 23, 6.
REID, K., HOPKINS, D., HOLLY, P.J. (1987) *Towards the Effective School*, Basil Blackwell.
REVANS, R.W. (1980) *Action Learning*, Blond and Briggs.
SCHON, D. (1983) *The Reflective Practitioner*, Temple Smith.
SCHMUCK, P.A. and R.A. (1974) *A Humanistic Psychology of Schooling*, National Press Books.
SHIPMAN, M. (1979) *In-School Evaluation*, Heinemann.
SIMONS, H. (1980) 'The evaluative school', *Forum*, 22(2)
SIMONS, H. (1981) 'Process evaluation in schools', in LACEY, C. and LAWTON, D. (Eds.) *Issues in Evaluation and Accountability*, Methuen.
SIMONS, H. (1984) 'Against the rules: Procedural problems in institutional self-evaluation', AERA Conference Paper.
SOUTHWORTH, G.W. (1987) 'Management roles and responsibilities: The primary school', Part 2, Block 2 Open University E325 *Managing Schools*. Open University Press, (forthcoming).
STENHOUSE, L. (1975) *An Introduction to Curriculum Research and Development*, Heinemann.
TANGERUD, H. (1986) 'The development and Implementation of school improvement policies by education authorities', (OECD/CERI) ISIP Conference Paper.
WALKER, R. (1985) *Doing Research: A Handbook for Teachers*, Methuen.

Endpaper

Geoff Southworth

The Introduction notes a number of themes which with some consistency occur across the readings. These themes are development, people, values, teachers working together, the agenda for change and the appropriateness of management theory and thinking for primary schools as organizations. These themes arise from such issues as:

roles and responsibilities	curricular plans
leadership	curricular practices
membership	understanding children
selection	understanding adults
learning the job	framing and agreeing educational aims
relationships	appraising teachers
group processes	the development of ownership
supporting colleagues	evaluating all of these (and more)
individuality	determining school effectiveness

All of these issues have been touched upon and discussed in the readings. If the themes act as the warp, these issues are the weft. Together they constitute the fabric of this book. More significantly, I believe they also constitute part of the fabric of primary school management. This is true in the sense that management has to address each and all of these issues and themes.

Even as just a part of the fabric of primary school management these themes and issues form a considerable array of forces and changes. For some the themes and issues of this book will appear too diverse, if not sprawling. Others may feel that there are inconsistencies between some of the chapters. I acknowledge both of these sets of feelings but I have not tried to make the book either wholly consistent nor narrow and 'tidy'; even assuming that the contributors would have accepted such an editorial stance. My experience of primary schools and of primary school management is neither that of consistency nor of narrowness. Whilst some management pundits are attracted to systems and management-by-objectives I am

Endpaper

not. Teachers who play a part in the management of their school know that however structured and systematic their approach is to the curriculum, or any other aspect of the school, each of these aspects of the school involves many things. These 'many things' are represented in the above list of issues. It is therefore not surprising that headteachers and teachers consequently experience a sense of pressure : not least because not only is there this array of forces acting upon and within the school but there is also so little time available for staff to begin to respond to all of these pressures. Yet despite the oppresive scale and scope of this agenda for change, and even with so little time available, all of these forces need to be managed: or do they? Do they need to be managed? Is 'managed' the right word?

In the Introduction I talked about the need to synthesize all the elements of a primary school. This idea of synthesizing is significant. Some reasons for claiming this have already been outlined in the Introduction but there are other reasons too. First, primary school teachers are not so much 'specialists' as 'generalists'. Few primary teachers would claim to be 'curriculum specialists' or 'subject experts', nor in terms of the above listed issues would they claim to be 'expert' (although I do think primary teachers are enormously skilled at understanding children). The consequence of being 'generalists' is that they are probably already skilled at responding to and working with diverse and multilateral forces. In other words primary heads and teachers *are* synthesizers: it goes with the job.

Second, in an earlier chapter ('Perspectives on the primary curriculum') I quoted from Pascale and Athos (1981). It is a quote which I have found tremendously helpful in making sense of schools as organizations:

> The inherent preferences of organizations are clarity, certainty and perfection. The inherent nature of human relationships involves ambiguity, uncertainty and imperfection. How one honours, balances and integrates the needs of both is the real trick of management.

Pascale and Athos suggest that integration is necessary; I take their integration to be akin to my notion of synthesizing. Importantly though, management is used as a *noun*, not as a *verb*. Pascale and Athos do not say how one *manages* the needs of both. I find management perfectly acceptable as a noun, but also find the verb to manage less acceptable. Manage as a verb is, in Roget's Thesaurus (Penguin Edition, 1984, p. 302), equated with 'manipulate, pull the strings, have taped, have the measure of', whilst The Concise Oxford Dictionary lists, 'control, take charge of, subject to one's control, gain one's ends with, cope with.' I do not find these meanings particularly appropriate. Synthesize, however, begins to point in a different direction, away from manipulation and control towards composing, or as I prefer *orchestrating*.

School management is important but as 'managers' proceed the process of management is not that of 'managing' but of 'orchestrating'. All of the forces, changes, skills and pressures identified in this volume (plus a lot of other things not included) need orchestrating. The idea of orchestrating might imply that there are leaders of the orchestra, and parts of the orchestra, and that there are conductors and players, rehearsals and performances. I suppose a whole metaphor could be developed. I will resist that and simply say that in order to respond to the range of issues which currently confront and affect the workings of primary schools all staff have a part to play in the orchestration of their school. It is a shared task because the scale and scope of the changes and forces require everyone to play a part. Moreover, a number of the writers in this volume point to the benefits of working together, teamwork, being a member of a group, learning from others and operating in a collegial way chiefly in order to develop ownership. Lastly, the size of the task of primary school management in the 1980s is such that no single person can 'manage' all that is demanded. Attractive as certainty, clarity and perfection are, they are aspirations rather than achievements. And a danger is that those who avidly seek them, to the exclusion of all else, manage to 'achieve' them only through uncreative control and manipulation. Rather, in these turbulent times, when there is much uncertainty and ambiguity it may be more appropriate to seek an orchestration of energy, effort and development. If management is the noun, I suggest orchestration is the main verb.

Contributors

Jim Campbell is Senior Lecturer in Education, Department of Education, University of Warwick.

Alan Coulson is Senior Lecturer in Education Management, Education Management Centre, North East Wales Institute of Higher Education, Cartrefle, Wrexham.

Marion Dadds is Tutor in Education of Children 3 to 13, Cambridge Institute of Education.

Peter Holly is Tutor in Curriculum Studies, Cambridge Institute of Education.

Jennifer Nias is Tutor in Curriculum Studies 3 to 13, Cambridge Institute of Education.

Colin Richards HMI is Staff Inspector for Curriculum, Department of Education and Science.

Geoff Southworth is Tutor in Primary Education and Management, Cambridge Institute of Education.

Robin Yeomans is Research Fellow to the Primary School Staff Relationships Project, funded by ESRC based at Cambridge Institute of Education.

Index

action research 210–12
  see also self-evaluation
Adelman, C. 210
Adelman, C. and Alexander, R. 213
Alexander, R. 3, 66, 71
  see also Adelman and Alexander
Argyris, C. 21, 27
Ashton, P. 100, 175
Aspin, D. 163
Athos, A.G.
  see Pascale and Athos

Bailey, C. 149
Ball, D.
Barry, G.H. and Tye, F. 105, 112
Benyon, L. 155
Berne, E. 82
Better Schools 9, 69, 143, 161, 162,
  171–4 passim, 176, 181–5
Blakeslee, T.R. 23
Blenkin, G.M. and Kelly, A.V. 63, 173,
  174, 176, 178, 186
Blythe, W.A.L. and Derricott, R. 70
Bollen, R. and Hopkins, D. 226
Bolton, E. 169
Bourdieu, P. 144
Brown, L.D. 26
Bruner, J. 151, 156, 174
Buckley, W. 51
Bullock Report 132
Burgess, R. 33
Burn, M. 99
Burnham, P. 31
Bush, T. 65, 106

Campbell, R.F. 22, 55, 67, 68, 108,
  130–1, 134, 184

Carnegie Report 231
Clift, P.S. 212, 213, 223
Clift, P.S. and Turner, G. 213
Cockcroft Report 132, 161
Cohen, L.
  see Finlayson and Cohen
collaboration 108–9, 184–5
collegiality 6–7, 15, 26–7, 61, 67–73,
  84, 138–9, 167–9, 231–2, 234–5
Cooley, C. 90
Cooper, D. 210
Corey, S. 210
Coulson, A.A. 17, 26, 31, 49, 50, 62,
  63, 64, 65, 67, 84, 108, 134, 138
  see also Gray and Coulson
Coulson, A.A. and Cox, 31, 49
Craig, I. 18
curriculum 8–9, 55–9, 144–58, 171–87
  and children 151–2
  and teachers 148–50, 175–6
  balance 150–1, 166
  continuity 154–7, 166
  documents on 171–85
  in practice 152–3
  materialistic 147–8
  orthodox perspectives 144–7
  outside school 156–7
  subjects 178–9
Curriculum from 5 to 16, The 8–9,
  142–3, 160–9, 171–3 passim, 176–81,
  183–5, 192
  content 162–7
  context 160–2
  implications 167–9
curriculum postholders 6, 8, 14–15,
  130–4 passim role 54–9
Cyert, R. and March, 51

Index

Day, C, Johnson, D. and Whitaker, P. 106
Dean, J. 155, 175
Dearden, R. 63, 150–1, 178
deputy head 6, 133, 203
  and head relationship 30–53, 64
  expressive functions 42–4
  instrumental functions 36–42
  role 49–53, 65
Derricott, R. 70
  see also Blythe and Derricott
DES 31, 59, 61, 66, 68, 69, 70, 72, 83, 97, 98, 99, 108, 132, 144, 145, 146, 149, 150, 171–8 passim, 182, 186, 208
developing school 230–5
  collegiality and 231–2, 234
  management 233–4

Ebbutt, D.
  see Elliott and Ebbutt
Education Act 1980 62
Education for All 165
Education Observed 2 (DES) 175
Eisner, E.W. 73, 151, 154
Elliott, G. 212, 213
Elliott, J. 27, 149, 208, 210, 211, 213
Elliott, J. and Ebbutt, D. 211
Elliott, J. et al 67
Etzioni, A. 30
evaluation 208–35
  see also self-evaluation
Evans, H.K. 22–3

Fairs, G.F. 87
Festinger, L. 99
Ferguson, S. 106, 107
Fiedler, F.E. 17, 85
Fieldler, F.E. et al 17
Field, D. 179
Finlayson, D. and Cohen, L. 102
Framework for the School Curriculum, A 173
Fullan, M. 73, 90, 230, 231, 233–4, 235

Galton, M. and Willcocks, J. 155
Getzels, J.W. and Guba, E.G. 85
Gibson, R. 145, 153, 173
Gilbert, D.J.D. 130
Goodacre, E. 130, 134
Gray, D.W.S. 145
Gray, H.L. and Coulson, A.A. 23
GRIDS (Guidelines for Review and Internal Development in Schools) 209, 219–30

guiding principles 219–20
LEA co-ordinators and 228–9
Guba, E.G.
  see Getzels and Guba
Gulbenkian Report 146, 153

Hall, V.
  see Morgan, Hall and Mackay
Halpin, A.W. 85
Halsey, A.H. 210
Handy, C. 2, 67, 71
Hargreaves, A. 55, 67, 222
Hargreaves, A. and Woods, P. 125
Harris, J. (deputy head) 30–53
Hartley, D. 136
headteachers 6
  and collegiality 61, 67–73
  as leaders 129–39, 202
  expressive functions 42–4
  in-post training 17
  instrumental functions 34–6
  managerial roles 18–19, 84–6
  perceptions of 62–7
  personal development 22–4
  recruitment 17–19
  see also management training
Herzberg, F. 67
Hilsum, S. and Start, K.B. 106
Hirst, P. 178
HMI 59, 68, 69, 70, 72, 83, 99, 132, 144, 145, 146, 160, 161, 171, 172, 175, 176–87, 208
Holly, P. 149, 209, 210, 211, 213, 220, 222, 229, 230, 231, 232, 234
  see also Reid, Hopkins and Holly
Hopkins, D.
  see Bollen and Hopkins; Reid, Hopkins and Holly
Hoyle, E. 183

ILEA 18, 61, 65, 69, 70, 83, 108, 129, 190, 201, 212
Improving Primary Schools (ILEA) 129, 132–5 passim, 139, 171
International Labour Office 12

Jentz, B.C. and Wofford, J.W. 20, 21
Johnson, D.
  see Day, Johnson and Whitaker
Joyce, B. et al 211
Junior School Project (ILEA) 129, 133, 190, 201–7

Kaplan, R.E. 25

243

Index

Katz, R.L. 17, 90, 99, 100
Keddie, N. 55
Kelly, A.V.
 see Blenkin and Kelly
King, R. 62, 63, 66, 100

Lacey, C. 101
Lancashire LEA 64
Landau, M. 51
La Porte, T. 51
Lawton, D. 175, 176, 182
learning
 and teacher appraisal 192–9
 behaviourist theory of 197
 environment 204–5
 self-initiated 195
 single-activity 205
 through challenge 204
Lewin, K. 210
Lieberman, A. 231
Little, J. 231, 232
Lortie, D. 91, 93, 94, 97, 100

McCall, G. and Simmonds, J. 33
McCall, M.W. 26
McGregor, D. 67
McIntyre, D.
 see Morrison and McIntyre
Mackay, H. 107
 see also Morgan, Hall and Mackay
McMahon, A. et al 68, 184, 211, 226
management training 5, 22–8, 66
 courses 16, 20–1, 66, 73
 see also headteachers
Management and the School Course
 Team 31, 49, 50
March,
 see Cyert and March
Mead, M. 90
Mintzberg, H. 17, 24
Morgan, C. 22, 106, 112
Morgan, C. and Hall, V. 17
Morgan, C., Hall, V. and Mackay, H.
 17, 106, 107, 112, 125
Morrison, D. and McIntyre, D. 102

NAGM (National Association of
 Governors and Managers) 62
Naisbitt, J. 234–5
Newcomb, T. 102
Nias, J. 31, 32, 33, 34, 51, 81, 91, 93,
 94, 98–102 passim, 125, 175
Nias, J. et al 52
Nugent, P. 23, 24

Nuttall, D. 209

Oldroyd, D. 62, 71, 72
Olsen, T.P. 149
Ornstein, R.E. 23, 158
Osborne, F. 229

Packwood, T. 71
Parental Influence at School (DES)
 148–9
parental involvement 206
Pascale, R.T. and Athos, A.G. 125, 154,
 239
Peters, T.J. and Waterman, R.H. 186
Phenix, P.H. 178
Phipson, G. 107, 112
Piaget, J. 196
Playfoot, D. 179
Plowden Report 59, 131–2, 169, 193
Pollard, A. 33
Poster, C. 105
Practical Curriculum, The (Schools
 Council) 145–6, 154
Primary Practice 146, 148, 149, 152,
 154, 161
Primary School Staff Relationships (PSSR)
 project 105, 109, 110, 125
Primary School Survey (1978) 132, 144,
 145, 150, 154, 163, 183
Procter, A. (head) 30–53
Project on the Selection of Secondary
 Headteachers (POST) 106
Purkey, S.C. and Smith, M.S. 231

Rapoport, R.N. 210
record keeping 202, 206
Reid, K., Hopkins, D. and Holly, P.J.
 230, 231, 233
Revans, R.W. 210
Richardson, T.E. 62
Riches, C. 107
Robey, D.
 see Taggart, Robey and Taggart
Rogers, C. 24
Rokeach, M. 100

Sallis, J. 62
Samuel, G. 106
Sarason, S.R. 26
Schmuck, P.A. and Schmuck, R.A. 208,
 234
Schon, D. 210
School Curriculum, The (DES) 145,
 148, 152, 163, 173

244

Schools Council 144, 145, 146, 209, 210, 211, 219
self-evaluation
 classroom 209–12
 school 212–20
  criteria for 220–2
  definition 222–3
  developing school and 230–5
  LEA checklist approach 212–13, 233
  'school profile' 213–19
Shaw, K.E. 72
Sherif, C. and Sherif, M. 97
Shibutani, T. 102
Shipman, M. 101, 213
Sikes, P. et al 100, 125
Simons, H. 213, 222
Skelton, M. 179
Skilbeck, M. 58
Small, N. 62
Smith, M.S.
 see Purkey and Smith
Southworth, G.W. 65, 67, 70, 72, 73, 108, 125, 147, 149, 150, 153, 171, 179, 183, 232
staff selection 105–26
 collaboration and 108–9, 124
 governors and 119, 121, 123
 interviewing and 107
 research into 109–23
 staff involvement in 116–18, 124
 values 112–16, 124–5
 visits 119–21, 122–3, 125
staffrooms 83, 97–8, 128–9
Start, K.B.
 see Hilsum and Start
Stenhouse, L. 103, 153, 176, 210
Suffolk Education Authority 64
Swann Report 165, 171

Taggart, W., Robey, D. and Taggart, B. 24
Tangerud, H. 234
Taylor, P.H. et al 26

teacher appraisal 192–9
 and children's learning 192–5
 external 196–7
 self-initiated 197–8
teachers
 and curriculum 148–50, 175–6
 as a group 135–8
 as a team 131–5
 as people 80–9, 90–1, 98–102
 comunication with pupils 205, 206–7
 continuity of 201–2, 203
 early development 5, 7, 90–103
 involvement 203
 support 94–8
 see also collegiality; staff selection
Thomas Report 168, 169
TIQL (Teacher-Pupil Interaction and the Quality of Learning) 211, 230
Turner, G.
 see Clift and Turner
Tye, F.
 see Barry and Tye

View of the Curriculum, A (HMI) 145

Walker, R. 232
Waller, W. 97
Warnock Report 163
Webb, D. 178
Whitaker, P. 31, 49, 63, 65, 107
 see also Day, Johnson and Whitaker
Whitbread, N. 185
Willcocks, J.
 see Galton and Willcocks
William Tyndale School 85
Winkley, D. 66
Winnicott, D. 99
Witkin, F. 153
Woods, P. 87, 100
 see also Hargreaves and Woods
Wragg, E.C. 81

Yeomans, R.M. 83, 108, 124